THE RED WEB

THE RED WEB

THE STRUGGLE BETWEEN RUSSIA'S

DIGITAL DICTATORS *and*

THE NEW ONLINE REVOLUTIONARIES

ANDREI SOLDATOV *and*

IRINA BOROGAN

PublicAffairs

New York

PublicAffairs books are available at special discounts for bulk purchases in
the U.S. by corporations, institutions, and other organizations. For more
information, please contact the Special Markets Department at the Perseus
Books Group, 2300 Chestnut Street, Suite 200, Philadelphia, PA 19103, call
(800) 810-4145, ext. 5000, or e-mail special.markets@perseusbooks.com.

Book Design by Cynthia Young

Library of Congress Cataloging in Publication Control Number:
2015015850
ISBN 978-1-61039-573-1 (HC)
ISBN 978-1-61039-574-8 (EB)

First Edition

10 9 8 7 6 5 4 3 2 1

"Information wants to be free."

—Futurist Stewart Brand

"This is not a phone conversation."

—a Russian expression meaning a wish to
discuss something in person because somebody
else might be listening

CONTENTS

PROLOGUE

In an otherwise residential district of southwest Moscow, a nineteen-story gray-and-white high rise, surrounded by a modest fence, could at first glance be mistaken for an average apartment block. But there is something odd about it: Only twelve of the floors have windows.

This building is the heart of the Russian Internet: phone station M9, containing a crucial Internet exchange point known as MSK-IX. Nearly half of Russia's Internet traffic passes through this structure every day. Yellow and gray fiber-optic cables snake through the rooms and hang in coils from the ceilings, connecting servers and boxes between the racks and between floors. Google rents an entire floor on M9 so to be as close as possible to the Internet exchange point of Russia. Each floor is protected by a thick metal door, accessible only to those with a special card.

On the eighth floor is a room occupied by the Federal Security Service, or *Federalnaya Sluzhba Bezopasnosti*, or the FSB, the main successor organization to the KGB, but the FSB's presence is evident on all the floors. Scattered among the communications racks throughout the building are a few electronic boxes the size of a video player. These boxes are marked SORM, and they allow the FSB officers in the room on the eighth floor to have access to all of Russia's Internet traffic. SORM stands for the Russian words meaning "operative search measures." But the words imply much more.

SORM boxes once intercepted just phone calls. Now they monitor e-mails, Internet usage, Skype, cell phone calls, text messages and social networks. It is one of the world's most intrusive listening devices, and it is the Russian government's front line in a monumental battle for the future of the Internet. The battle has stakes for everyone who ventures into the digital universe.

This book is a journey through this conflict as it has unfolded in Russia during recent decades, a quarter century of tumult from the Soviet Union, which sought to put information in a kind of prison, to the emergence of a new Russia. The book shows that in some ways, Russia did not break entirely with its Soviet past; the SORM boxes, invented by the KGB, have been constantly updated ever since and are used to this day against political opposition. In other ways, however, Russia has become an entirely new country of digital revolutionaries who have learned to thrive on free information at their fingertips, communicate on social networks, and read headlines about the world. In 1991 Russia inherited a dysfunctional and broken communications system with barely a connection abroad, and today it stands in the top ranks of those developing countries that are wired to the world. In a global survey by the Pew Research Center, 73 percent of those questioned in Russia said they had online access, compared to 63 percent for China and 87 percent in the United States.[1] The book is an investigation into these two great forces—surveillance and control on one side, and freedom on the other—and what happens when they collide. It does not yet have a definitive ending.

But the significance of these events extends far beyond Russia, and not only because the Kremlin has repeatedly attempted to change the global rules of the Internet, to build national frontiers in what today is a wide open space.

We have interviewed dozens of participants in the events described and examined thousands of pages of documents. In a nation with a strong tradition of secrecy, even today, it is very difficult to find the truth or people to talk about it. This wall of silence became more pronounced after President Vladimir Putin returned to power in 2012 in the face of popular protests and tightened the flow of information by new laws and practices of censorship and intimidation.

Part I of the book covers the Soviet collapse and the nearly two decades leading up to the Moscow protests of 2011–2012. Part II takes a closer look at some of the forces driving the conflict and what has happened since Putin's return and the outbreak of violence in Ukraine. As co-authors, we wrote the book together and refer to ourselves in the narrative by our first names. We researched and wrote this book not only as journalists but also as insiders and participants in the events we chronicle, as well as products of both the last of the Soviet years and the digital revolution itself.

Part I

CHAPTER 1

The Prison of Information

In January 1950 Abram Trakhtman, a thirty-two-year-old major of the Ministry of State Security, a forerunner of the KGB, faced a personal crisis that threatened his entire career in Stalin's secret police. For days he had sat alone in his office, located in a three-story, red-brick building in northeast Moscow.

The building on the compound was first erected in 1884 for a Russian Orthodox Church seminary. In the early 1920s, after the Bolshevik Revolution and the rise of an officially atheist state, the seminarians were expelled. The seminary was turned into a prison for adolescents. Then, in the 1940s, it was transformed again.

The building stood on the outskirts of a small village, Marfino, which had just one cobblestone road. Bus no. 37 from city center stopped there twice a day. In 1947 the village was suddenly surrounded by newly erected walls and transformed into a Soviet secret research facility. It was named Object Eight and known informally as the *sharashka* of Marfino. A *sharashka* was a prison camp that held scientists who were put to work using their expertise for the state. They could not leave, but their conditions were better than the rugged prison camps of the Soviet gulag. At

Marfino the rooms were filled with convicted and imprisoned engineers, mathematicians, and linguists who were working to help
the secret police find ways to provide secure telephone technology
for Joseph Stalin.

Down the corridor from Trakhtman's office was a large room, a
former church cupola that had been subdivided so it looked like a
half-moon chamber. On the ceiling the original church paintings
were still visible, but down below it was crowded with radio and
telephone equipment.

Trakhtman, thin-faced, with round, owlish eyeglasses and a
head of naturally curly hair, was reluctant to go to the round room
just now, even though he knew his subordinates were waiting
for him.

Abram Trakhtman was the chief of the acoustic laboratory.

He wore a green uniform with gold shoulder straps and a cap
with a blue crown. The blue had been embraced by Russian secret services since the days of the tsars. An engineer by training,
Trakhtman had enjoyed a very successful career up until January
1950. He was born to a Jewish family in a small Ukrainian town
in the Pale of Settlement. He survived the pogroms, made it to
Moscow, and entered the Moscow Communications Institute,
graduating just before World War II. He then joined the Central
Research Institute of Communications, where he was noticed by
Alexander Mints, a prominent Soviet physicist and radio engineer
highly regarded by the Soviet authorities. Mints made him part
of his entourage, and Trakhtman earned two Stalin Prizes during
the war.[1]

When the Ministry of State Security decided to launch the
Marfino project in 1947, Mints was asked to lead it, but he declined.[2] Trakhtman got the job, which he eagerly accepted. He
was given his own laboratory. He always wore the gold insignia of
his Stalin Prize on his uniform. Yet now Trakhtman found himself
in a dangerous situation—just when he thought he was on the
verge of advancement.

Only two months before, Trakhtman's laboratory had achieved a major success. They helped catch a government official who was providing sensitive secrets to the Americans. The laboratory consisted of five people; three of them were inmates, including the writer Alexander Solzhenitsyn and his close friend Lev Kopelev. (Solzhenitsyn was later sent off to a labor camp.) A gifted philologist, Kopelev was a big, flamboyant man with thick black hair, a black beard and mustache, and large, expressive eyes—a real firebrand. It was Kopelev who had identified a Foreign Ministry official who made a phone call to the US Embassy in Moscow, thereby revealing the existence of an undercover Soviet spy who was headed to New York to steal atomic bomb secrets. To accomplish this, Kopelev had analyzed the recording of an intercepted phone call and fingered one of five suspects. The suspected caller was arrested. Kopelev, excited by this success, thought he had created a new scientific discipline and gave it a name: phonoscopy.

With Kopelev by his side, Trakhtman made contact with a high-ranking general and won permission to establish a new research institute that would work specifically on speech recognition and speaker identification. Excited, Trakhtman told Kopelev that they would have a promising future together and asked Kopelev to think about what kind of equipment they would need for the new institute. A location for the sharashka was found in the center of Moscow.[3]

But January 1950 was an unfortunate time for an engineer with a name like Abram Trakhtman, even within the state security apparatus. A year before, the Communist Party newspaper *Pravda* had accused Jewish theater critics of unpatriotic behavior in an article edited personally by Stalin, and the Soviet press launched an orchestrated campaign against "cosmopolitanism," which was essentially an attack on prominent Jews.[4] The Jewish Anti-Fascist Committee was disbanded, many of its members arrested, and Jewish newspapers and publishing houses were closed. The campaign then turned into something akin to a witch hunt, with

Jewish doctors being accused of poisoning Soviet leaders. In 1950 the anti-Semitic campaign reached the ranks of state security. Just a few days after Trakhtman had secured the general's approval, he was told that the building chosen for the new sharashka was not sufficiently secure. Then he was told that Marfino's prisoners could not be moved to this building because it was too risky to have them in the center of Moscow. It was clear to him that his plans were being deliberately and repeatedly delayed. Days passed without any decisions being made. Trakhtman was rarely seen in his laboratory, the half-moon chamber. His subordinates concluded that he was afraid to address their questions about the fate of the new project. They were right.

Finally Trakhtman was told he would not get any convicted engineers for his new sharashka. Despairing, Trakhtman tried to raise the stakes. He refused to be a director of the new institute without his prisoners and declared that the entire project was doomed without them.

That was a mistake. The general who had given him permission for the new institute proceeded to cancel it. Trakhtman was stripped of his rank of major and expelled from Marfino. In late January he went back to the compound one last time.

After much anxiety, he walked into the laboratory and then turned to Kopelev and said, "Now, strictly between us—it's impossible to be a director of the institute with such a name," meaning a Jewish name like Trakhtman. He then squeezed Kopelev's hand, smiled sadly, and left.[5]

With his ambitious plans for a new sharashka destroyed, Trakhtman soon relocated to another top-secret facility, working on missile guidance systems, a part of the Soviet space effort. For Trakhtman, research on speech recognition was over. The most promising project of his life was ruined.

But the general did not forget about Trakhtman's subordinates at Marfino's acoustic laboratory. They remained locked up at Marfino for another three years until December 1953, when eighteen prisoners were transferred from Marfino to a sharashka outside of Moscow. It was called Kuchino, another compound of the security service, and the talented Lev Kopelev followed them in January 1954. The compound was controlled by the Soviet secret police and intelligence service, which was renamed that year the *Komitet gosudarstvennoi bezopasnosti*, or, simply, the KGB.

Kuchino, about twelve miles east of Moscow, was set on an old prerevolutionary industrialist's estate. It became the KGB's main research center for surveillance technologies, including the all-pervasive Soviet system of phone tapping and communications interception. From this day forward, speech recognition research and telephone wiretapping were bound together, funded and directed by the KGB.

The Soviet secret services wanted to make sure they could properly intercept any call, and identify the person who made it. They wanted to make sure that information in the Soviet Union—all kinds of information, including communications between people—was under their control. Long before the term was fashionable, they determined that they wanted to be the dictators of data.

When Vladimir Fridkin graduated from the physics department at Moscow State University in December 1952, he earned a diploma with honors in physics. A thin-faced but earnest young man, he could not land a job in physics, despite months of searching. He was repeatedly turned down. He knew the reason: he was a Jew, and the anti-Semitic campaign launched by Stalin had erased all the advantages Fridkin might have expected with his degree.[6]

He gave up hopes of becoming a nuclear physicist and finally landed a job at the Scientific Research Institute of Polygraphic Engineering. The institute occupied a few miserable barracks in the rear of a large factory in the west of Moscow. When Fridkin first opened the door of his small office, it was almost empty—there was nothing but a table and chair. It was an inauspicious beginning: he could hardly carry out scientific research in the barren little room.

Instead, he went every day to sit for hours under a green-shaded lamp in the vast, high-ceilinged reading room of the Lenin Library near the Kremlin. The library held the largest collection of books, documents, and dissertations in the country, in hundreds of languages. One day, while there, he discovered an article written by Chester Carlson, an American physicist, about the process of electrophotography, or, more simply, photocopying.[7]

There was nothing like photocopying in the Soviet Union. Fridkin was intrigued by the possibility that he could build a Soviet copying machine. First, he went to the institute's department of electrical equipment and asked them to get him a high-current generator. Then he went back to the physics department where he had studied at the university and obtained sulfur crystals and a photographic enlarger. In his small office he experimented. He tried to make a copy of a page, then of a photograph. One day he succeeded in duplicating an image of Mokhovaya Square, a well-known landmark in front of the Kremlin. When the director of the institute saw this he exclaimed, "You do not understand what you invented!" The director immediately ordered the institute's designers to take what Fridkin had done and transform it into a single machine that could make photocopies. When they managed to do this, the first copying machine in the Soviet Union was born. It was box-like, more than three feet high and two feet across, with two cylinders on the top and the high-current generator attached. It was named the Electrophotography Copying Machine No. 1.

Even though the machine was primitive, nobody doubted the significance of the invention. The institute director called the ministry—in the Soviet centrally planned economy, a government ministry oversaw every such institute. Soon the minister himself came to the Institute of Polygraphic Engineering to see the machine, and he was so impressed that he ordered it into mass production. A factory in Chisinau in the Soviet republic of Moldova was selected to produce the new machines, and a special electrophotography research institute was established in Vilnius. At twenty-four years old, Fridkin was appointed deputy chief. He was featured in a television show praising the Soviet achievements in science. He was also paid a bonus for his accomplishment.

Although Fridkin felt much better, he still wanted to be a physicist. At last, in 1955 he was given a job at the Institute of Crystallography. When he moved there, his copying machine followed him. For two years his colleagues at the institute came to his room every day to use his machine to copy articles from foreign journals. Fridkin became a very popular person in the institute. Then, one day in 1957, a nice young woman from the KGB section walked into his room. Fridkin had known her. She had a pretty face, wore plain clothes, and Fridkin often spent time drinking tea and chatting with her. But she brought bad news. "I have to take away your device and destroy it," she said. Fridkin asked whether she knew that this was the first copying machine in the Soviet Union. "I know, but people who come over to you can copy some prohibited materials," she replied.

The first copying machine in the Soviet Union was smashed to pieces, and the parts were taken to a dump. One critical part of it, a slab of mirror, was salvaged and put up in the women's restroom. Fridkin's institute did not carry out secret research, so the decision to destroy his machine was not protecting anything at the institute; rather, it reflected the broader and deeper paranoia of the Communist Party. The party maintained a stranglehold on power and a chokehold on information. It could not tolerate the possibility that Fridkin's invention might be used to freely make copies of unapproved documents and allow them to be easily distributed.

In a few years the factory in Chisinau ceased production. Fridkin knew that the quality of the machines produced by the Chisinau factory was not very high. But it was hardly a reason to stop
making them. Later, when photocopying became routine in the
West, the Soviet Union bought Western Xerox machines, but its
attitude to information remained unchanged. The few photocopi-
ers that were brought from abroad were kept under lock and key
in party offices or in the Academy of Sciences. In many factories
and institutes a special staffer operated the photocopier under the
watchful gaze of the KGB. It happened in Fridkin's institute too.
He seethed with anger at the sight of the photocopying machines
in his own institute being locked in the prison of information.

Stalin died in March 1953, and the brutal, totalitarian system
of mass repression slowly began to relax. The mood in Soviet
society started to change. Many gulag prisoners were released and
returned home by 1955. In February 1956 Nikita Khrushchev, the
new Soviet leader, made a speech at a closed session at the 20th
Party Congress denouncing Stalin's crimes. The "secret speech"
lasted four hours. In a few years Khrushchev loosened state controls in a period that became known as the Thaw. Dozens of different freethinking groups blossomed in the Soviet Union, including
Moscow intellectuals, artists and writers, all kinds of nationalists,
and Jews who had been denied permission to emigrate, known as
"refuseniks." It was a time when many were optimistic, especially
young people who yearned for better lives after the deprivations
of war and Stalinism. But the Thaw did not last. In 1964 Khrushchev was ousted and replaced by Leonid Brezhnev, who effectively
ended reforms. In the autumn of 1965 arrests of intellectuals and
writers began in Moscow and Ukraine, and censorship tightened.
The Soviet invasion of Czechoslovakia in August 1968 effectively
marked the end of the Thaw.

But one feature of the period did not disappear. The circulation of uncensored information became an essential part of the dissident movement, if not its main goal. This included the circulation and copying of manuscripts, known as *samizdat*, or self-published, and it covered a wide horizon of material: banned works of literature, social and political commentary, open letters, Solzhenitsyn's novels, and, from 1968 to the early 1980s, the *Chronicle of Current Events*, which reported human rights violations in the Soviet Union. Soviet dissidents didn't have Fridkin's machine nor a Western-made Xerox. They hammered out their works on carbon paper with a typewriter known as the Erika, made in Eastern Germany, which could produce only four copies at a time.

In the Soviet Union the state had always held the upper hand when it came to distributing information. All other sources, like independent media or the church, were outlawed. "A newspaper is not only a collective propagandist and a collective agitator, it is also a collective organizer," Lenin wrote in 1901 in the fourth issue of *Iskra*, the main Bolshevik newspaper. The Bolsheviks wanted newspapers to organize and mobilize the masses, not to inform them. They could not tolerate an independent press after the 1917 revolution: from their point of view it was impossible to let the enemy—a capitalist, free press—present an alternative worldview to the masses. Stalin repeated Lenin's words in 1923 in an article, "The Press as Collective Organizer," in *Pravda*.[8] In the 1930s all Soviet cities were filled with street loudspeakers, spreading propaganda. Just like in the Middle Ages, when the church bells defined the day, in Stalin's Soviet Union the day started with a national anthem broadcast by a loudspeaker on the street, and it ended with the anthem. There was no way to turn the loudspeakers off. For many decades Soviet citizens had no choice in what they could listen to or read. By the end of World War II an entire generation had come of age not knowing anything else, let alone what they had lost. They lived all their lives to the echo of the words and formulas dictated by the state.

The Soviet regime rigidly controlled public space. Newspapers and television were put under prior censorship by the general directorate for the Protection of State Secrets in the Press, known as Glavlit, which reported to the Council of Ministers. From March 1961 Glavlit was also put in charge of controlling communications (telex and phone conversations) of foreign correspondents in Moscow.[9] Another government committee, known as Goskomizdat, censored fiction and poetry. Radios were jammed, and dozens of jamming transmitters were positioned along the borders. It was a fast-growing industry. In 1949 350 short-wave transmitters tried to jam the Western radio broadcasts. In 1950 there were 600 of them; in 1955, about 1,000, with 700 in the Soviet bloc countries. All of them were erected to jam what amounted to no more than 70 Western transmitters. By 1986 the Soviet Union had thirteen powerful long-range jamming stations, and local city jamming stations were established in eighty-one cities, with 1,300 transmitters in total. The radio jamming was stopped only in November 1988 by the Soviet leader Mikhail Gorbachev.[10]

For most of the seven decades of Soviet rule to seek information was a risky and dangerous game for ordinary people. Soviet-produced radio sets had some frequencies disabled. To be found in possession of a quartz with the wrong frequencies was a potentially criminal offense. Soviet-made radios were required to be registered with the government, a rule that was canceled only in 1962. The authorities wanted to be able to track anyone who copied information; the KGB required that samples taken from all typewriters be kept on file in case one had to be identified.

The ordinary and casual exchange of news with foreigners was also restricted. With the borders closed, Soviet citizens needed an "exit visa" to go abroad, a long-cherished dream that could be granted only after a long talk with a KGB officer. When abroad, Soviet citizens were requested to walk in groups so to exclude any contact with locals, including informal conversations. Soviet citizens who were allowed to go on business trips were requested to present reports of their encounters with foreigners.

Not surprisingly, the Communist Party wanted to force Soviet citizens to censor themselves. And the intimidation was effective. Everybody in the Soviet Union knew the expression "this is not a phone conversation," which expressed a wish to discuss something in person because they were afraid somebody else might be listening. The "somebody else" was the state and its vast networks of informers.

The Soviet Union was not an occupying regime; instead, the regime attempted to make everyone complicit in its goals. The peculiar structure of Soviet society helped the authorities in this. The military-industrial complex was an enormous archipelago of institutes, factories, and government ministries. By some accounts, it made up 30 to 40 percent of the Soviet economy. Within it the Soviet Union employed a vast army of engineers at secret military and security research facilities, known colloquially as "post office boxes." These laboratories and offices were known only by a post office box number, such as NII-56. Any mail would be addressed to that box number, not to the real name of the facility. One purpose of the zip-code-style number system was to hide the secret facilities from the prying eyes of foreigners, who were prohibited from going near them. Often the state designated an entire city "closed." Both of Irina Borogan's parents, engineers by training, worked at the post office box in the tiny town of Electrougli: foreigners were not allowed into the town, although it is located only twelve miles from Moscow. There a certain kind of vague doublespeak took hold and became part of everyday conversations. A person might say they worked at a "post office box" developing a "device," but their meaning was immediately clear. In this way the Soviet population was co-opted into becoming a part of the system. Even if an individual didn't work at a "post office box" or in the military, it was likely that someone else in the family did so, and the rules covered everyone.

In such a system the government did little to encourage telephone use. Officials at the Soviet Ministry of Communications loved to recall Khrushchev's statement that Soviet citizens did not need home phones because, unlike in the United States, there was no stock exchange in the Soviet Union, and therefore they don't need so much information.

When dissidents tried to use telephones to exchange information and contact each other, the KGB was quick to react.

Kopelev, who left the Kuchino sharashka in December 1954, became a passionate Soviet dissident in the 1970s. He turned his two-room apartment, on the sixth floor of an apartment building in the north of Moscow, into a gathering place for dissidents. Dozens of phone calls were made from there every day. But when the KGB found out, they cut off his home phone line. After that, his son-in-law brought him a handset from a phone station he worked at, a plastic black piece with a white disk, a dial, and a cable. Every night Kopelev walked down the stairs to the first floor of his apartment building. There was a room there for a *de-zhurnaya*, a person on duty, usually a woman, whose job was to control who came into the building. Inside the room there was a phone, but the room was locked. However, outside there was a phone socket on the wall, and when the *dezhurnaya* was off, Kopelev got the device connected to the socket—and spoke for hours.[11]

In 1972 the KGB requested the Soviet Council of Ministers to adopt a new rule prohibiting the use of international phone lines "in a manner contrary to the public interest and public order of the USSR."[12] It was a typical KGB move to keep tight control. Even though the restriction was approved, it was not enough for the KGB; they wanted still more restrictions. In June 1975 Yuri Andropov, then chairman of the KGB, reported to the Central Committee about a new threat. He said that Jewish refuseniks were making international phone calls. In his letter to the Central Committee marked "Secret," Andropov reported that in 1973–1974 more than one hundred phone customers were identified and their phone lines turned off, which, according to the KGB chairman, "caused a severe blow to the foreign Zionist organizations which consider regular telephone as the most important way to get information of interest from the Soviet Union."[13]

Andropov warned, however, that the Zionists were bypassing the KGB by actively using automated international telephone lines as well as telephone booking offices to make international calls using bogus names. The KGB lamented that the Zionists had delivered to the West a series of appeals to the international community, demanding that the Soviet authorities restore their disconnected phones. Andropov's recommendation was "to suppress the use of international communication channels for transmission abroad of biased and slanderous information."[14]

The policy remained that information was to be locked away. But Andropov could not keep it all imprisoned.

The same month that he reported his concern to the Central Committee, a samizdat book was passed around a small town outside Kharkiv, 460 miles west of Moscow. The book was essentially a stack of tissue paper, bound by coarse thread, containing a collection of articles written by Vladimir Jabotinsky, a prominent Zionist in the early years of the twentieth century.

The samizdat book was passed to Alexander Paritsky, who was then thirty-seven years old. He lived with his wife, Polya, and two daughters in a small apartment. Kharkiv was mostly known for a huge tank factory. Paritsky's father and brother were both imprisoned under Stalin, but he was by no means a dissident. He was constantly reminded, however, that he was a Jew. He had a modestly successful career as an engineer at a local research institute.

Paritsky's sister, Dora, brought the dog-eared samizdat manuscript to him. "As usual, we had it for only the one night and then it goes further on the chain," Paritsky recalled. This was the usual procedure for samizdat—you could read it for one night and you had to pass it on.[15] The night turned into a marathon reading session. By the next morning "Polya and I became Zionists. We decided to emigrate to Israel," Paritsky recalled.

The next day he announced their decision to an astonished Dora. However, there was a problem: Paritsky worked on radars for the Ministry of Defense, and that made all his work top secret. Soon he left his job and became an elevator repairman. In July 1976 he applied for an exit visa for himself and his family. He also tried to find a way to contact Moscow's community of refuseniks, hoping to make his case public. Paritsky began getting letters from Jews in Israel and soon got his first phone call from abroad. When he received his second international call, from London, the phone was turned off right in the middle of conversation.

"I was told that my phone was turned off by the order of the chief of Kharkiv's communications center," he recalled. "My wife and I arranged to see him, to find out the reasons."

When the pair went to the communications center, the chief just gave the Paritskys a brochure, which turned out to be the Charter of Communications. The chief pointed to the article that had been inserted in 1972 prohibiting the use of the phone to do harm to the Soviet state. To drive the point home, a few days later Paritsky got a formal summons to the city council offices, where he was given a warning about his anti-Soviet activities. However, Paritsky didn't stop, and after that he made his calls from special offices where citizens could book calls through telephone operators.

On August 27, 1981, Paritsky was arrested near his apartment in Kharkiv. The *Chronicle of Current Events* reported his case. The KGB first hinted at accusations of espionage, knowing of Paritsky's past secret work, but then they changed tactics. The KGB added to his indictment that Paritsky was using international telephone lines for spreading anti-Soviet information. "At the court, the prosecution presented a woman, an operator at the international telephone communications hub. She testified that during her duty her client complained about the poor quality of the line. Then she gave my name, so she identified me by my voice heard on the phone five to seven years earlier," Paritsky recalled. "She then explained that she connected the line to check the quality and heard me speaking all possible defamation of the Soviet system."

He was sentenced to three years in jail and sent to the labor camps. Only in April of 1988 were Paritsky and his family allowed to leave the Soviet Union.

With the approach of the 1980 Olympic Games in Moscow, the Soviet Union needed international telecommunications to host the Games properly. In 1979 the number of international lines was significantly increased. An international telephone exchange station, known as M9, was launched, located in two tall buildings on Butlerova Street in Moscow's southwest.

When, on July 19, 1980, the Games opened in Moscow, Gennady Kudryavtsev felt especially proud. Kudryavtsev had carried out a project to expand the international phone lines. He had delivered them on time. There were sixteen hundred new channels and a whole floor of M9 for international calls.[16] These channels provided automatic connection, without an operator, which was hitherto unheard of in the Soviet Union.

The KGB had resisted the expansion. To mollify them, the Ministry of Communications suggested that callers would have to dial not only the number they wanted to call but also their own number so no one would go unidentified. The KGB was still reluctant to allow more phone lines to contact the outside world. Then Kudryavtsev suggested adding another way for the KGB to control conversations. "There was a specialist who told me that there was a way to add a special programming loop to get all calls intercepted," said Kudryavtsev. The method of intercepting all calls was introduced, and the KGB was finally satisfied. No matter how many more lines were opened, they could listen to any call.

The sixteen hundred channels turned out to be quite enough, and there were no complaints from the participants and visitors. "All passed with the first call attempt, because there was almost nobody to call, to be honest," Kudryavtsev recalled. The Games were boycotted by sixty-five countries in response to the Soviet invasion of Afghanistan.

Still, the regime did not want to let people have the option for long. A few months after the Olympics, in early 1981, Kudryavtsev, who had been appointed the first deputy minister of communications, was called to the offices of the Central Committee of the Communist Party.

He was uneasy. Just a few days before, he had learned that part of his responsibilities as first deputy minister was to oversee the system of Soviet jamming stations. He knew that the summons to the Central Committee had to do with the international lines. "I heard already that the KGB people went around complaining about international phone lines," he said. But when he arrived, it was worse than he predicted; he was given a secret decision approved by the secretariat of the Central Committee to reduce the amount of automatic international lines. The lines had been his triumph, but now he was being asked to take them down.

The decision was presented as coming from the Central Committee, but in fact it was written at KGB headquarters. Kudryavtsev was put in charge, and the scale astonished him: the order was to reduce the number of overseas channels from sixteen hundred to only one hundred. For channels to some countries, the cut was even more drastic. "We had eighty-nine channels for the United States, and I was told to reduce the number to only six," Kudryavtsev said. He was clearly upset, "Of course it hurt me—I made it, I saw that it was necessary, that it was impossible to go without it."

In a month Kudryavtsev destroyed his own creation. The changes made automatic connection almost impossible, and customers, including foreign embassies, noticed it. On a small sheet of paper Kudryavtsev wrote out an explanation that it was due to "technical problems," but he blushed every time he was forced to explain.

Finally Kudryavtsev found a way to take control of a telephone station on Leninsky Prospect. He redirected the lines of those who were allowed to use automatic international connection to this single station. In a year the chosen organizations, approved by the authorities, found that automatic international connection was restored.

For the rest of the country it was not—and remained that way for many years.

Kudryavtsev was angry because the KGB was given everything they demanded for the Olympics, but after the games were over, they forced everything to go back to the way it was before. As a Soviet official, Kudryavtsev completely accepted that the KGB needed to possess the means for intercepting calls, but he didn't understand why they needed to cut the lines. It was against his engineer's nature, and it tortured him for years. His usual sad joke was to tell his friends that he got his first government award for increasing international communications capacities, and his second award came for cutting off those capacities.

For many years after 1981 Kudryavtsev tried to talk some sense into the KGB, but the generals would not listen. They believed he was behind the expansion of the phone lines before the Olympics—and in this they were right—and they told him only one thing: "Gennady Georgievich, you had f—ed us when you were leading to the Olympics. Now shut up."

Kudryavtsev took that rather seriously. In the massive building of the Ministry of Communications on Tverskaya Street, known as the Central Telegraph, he was given an office once used by Genrikh Yagoda, a chief of Stalin's secret police, the NKVD, who was also a commissar of communications. "All the furniture was from Yagoda's times—his table, his safe—only his lift was blocked, which used to lead to the basement and then to the metro. But I checked—the lift shaft was still there."

In 1988 Kudryavtsev went to the Politburo to explain a minor issue of international connection between a factory in Ivanovo, not far from Moscow, and its Bulgarian partners, and Mikhail Gorbachev was present. When Gorbachev asked him what should be done to improve the line, Kudryavtsev replied, "Cancel the decision of the secretariat of the Central Committee on restrictions of international communications." Gorbachev said, "But what should be done specifically for Ivanovo?" And thus the question was postponed again.[17]

Ed Fredkin, a leading computer authority at the Massachusetts Institute of Technology and a jovial and energetic former Air Force fighter pilot, had worked for years developing contacts inside the Soviet research community. He was fond of big ideas and, in 1982, at forty-eight years old, went to Moscow to attend a physics conference with the notion, as he recalled it, to "infect the Soviet Union with personal computers."

"Since we arrived a few days prior to the start of the meeting, I immediately went to the Academy of Sciences Computation Center to reconnect with old friends and explain what I wanted to do," he told us. "My friends told me that I had to talk to Yevgeny Velikhov. I called him, and he came over to the Computation Center."[18]

Velikhov, then forty-seven years old, was an open-minded and ambitious nuclear physicist and a deputy director of the Kurchatov Institute of Atomic Energy. Velikhov had recently been elected a vice president of the Soviet Academy of Sciences, the youngest ever. Fredkin had known Velikhov for years, and he spoke openly with him, arguing that the widespread adoption of

computer technologies was vital to the future of the Soviet Union and that better times could be realized only if the authorities gave up rigid control of information. Fredkin suggested that personal computers could fit with socialism even better than with capitalism, and Velikhov, an enthusiast of personal computers since the late 1970s—when he had bought for himself one of the first Apple models—arranged for Fredkin to speak before Soviet scholars at the presidium of the Academy of Sciences. "We needed this talk at the presidium to overcome the resistance," recalled Velikhov.[19] The goal was to change the Soviet government's position, which was then geared toward developing information technologies by using a rigid hierarchical scheme with massive, central computers, and terminals, not personal computers.

Two days before the talk Fredkin was in his room in the Academy of Sciences Hotel when he got a phone call from someone. The person spoke English and didn't introduce himself:

"I understand that you have been told by Velikhov that you will be allowed to give a talk at the next meeting of the presidium."

"Yes, that is correct."

"Well, we have looked into the matter, and to this date, no foreign person has ever made a presentation at a meeting of the presidium. It's true that Vice President Velikhov is an important man, but he is not important enough to overcome such a lack of precedence."

Fredkin was speechless.

"So, you will not address the meeting of the presidium."

Not knowing how to reply, Fredkin simply said, "Thank you."

But the next day Fredkin got another call from the same person, who now told him that the talk was approved. Still, it was not easy. "When I arrived to give my talk, the acting president of the Academy of Sciences, someone whom I knew well and considered to be a friend, pointedly stood up, put his papers into his briefcase, slammed it shut, and stormed out, just as Gromyko had done, on occasion, at the United Nations."

Fredkin made every effort to break the ice. He told the audience about his family ties to Russia; his parents had been suppliers of wood for the imperial palace in St. Petersburg. He spoke of the large technology gap between the Soviet Union and the United States. He said computers were different: the performance-to-cost ratio improved by more than a factor of two every two years, making it uniquely different from any other kind of technology. But the suspicious audience first asked him why he cared about Soviet technological problems. Fredkin had a ready response, "My wife and I would feel safer back in Boston if the world remains relatively balanced."

Fredkin impressed the audience. Next Velikhov went to Staraya Ploshad, a city square where the headquarters of the party's Central Committee is located. He headed to a building right on the square, a big six-story neoclassical edifice with giant windows, built in 1914 for an insurance company. The top officials of the Central Committee had their offices there, and Velikhov had an appointment on the fourth floor to see Yuri Andropov. At the time Andropov, the KGB chief, had been elevated to become a secretary of the Central Committee, responsible for ideology; he was also sitting in for Brezhnev temporarily while the ailing general secretary was on holiday in Crimea. Velikhov asked for the meeting, an effort to overcome the resistance he faced to adopting personal computers in the Soviet Union.

The meeting with Andropov lasted an hour. "He was well prepared for the meeting, and he had his information from the foreign intelligence; it was obvious I didn't need to explain to him things from scratch," said Velikhov. He persuaded Andropov to form a new branch inside the Academy of Sciences, a section of information technologies and computation systems.

It was the same Andropov whose subordinates, a year before, had Kudryavtsev cut international phone lines. At that time nobody—and least of all Andropov—thought personal computers should be made available to ordinary Soviet citizens.

Back home Fredkin worked on lifting the US export controls on sending personal computers to the Soviet Union. He argued that personal computers would force the authorities to give up control over information, that they would jailbreak the prison. "I realized that nothing would happen until someone 'broke the ice.' I created 'Computerland USSR,' called Velikhov, and told him that if he would produce a purchase order for a small number of IBM PCs, I would arrange for them to be delivered and that that would open the floodgates," Fredkin recalled.

Velikhov immediately produced the purchase order. "Computerland USSR" ordered about sixty computers from IBM in Europe, and Fredkin got friends at the Academy of Sciences Computation Center to make sets of chips that would allow the computers to display Cyrillic characters on the screen (as they had already done for one PC smuggled earlier into the Computation Center). Fredkin's company took delivery in Europe, modified the keyboards and displays, got official clearance from the US Commerce Department, and delivered them to the Academy of Sciences. "The dam was broken," Fredkin recalled. "Computerland USSR may be the only computer company in history that received and delivered one single order . . . then went out of business!"

For almost the whole of its history the Soviet Union had been a prison of information. But the prison, like so many other edifices of the Soviet state, was finally breeched in August 1991. Then the information finally broke free.

CHAPTER 2

The First Connection

In the far north of Moscow the Kurchatov Institute sprawls over nearly 250 acres. Once an artillery range, the institute was founded by Igor Kurchatov, who developed the first Soviet atomic bomb within its walls. For decades since, the institute has also served as a preeminent nuclear research facility. The compound is dotted with dozens of buildings, including a collection of impressive two-story mansions built for Kurchatov and his fellow researchers in the late 1940s. A small and unobtrusive barracks-like building houses the first Soviet nuclear reactor, still operating. The institute has always been a closed, heavily guarded facility and to this day is protected by multiple guarded gates. When a visitor arrives, documents are checked and the car trunk is inspected by a guard carrying a Kalashnikov assault rifle. A second gate opens only when a first one is closed.[1]

The Kurchatov Institute held an exalted and exceptional status in the Soviet Union. It was at the forefront of research in the Soviet military nuclear program. In addition to work on the atomic bomb, scientists were involved in many crucial defense projects, ranging from Soviet nuclear submarines to laser weapons. The KGB not only supervised the institute but, in a broad sense, was "one of the shareholders," as Yevgeny Velikhov, who served as director from 1988 to 2008, recalled it.[2] At the same time, the institute enjoyed a degree of freedom unthinkable for others at facilities far less important. Contacts with foreigners were allowed, including trips abroad, and the institute's leaders took advantage of the fact that the Soviet state highly valued and desperately needed their work—they demanded special treatment and got it.

The institute exploited this elite status to the full. In November 1966 more than six hundred people, mostly young physicists, gathered at Kurchatov's House of Culture, the institute's club, to listen to Solzhenitsyn, a writer of growing prominence. His first published work, *One Day in the Life of Ivan Denisovich*, had caused a sensation for its frank depiction of Stalin's prison camps when it appeared in the literary journal *Novy Mir* in 1962. Velikhov, who was then a deputy head of the institute as well as a broad-minded scientist who had traveled across the United States a few years before, invited Solzhenitsyn to the Kurchatov Institute. The institute was the very first venue that invited Solzhenitsyn to speak publicly. "Everything went well," he recalled.[3] "He told his story. How he found himself in the camp." Solzhenitsyn also read aloud from a still-unpublished novel, *Cancer Ward*, which he hoped still had some chance to get approved by the Soviet censors. (In the end it was not.) Then he read the excerpts from *The First Circle*, his novel of the sharashka at Marfino, which also had not been published. The KGB had confiscated the manuscript in 1965, and reading it aloud at Kurchatov was a brave act for both Solzhenitsyn and his hosts. "The collective liked him very much," Velikhov said. Later, in 1970, Solzhenitsyn won the Nobel Prize for literature; four years after that he was stripped of citizenship and expelled from the Soviet Union. But the Kurchatov Institute did not change course and kept inviting dissident writers.

It was in this elite environment of relative freedom that programmers and physicists first connected the Soviet Union to the
Internet.

By the mid-1980s the computer revolution in the West was rac-
ing ahead, and the Soviet Union lagged behind. The country
struggled with the manufacturing challenge of computer chips,
and Soviet personal computers were bad imitations of Western
models. The Cold War persisted, and the astounding leaps in
computer technology in the West were catching the attention
of younger Soviet scientists, including Velikhov, but older party
leaders and industrialists—Brezhnev and Andropov's generation—were frustratingly indifferent. The technology gap between
East and West continued to widen. In 1985 Alexey Soldatov, then
thirty-four years old, was named director of the Computation
Center at the Kurchatov Institute. He got the job because Anatoly
Alexandrov, the Kurchatov director, wanted someone who could
explain to computer programmers what the Kurchatov Institute
needed from them.[4] Soldatov, Andrei's father, was a serious, heavily built scientist, spoke slowly because he stuttered badly. In a
determined effort to overcome it, he had developed a method to
think in advance what he wanted to say, and his speech became
very precise, if rather colorless.

Soldatov had a promising career in nuclear physics. He had
graduated from a prominent Moscow institute in 1975, defended
his doctoral thesis in 1979, then held an internship at the Niels
Bohr Institute in Copenhagen. He was known at the Kurchatov
Institute for using more computer time on his work than anyone else.

The Kurchatov Institute had, by that time, assembled a team
of skilled programmers working to adapt the Unix operating
system to the Soviet Union, a copy of which had been smuggled
to Moscow two years earlier. Unix is machine-independent, so it

could be used on any of the computers at Kurchatov, including Elbrus, the first Soviet super-computer, and the ES, a Soviet-made replica of the IBM mainframe. But what made Unix significant was that it made networks possible. In the autumn of 1984 the programmers demonstrated at a seminar the first version of a modified Unix.

The visionary behind the programming team, and one of the prize winners, was Valery Bardin, thirty-one years old, who was frequently overwhelmed by great and sometimes odd ideas, some of them truly brilliant.[5] When Soldatov heard about the adaptation of Unix and Bardin's band of programmers, he recalled how a network connected computers at the Niels Bohr Institute. Soldatov then proposed building a computer network, based on Unix, at the Kurchatov Institute.[6]

Over the next four years programmers from Kurchatov built a Russian version of Unix and applied it to a network.[7] It was named Demos, an acronym for the Russian words meaning "dialogue united mobile operating system," and the team was rewarded with a prize from the Soviet Council of Ministers. The prize, however, was classified as secret. The local Kurchatov network was created on some of the same protocols the Internet is built on today. While Bardin's programmers brought their brains to the project, Soldatov contributed his substantial administrative skills to persuade the institute's leaders to buy equipment they needed for the network. The Kurchatov Institute was so vast that it was easy to explain why it would be better to have computers in different buildings connected through a network than to install all the machines at the Computation Center. However, networks were rare then in the Soviet Union, which favored large, mainframe computers that were easier to control than a network of smaller, spread-out machines.

Over time the Kurchatov computer team split into two separate groups. Programmers wanted to seize the opportunity Gorbachev had provided when he agreed to launch "cooperatives," the first private businesses. They wanted to sell the Demos operation system, and for that they needed to be outside the heavily guarded Kurchatov compound. One group moved out of the institute and set up their computers on the second floor of a spacious two-story building on the Ovchinnovskaya Embankment along the Moscow River. In 1989 the group founded a cooperative, naming it Demos.

The second group remained at the Computation Center at the Kurchatov Institute, led by Soldatov. Despite the split, the two teams were closely interconnected—including by a network connection—as people moved constantly back and forth between the mansion and the institute.

In 1990 Soldatov and his team began to imagine they could get the institute connected with other research centers in the country. When they needed a name for this network, they asked a young programmer, Vadim Antonov, to run a random word-selection program in English. He came up with Relcom. When Antonov suggested this could signify "reliable communications," the name stuck.

In August of that year the Relcom network became a reality, making a connection between the Kurchatov Institute in Moscow and the Institute of Informatics and Automation in Leningrad, 460 miles away. After that, connections were established with research centers in Dubna, Serpukhov, and Novosibirsk. The network used ordinary telephone lines, and the bandwidth was extremely narrow—the network was capable only of exchanging simple e-mails. Nevertheless the Relcom team dreamed of connecting with the world. Soon after the first connections were made, Soldatov went to Velikhov, who became director of Kurchatov in 1988. He told Velikhov that he needed his personal help for a nationwide network that would connect the most important research centers in the country and beyond. Velikhov was skeptical at first. He recalled clearly how such initiatives had failed in the past. Nonetheless, when Soldatov told Velikhov he wanted to appropriate his personal phone line for the network, as it was the only direct line from the institute capable of making international calls, Velikhov agreed, along with helping them acquire modems.[8]

On August 28, 1990, the very first Soviet connection to the global Internet was made when the Kurchatov programmers exchanged e-mails with a university in Helsinki, Finland. Soon they were given access to EUnet, a European network. Finland was chosen for a reason: Finland was the only country after the Moscow Olympics in 1980 whose automatic international telephone connection remained. Then, on September 19, Antonov registered the domain .su on behalf of the Soviet association of Unix users, and a new frontier on the Internet was born.

At the end of 1990 Relcom connected thirty research organizations in the country. By the summer of 1991 it had a leased line to Helsinki, and the internal Soviet network had reached seventy cities, with over four hundred organizations using it, including universities, research institutes, stock and commodity exchanges, high schools, and government agencies. Relcom got its first client in the news media too: the young news agency Interfax.

Technically Relcom still had two headquarters. There were a few rooms on the third floor at the Computation Center at the Kurchatov Institute, which housed the main server, built on the IBM 386 personal computer. Modems at 9,600 bits per second—the baud rate—were permanently connected to the international phone line. The other headquarters was located in the nondescript mansion on the Moscow River embankment, with the second floor housing the team of fourteen Demos programmers, working night and day repairing and improving software and maintaining the network. They also had a backup server and a 9,600-baud modem.[9]

Early in the morning on August 19, 1991, a phone call woke Bardin at home. A journalist friend said he had heard from

Japanese contacts of an attempted coup against President Gorbachev. The news about the putsch broke first in the Far East, then rolled westward across the time zones before hitting Moscow. Hours after the announcement was first broadcast in the Far East it aired on television in Moscow.

Bardin's first reaction was to check the group's server from home. There was no connection. He went out to buy cigarettes.

On his way he met a friend from Leningrad (now St. Petersburg), Dmitry Burkov, a programmer and cofounder of Demos. Together they rushed to the Demos building, knowing there was always someone sitting there, day and night. They saw tanks on the streets of Moscow. Around 7 a.m., on the orders of the defense minister, Dmitry Yazov, who had joined the coup plotters, both tank units began moving into the city along parachute regiments in armored troop carriers. Strict censorship was imposed on the news media.

State television introduced Gennady Yanayev, a Soviet vice president and gray, unremarkable figure, as the new leader of the country. In fact, Yanayev was given this role only to make the ousting of Gorbachev look more legitimate. The real mastermind was Vladimir Kryuchkov, the chairman of the KGB, and the KGB had a prime role in orchestrating the coup. KGB special operations forces were dispatched to Crimea, where Gorbachev was on vacation. The KGB cut off Gorbachev's personal phone line from his vacation compound, then the local phone lines. He was totally isolated.

At the corner of Bolshaya Lubyanka Street and Varsonofyevsky Lane stands a six-story, gray building. It was built in the 1970s in the Soviet architectural style of that period for important government offices—monumental and gloomy, with the first floor in cold granite. Local residents knew that the building belonged to the secret services. After all, KGB buildings dotted the district of Lubyanka—just across the street there is a two-story mansion that housed the very first headquarters of Lenin's secret police, and in Stalin's times it was the location of a much-feared toxic laboratory tasked with developing poisons. Nobody dared ask what was going on inside the building at Varsonofyevsky Lane, assuming it could house one of the departments of the KGB.

But it was not a just any department; it was the KGB's telephone eavesdropping center. Underground cables ran from it to a neogothic, red-brick building two hundred meters away on Malutinsky Lane, Moscow's central and oldest phone station.[10]

In mid-August 1991 the building saw feverish activity. Similar frantic movements were also happening at the central phone station, where the Twelfth Department [eavesdropping] occupied a few rooms.

On August 15 Kryuchkov urgently summoned Yevgeny Kalgin, head of the Twelfth Department, from his summer vacation. Kalgin was promoted through the ranks of the KGB primarily for his personal loyalty to the chairman. Initially he had been Andropov's driver and later was made his personal assistant. When Kryuchkov, a close pupil of Andropov, had been appointed chairman of the KGB, he entrusted Kalgin, now a major-general, with running the Twelfth Department.[11] Kalgin went to KGB headquarters and received classified instructions from Kryuchkov to listen in on the phone conversations of people around Boris Yeltsin, who in June had been elected president of the Russian Federation, then still one of the internal republics of the Soviet Union, thrusting him into the forefront of the reform movement and into competition with Gorbachev for leadership. The KGB instructions were to eavesdrop on members of Yeltsin's government and friendly members of the parliament—both their offices and home lines. Kalgin was told to learn how Yeltsin's people reacted to events and to control their contacts. This eavesdropping was illegal even by Soviet standards: the KGB could not spy on high-ranking officials. However, in late

July the KGB had overheard Gorbachev speaking with Yeltsin, and they had agreed to dump the head of the KGB. Kryuchkov intended to get rid of Gorbachev first.

Kalgin agreed to make preparations. That would require a lot of work for the sixth bureau of the Twelfth Department—the "controllers" in KGB slang—mostly women in headphones whose work was to listen to and record telephone conversations. The next day, on August 16, Kalgin briefed the female colonel who was chief of the bureau, and she in turn recalled her subordinates from summer leave.

On August 17 Kryuchkov personally called Kalgin and ordered him to put Yanayev's phone line "under control" to make sure he stayed loyal to the cause. On August 18 Yeltsin returned to Moscow from Kazakhstan, and Kalgin was then told to put all of Yeltsin's phone lines "under control."[12] The chief of the bureau explained to the hand-picked controllers that information from intercepted calls was to be reported via the internal phone line personally to Kalgin. They were given 169 phone numbers. The fifth bureau of the Twelfth Department, in charge of listening to foreigners, were given 74 numbers.[13] With that, the eavesdropping operation had begun.[14] The same day Gorbachev was locked away in Crimea.

On August 19 the plotters declared emergency rule and took charge of the country, but Yeltsin and his supporters slipped through KGB security cordons and made it to an enormous white government building on the Moscow River, where they barricaded themselves inside. The building, which became known as the Russian White House, housed the Yeltsin government.

Andrei Soldatov, then fifteen years old, was in his last year of school before university when he heard the news of the coup. Ever since he was young Andrei had been interested in political history. His grandfather had been a Soviet Army colonel and a deputy commandant in Moscow whose duty was to march before the gun carriage bearing the body of a Politburo member during a state funeral, leading the procession to the Kremlin wall. Andrei remembered seeing his grandfather in full uniform on state television broadcasting the funerals of Brezhnev and Andropov. The advent of Gorbachev's *perestroika*—reform movement—had provoked vigorous arguments and debates in Andrei's family. His uncle was an Air Force colonel who had served in Afghanistan and was outraged by dissident physicist Andrei Sakharov's opposition to the Soviet invasion of Afghanistan. Soldatov's father, Alexey, the nuclear physicist, was a prime but cautious source of information about the Chernobyl nuclear accident, as the Kurchatov Institute remained the leading atomic research center of the Soviet Union. Andrei and his mother, a physician, were always the most liberal voices at the table.

On hearing news of the putsch, Andrei rushed to Manezhnaya Square, a traditional place for rallies by democrats and the reform movement. Tanks were lined up on the square, facing the Hotel Moskva. On the opposite side, close to the old Moscow State University building, students had gathered, shouting, "To Presnya, to Presnya"—the district where Yeltsin's supporters had taken their stand. Andrei and his schoolmate walked over to the tanks, trying to engage the soldiers in conversation. The soldiers, surrounded by civilians, were obviously confused. Their officers, also confused, did not interfere.

The last thing Andrei Soldatov was thinking about was calling his father, Alexey Soldatov; his parents had divorced when he was eight, and his relationship with his father was strained. But Andrei sensed the significance of what was happening and collected every piece of evidence he could. He saved issues of the newspaper *Moskovsky Komsomolets*, the most popular liberal daily in town. He grabbed a cover from a smoke-grenade discharger on the turret of the tank and took it home. He collected one of Yeltsin's leaflets.

"The country is in mortal danger!" it declared. "A group of Communist criminals has carried out a coup d'état. If today citizens

of Russia do not counter the activities of the putschists with conscience, determination and courage, then the dark days of Stalinism
will return!"

If you do not resist the state criminals—

—you betray FREEDOM!

—you betray RUSSIA!

—you betray YOURSELF!

At home Soldatov's mother had the radio tuned day and night
to Echo Moskvy, the radio station founded by democrats on the
Moscow city council and a primary source of information about
the events unfolding.

Irina Borogan also rushed to the square on her way home from
taking her university entrance examinations.

For Irina, perestroika had been a time of personal excitement.
She had been only eleven years old when it began, but it felt like
a breeze of fresh air. In her school rules were relaxed, making it
possible to voice personal opinions and have discussions about
politics and Soviet history with teachers. One day Irina, emboldened by the new atmosphere, began a fierce dispute with a deputy
principal in charge of ideology, a woman with strong communist
views. Irina felt the new mood everywhere—in a bus, on a com-
muter train, in the metro. For the first time in their lives, she noticed, many people were talking openly and freely not only about
their private lives but about everything, from the misery of living standards to Stalin's repressions and modern music. Western
movies, books, and music that for years had been prohibited now
flowed to the country. For Irina, newspapers and magazines became more breathtaking than crime novels. At the age of thirteen
she made a decision to become a journalist. She felt Gorbachev's

glasnost—policy of openness and transparency—was a great gift
to her generation.

When she learned of the putsch, she feared that the coup leaders might destroy all the good things Gorbachev had done over
the last five years. Her father, who worked at a closed facility in
the military-industrial complex, said, "If they ban us from getting
Western investments, our economy will die." Irina didn't care a
lot about the investments, but she felt angry with the coup leaders
who threatened to turn back the clock and suffocate her generation. During the coup attempt she was out and about among
Moscow's squares, where people gathered and talked. On the second day she took her university entry exam on history, and the
question posed to her concerned Stalin's repressions. The teachers were liberal and talked angrily about the putschists. So Irina
asked, with a smile, "Do you want me to answer in the old way or
in the new one?"

They all laughed, and she passed the exam.

By coincidence, the putsch began on the opening day of a Moscow computer expo. The nascent business of Relcom/Demos
had a stand at the show, and some programmers were milling
about there. The first thing Bardin did when he arrived at the
Demos two-story building was to call the expo and order everyone to return to the office as quickly as possible with their equipment. The network connection had been off because of technical
problems, but it was soon restored. As chief of the team based at
the Demos building, Bardin took over.

That day Alexey Soldatov, head of the Kurchatov office, was
far out of town, in Vladikavkaz in the North Caucasus. When he
heard of the putsch, he called Bardin at once and asked, "What's
going on?"

"The network is running like clockwork," Bardin replied.

"Look, you do understand that we all could go to jail, don't you?"

"Sure. We are working as always," Bardin said.

"Great," said Soldatov. They understood each other. Then Soldatov called his people at the Computation Center. To both teams he insisted on one thing and one thing only: *keep the line open!* Someone at the Computation Center suggested they attempt to print up Yeltsin's proclamations, but Soldatov was adamant: focus on maintaining the connection—this was vital. Velikhov, the Kurchatov director, was on trip to a physics conference in Sicily, and there was no way to get in touch with him.

A few hours later Bardin received a call from a friend in Vienna who had sold computers to their business. "Look, Valery, I don't think they can really make the coup stick," the friend asserted.

"Why?" Bardin asked.

"Because we are talking on the phone," the friend said. "And all coups begin with cutting off telephone lines."

In an hour a guest knocked on the door of the office at the Demos building and said he was a representative of the Yeltsin team. He said he was looking for the commercial offices that had Xerox machines to help them disseminate Yeltsin's appeals. The man had no idea what kind of office he had just entered.

"Forget about Xerox," Bardin told him. "We are connected with all big cities, plus with the West."

The Yeltsin man slipped away, without another word. Then another Yeltsin envoy appeared at the building and declared authoritatively that they were now all under command of Konstantin Kobets, who had been deputy chief of the Soviet general staff for communications, a Yeltsin supporter, now appointed to lead the resistance. However, Bardin had no idea who Kobets was, and it was the first and last time Bardin heard of Kobets during the three days of the putsch attempt. This second envoy also brought with him some copies of Yeltsin's statements and asked Bardin to distribute them through the Relcom channels. Simultaneously a direct line was opened with the St. Petersburg government, which supported Yeltsin.

The Internet connection to cities outside of Moscow and beyond the borders of the Soviet Union proved extremely important, circulating proclamations from Yeltsin and other democrats around the world. The main channel was a user group, talk.politics .soviet, available on UseNet, one of the first worldwide collections of Internet newsgroups, built on many different servers and thus not reliant on just one. It was full of angry and worried messages posted by Westerners. From Moscow, at around 5 p.m. on August 19, Vadim Antonov, the bespectacled twenty-six-year-old senior programmer who had helped Relcom find a name, posted a message: "I've seen the tanks with my own eyes. I hope we'll be able to communicate during the next few days. Communists cannot rape Mother Russia once again!"[15]

Westerners sent messages of support to Yeltsin, and by that night in Moscow, or mid-day in the United States, American support was surging onto the network as more participants from the United States took part. The network soon became overloaded, causing the connection to drop momentarily. Alexey Soldatov, worried and obsessed, was hanging on the phone with Bardin and kept demanding that he must do anything to keep the connection alive. Antonov posted another message: "Please stop flooding the only narrow channel with bogus messages with silly questions. Note that it's neither a toy nor a means to reach your relatives or friends. We need the bandwidth to help organize the resistance. Please, do not (even unintentionally) help these fascists!"

By then Relcom was busy disseminating news releases from the independent Soviet news agency Interfax along with news from Echo Moskvy radio, the Russian Information Agency, Northwest Information Agency (Leningrad), and Baltfax, all outlawed by the putschists.

O n the morning of August 20 CNN carried a report that shocked Relcom's team. A CNN correspondent declared that despite censorship, a large amount of uncensored information was flowing out of the Soviet capital and then showed a computer screen along with the address of the Relcom news group. Bardin and Soldatov believed it was later pulled off the air only because someone in the United States explained to CNN that broadcasting their address could endanger the source of information.

The next morning Polina, Vadim Antonov's wife, also a Demos programmer, wrote to a worried friend, Larry Press, who was professor of computer information systems at California State University.

> Dear Larry,
>
> Don't worry, we're OK, though frightened and angry. Moscow
> is full of tanks and military machines—I hate them. They try to
> close all mass media, they stopped CNN an hour ago, and Soviet
> TV transmits opera and old movies. But, thank Heaven, they
> don't consider RELCOM mass media or they simply forgot about
> it. Now we transmit information enough to put us in prison for
> the rest of our life.
>
> Cheers,
>
> Polina

Polina at first intended to go to the center of the action—the White House—with her laptop to report from there, but decided against it because phone connections were unreliable. Instead, she began to translate the news from the West that Larry sent regularly about the coup for Russians.[16]

Around this time state television announced Decree No. 3 from the coup plotters, restricting information exchanged with the West. The decree called for all Russian television and radio suspended, including the new democratic radio station Echo Moskvy, which had been essential to the resistance. The coup plotters declared that radio and television broadcasts were "not conducive to the process of stabilizing the situation in the country." The decree was broad, intending to shut down all channels of communication in the country, and gave the KGB a role in enforcing it.

Despite the threat, at Demos there was no debate about Decree No. 3: they were determined to keep the line open, knowing they were taking great personal risks. "We were already on the losing side," Bardin recalled, "just because information exchange is what Relcom was all about. We would be the enemies of the regime anyway, no matter what we did."

Bardin, Soldatov, and their programmers, all in their late twenties and thirties, had accomplished significant career breakthroughs in the years of Gorbachev's revolutionary changes. Each of them knew they owed much of their success to Gorbachev's glasnost. They were furious that it could all be ruined by a bunch of backward-thinking generals and sclerotic bureaucrats who had locked up Gorbachev in Crimea and were trying to dispose of Yeltsin in Moscow.

At the same time, Yeltsin's people desperately exploited every opportunity to spread the word about resistance to Russian citizens. Vladimir Bulgak served under Yeltsin as the minister of communications for Russia. He had spent his career in radio, starting as a mechanic, and had risen to become chief of the Moscow radio network. In the 1980s he was put in charge of the finances of the Ministry of Communications and, as a result, saw the underside of the centrally planned economy. Bulgak despised

Soviet methods of managing the communications industry. In 1990 he joined Yeltsin's team.

On the day before the coup attempt, Bulgak went on holiday to Yalta, in Crimea. When he saw the coup plotters' announcement on television, he called Ivan Silaev, Yeltsin's prime minister, asking what he should do.[17]

"Where you think the minister should be at such a moment?" replied Silaev. "In Moscow!"

On August 20 Bulgak was on the first plane to the capital. When he landed, his driver took him from the airport to Yeltsin's headquarters at the White House, bypassing the main roads filled with tanks and troops. At the White House Bulgak was told that his main objective must be to turn on radio transmitters and broadcast Yeltsin's proclamation of defiance. "Yeltsin told me to turn on all middle-wave radio transmitters on the European part of Russia," Bulgak said. These middle-wave transmitters were the main broadcast option in the Soviet Union and, with coverage of 370 miles each, were installed all over the country.

It was a difficult task, as all radio transmitters were not under the control of Yeltsin's government but rather under the control of the Soviet Ministry of Communications, a higher level. "Only three people in the Union's Ministry knew the passwords, and without a password, a chief of a transmitter never turns on his station," Bulgak said. He was able to get the passwords from a personal friend.

Then, through his own contacts, Bulgak managed to get a mobile radio transmitter on a truck to be driven from Noginsk, thirty-seven miles from Moscow, right to the courtyard of the White House where Yeltsin was holed up. It was immediately turned on; in case all else failed, they could at least broadcast Yeltsin's appeal to the center of the Russian capital. However, the electronic warfare's detachments were urgently deployed in the southwestern district of Moscow to jam the broadcast of Bulgak's mobile station. Another military station, in Podolsk, was tasked to intercept broadcasts from Yeltsin's station and report them to the coup commanders.[18]

Bulgak worked feverishly through the night, using his personal contacts inside the union's ministry. By the morning of August 21 the transmitters were turned on. When Yeltsin walked down the steps of the White House, he spoke into a microphone that was directly connected to Bulgak's activated transmitters. The people at the Soviet Union Ministry of Communications were stunned—Bulgak had triumphed.[19]

On the afternoon of August 21 Kryuchkov told Kalgin to stop the eavesdropping on Yeltsin and his people and destroy all the records.[20]

As Bulgak got Yeltsin his transmitters, Relcom went further. On the first day of the coup someone in Bardin's team came up with an idea they called "Regime N1": to ask all subscribers of Relcom to look out the window and write back exactly what they saw—just the facts, no emotions. Soon Relcom received a kaleidoscopic picture of what was happening throughout the country, disseminating the eyewitness reports from subscribers along with news reports. It became clear that the tanks and troops were present only in two cities—Moscow and Leningrad—and the coup would not succeed.

The coup attempt collapsed on August 21. Overall, during the three days, Relcom transmitted forty-six thousand "news units" throughout the Soviet Union and around the world. Regime No. 1 was a revolutionary idea, although not everyone realized it. Radio transmitters spread information in one direction, outward. But Relcom worked in both directions, spreading and collecting information. It was a horizontal structure, a network, a powerful new concept in a country that had been ruled by a rigid, controlling clique. In the 1950s, the first Soviet photocopy machine had been wrecked because it threatened to spread information beyond the control of those who ruled. Now the power of those rulers was being smashed—by a network they could not control.

Another principle was also demonstrated during the coup: the programmers did what they thought was right and did not ask permission. Antonov didn't wait for Bardin to post his messages, Bardin didn't ask Soldatov what he should do, and Soldatov didn't seek Velikhov's authorization. The announcement that they were "under command" of Kobets was laughable to them. They were freethinking and spirited, and they never wanted to return to the stultifying command of party hierarchies in which everything required permission from above.

Bulgak, a member of Yeltsin's group, certainly played the game the old way. He used his position, his connections, and his power to support his leader. But Bardin, Soldatov, and Antonov were too far from the Kremlin to believe they were part of any power game. They acted because the free flow of information—their core conviction—was threatened. They also knew that they had the support of thousands of subscribers making the network stronger.

From the first day of the coup Bardin worried about the KGB. He was certain they had put the Demos building under surveillance days before the coup attempt began. He even saw a lone man standing out in front of the building. But the KGB never bothered once to interfere with Russia's first connection to the Internet, neither at Demos nor at the Computation Center of the Kurchatov Institute. But at that moment and in years to come the KGB never went away. They were always keeping an eye on this strange and powerful new method for spreading information—but had great difficulty understanding it.

CHAPTER 3

Merlin's Tower

The collapse of the August putsch freed Soviet citizens from Communist Party control. By December the Soviet Union dissolved. In the suddenness of the moment old Soviet rules seemed to be obsolete and new democratic rules were not yet established. At onc point the KGB organized excursions in its headquarters for foreign tourists, as if showing off a relic from another era. Foreigners flooded Moscow and other big cities, private businesses emerged everywhere, and for a while new "joint ventures" were being established at every turn with foreign investors.

Yet it was also evident in these turbulent times that freedom brought something to Russia not very familiar to its citizens from all the years of Soviet paternalism: the freedom to make choices. Few were prepared, including those engaged in the most Westernized area of business, the rapidly evolving technology of computers, networks, and communications.

The Russian minister of communications, Vladimir Bulgak, who had brought the radio transmitter to the courtyard of the White House during the coup, confronted a monumental

set of problems. He had taken over the Soviet ministry of communications, moving in to the same headquarters office used
by Kudryavtsev at the Central Telegraph building. Bulgak soon
faced the same cursed legacy of international communications
that had vexed Kudryavtsev for so many years.[1] New Russian
business enterprises were desperate for more communications
lines and connectivity, and their demands far outstripped the
existing analog infrastructure. The Soviet Union earlier and,
now, Russia, simply did not have enough lines to the outside
world. In 1991 Russia had only two thousand international lines
for the whole country, and all of these lines were analog, copper
cables.

Bulgak's first big headache was to acquire long-distance fiber-
optic cable. Bulgak realized that his only option was to build
fiber-optic lines with foreign money and foreign partners. He
moved quickly and secured from President Yeltsin the right to
sign off on government guarantees for foreign credits. Almost
immediately Bulgak got Japan and Denmark involved. The partners built a fiber-optic cable from St. Petersburg to Vladivostok
and from Moscow to Dzhubga near the Black Sea, and then the
cables were laid to connection points of international telecommunications traffic: from St. Petersburg to Copenhagen, from
Dzhubga under the Black Sea to Istanbul, and then to Palermo,
Italy, and from Vladivostok through Nakhodka to Tokyo and
Seoul. The whole project took three years and cost $520 million.
Of the total, $500 million came from Japan and the rest from
Denmark.

"The demand was huge. We thought these lines will be loaded
in fifteen years, and that happened in five years," Bulgak recalled.[2]
Sometime later, when Bulgak met Nikolai Ryzhkov, who had
served as prime minister under Gorbachev, Bulgak underscored
how he had done what the Soviet Union had not. "Look, you
know, what did it cost me? $520 million. That's for everything.
And you were the prime minister of the entire Soviet Union, and

what was $520 million to you? It was nothing! Why could you not do it?" Ryzhkov did not have an answer.[3]

In three years, during a period of intense upheaval, Bulgak managed to increase the number of international lines in the country to sixty-six thousand, all of them digital.

An even more trying problem was to install modern phone stations all over the country. "Our industry then lagged behind the West by twenty to twenty-five years in producing the local phone stations, both international and intercity," said Bulgak. "We came to think that our industry would never catch up, and that meant we had to go and buy." In three or four years over 70 percent of all Russian intercity phone stations were replaced by modern digital ones, made in the West.

By 1995 Russia had established modern, national communications.

Meanwhile, at the Kurchatov Institute, scientists faced their own obstacles. The phone bills for the open line to Finland were costing around 20,000 rubles a month—an ordinary Soviet-made car could be bought then for 45,000 rubles. Where could engineers and physicists go to find money to keep the connection open? These scientists were products of the Soviet Union, shaped by it, even though they recognized its failures and shortcomings. Private entrepreneurship had been outlawed in Soviet times, and the scientists had no concept of how to run a business. The two teams, one at Kurchatov Institute and the other at Demos, clashed constantly over the way to make the network profitable. Vadim and Polina Antonov, who were among the early participants at the Demos building, soon decided to move to Berkeley, California, leaving in December 1991, the month the Soviet flag came down over the Kremlin.[4]

Finally the two teams divorced. The group on the embankment, which had started the cooperative Demos, transformed it into an Internet service provider (ISP) of the same name. Demos had a special department in charge of selling personal computers, a very profitable business in the early 1990s, and the profits were used to fund the ISP.

The other team, headed by Alexey Soldatov at the institute, registered Relcom as a joint stock company—a company owned by its shareholders—in July 1992. The Kurchatov Institute was listed among the founders, and Velikhov was made chairman of the board. Soldatov, who kept his position as chief of the Institute's Computation Center, was elected president, and Valery Bardin became his deputy and a development director. The idea was to launch the company to provide access to the Internet as a nationwide service.

But in 1992 no one knew much about launching a private enterprise.

There was one person, however, who seemed to know. Anatoly Levenchuk, a flamboyant engineer from Rostov, was a libertarian, obsessed with the idea of a free market. Levenchuk was a sparkplug of a man—short, energetic, driven by ideas. He favored extravagant outfits and spoke in a high-pitched, rapid-fire voice.

Levenchuk was the most agile and informed expert in the nascent Russian stock market. He got connected to the Internet early, in the winter of 1990–1991. Because of his indomitable energy, many enthusiasts went to him with business ideas, often involving establishing computer networks. To all of them Levenchuk put two questions. First, could he subscribe immediately? Second, did the network have access to the IBM network VNET? (At the time the Internet was still a collection of smaller networks, and VNET, which was based on IBM technology, was one of them.)[5] Usually the response was that the network was to be started in a few months, access to VNET was impossible, and then the enthusiasts disappeared. Finally someone referred Levenchuk to a contact who could say "yes" to both questions and gave him the home phone number of Valery Bardin of Relcom—Levenchuk called that evening. Bardin said Relcom had access to VNET, but he didn't know how to sell to Levenchuk access to the network. It was a very basic business transaction, but the physicists simply did not have the know-how. Levenchuk subsequently helped write the contracts for Relcom to sell Internet access, and in the winter of 1991 he got an e-mail address provided by Relcom, one of the first 150 e-mail accounts in the country.

Levenchuk also showed up at the Relcom offices. Soldatov had wisely opened the office just outside the walls of the Kurchatov Institute, on the next street. Levenchuk told Soldatov how to write a development plan for the new company. The project attracted some investment—actually several tens of thousands of dollars—from Rinako, a large Russian investment firm, which, in return, got a share of ownership in Relcom, and Levenchuk was given a seat on the board of directors. Soldatov also asked Levenchuk to serve as a consultant. The first thing Levenchuk advised him to do was to look for serious Western investors—foreign investment could give the company a real chance to expand in the nascent Internet market.

But Soldatov was cautious. The unresolved question hung over them: Where to get money? Everyone sensed that the market for the Internet would be huge, but they weren't sure how to go about it. In 1992 a third ISP, Sovam-Teleport, entered the scene, backed by the billionaire George Soros and the British telecom company Cable & Wireless. Almost immediately the new provider captured a third of the market. Meanwhile Demos was churning profits by selling personal computers. Soldatov faced a question he didn't know how to answer: How could he turn Relcom into an expanding business?

Bulgak solved the problem of connecting Russia with the outside world, but there was something else Internet users in Russia urgently needed. The horizontal structure of the Internet meant that the networks needed common points to exchange traffic. Also, the users needed more sustainable connections with the West, as most traffic in those days went back and forth to Western countries. Although Bulgak had established the sixty-six thousand digital lines, connecting to them from inside the country was still cumbersome and not always reliable. In 1995 Relcom, Demos, and the Moscow State University's network went to M9, the very first Moscow station that provided automatic international connections for the 1980 Olympics. The ISPs asked for help.

Mikhail Elistratov, the main engineer of the Moscow Internet exchange point, who has worked in the M9 building since 1995, explained, "There is the ring of intercity phone cables around Moscow, and M9 sits on that ring—along with a few other hubs, like M10 or M5. Out of them there are rays of cables laid to the west, east and so on. These cables, then copper, were very thick underground cables and provided connection in the particular direction, so if you need Novosibirsk, which is on the East, you get to the M10, and if you need the West, you get to the M9. And the M9 could always be connected with M10 and so on." The fact that M9 was pointing toward the West and relatively new made it the logical choice to be the exchange point for the Internet in Russia.[6]

Relcom already had some modems at the station providing a direct connection to the Kurchatov Institute via copper cable, and the M9's main engineer, Vladimir Gromov, agreed to give the Internet networks space on the twelfth floor at the top of the building. "It all started on the twelfth floor, even the first Moscow mobile operator got a space there because everyone wanted to be close to each other to get interconnected," Elistratov recalled.

The gathering on the twelfth floor became Russia's first Internet exchange point, named MSK-IX. It was manned by a bunch of engineers who were given tables surrounded by telecommunications racks in a corner of the same floor. They were working for an organization, affiliated with Kurchatov, that was in charge of registering domain names in the .su and .ru zones of the Internet.

The MSK-IX was to become the main Internet exchange point in Russia for years to come.

Speed was everything for Bulgak. In the hurry to modernize, he bought equipment from abroad, bypassing old Soviet factories, which were forced to close. Bulgak didn't worry about their fate, but there was one organization that did concern him: the successor to the KGB, known in the early 1990s as the Ministry of Security. The ministry inherited the antiquated, analog systems of phone tapping from the Soviet KGB. The first time Bulgak went to the headquarters—located at the Lubyanka, the old KGB building—he pressed them for answers about modernizing the telephone lines. "I told them we are destroying analog lines and replacing them with digital lines. Understand? They said they understood," Bulgak recalled. Next he asked whether the ministry was ready to install digital interception equipment. The ministry responded by asking him to buy Western-made telephone stations that would have the intercept option built in, the kind available in the West for use by police departments. "We bought the stations, and the security service took them," Bulgak said. "What they did with them, I don't know." At a meeting with the minister of security Bulgak said he intended to keep modernization running at a fast pace. "Are you keeping up with our pace?" he asked. "If not, tell me and I will slow down."

The minister replied, "We will not slow you down. We can keep up with you."

The Ministry of Security got the job of phone and postal interception under a secret decree that was issued on June 22, 1992. Two days later Bulgak signed the paperwork giving the Ministry of Security access to communications cables and places where they could work to intercept calls.[7] When Bulgak went to Lubyanka again, he asked the same question: "Are you keeping up with us? Is there any direction where we need to slow down?" The answer was the same: "No, we are keeping up."

In fact, the security services were lagging way behind.

Ⅰn the aftermath of the Soviet collapse Yeltsin wanted to establish something like the West's intelligence community rather than just a purged version of the old KGB, which had been responsible for everything from counterintelligence to foreign espionage to government communications to guarding borders. In 1991 the KGB was split into a handful of independent security agencies. The largest, initially called the Ministry of Security, then the Federal Service of Counter-Intelligence, or FSK, would be responsible for counterespionage and counterterrorism. In 1995 it was renamed into the Federal Security Service, or FSB. Then the KGB's former foreign intelligence directorate was transformed into a new espionage agency called the Foreign Intelligence Service, or SVR. The division of the KGB responsible for electronic eavesdropping and cryptography became the Committee of Government Communication, later called the Federal Agency for Government Communications and Information, or FAPSI. Directorates that had once been in charge of guarding secret underground facilities and protecting Soviet leaders as well as a branch responsible for borders were made into independent agencies.

The names changed, but as we wrote in *The New Nobility* in 2010, the shift from "K" to "B" at the end of the acronym of the FSB was more than symbolic. The renamed service was given a broad mandate to become the guardian of "security" for the new Russia.[8] The FSB regained its investigative directorate, which it had lost after the Soviet collapse, and would function both as a secret service and a law enforcement agency. On July 5, 1995, Yeltsin signed an act into law giving the FSB even more powers to conduct surveillance and interception. The only external control over the security services was the General Prosecutor's Office, a special body responsible for overseeing all the secret services. But the prosecutor's jurisdiction was limited.[9]

The multiple security services that arose out of the Soviet KGB were, at first, in a state of uncertainty. No one had given them a real sense of mission. The job of protecting the Soviet party-state, so central to the KGB, was obviously gone, leaving only a vacuum of ideology and a clear loss of focus. By 1995, however, the agencies began to regain their footing. They also began to struggle fiercely with each other, provoked by the fractured, competitive system Yeltsin created to keep the services under control. After obtaining a report from the FSB director, Yeltsin often compared it with reports from other security services. The process was a far cry from the concept of intelligence oversight in democracies and more like the competition of viziers in the medieval Middle East or Napoleon's France, where several secret police agencies spied on each other.

As the 1996 elections approached, in which Yeltsin was running for another term against a Communist Party leader, Gennady Zyuganov, the security services competed with each other to keep Yeltsin in power, and their proposals were hardly democratic. The FSB and Alexander Korzhakov's service proposed that the election simply be canceled, which was not accepted. FAPSI, in turn, held a very strong card: the agency controlled the information system the Central Election Commission used to accumulate data from polling stations during national elections, built in 1995.

At Relcom Soldatov and Bardin were constantly arguing about the company's future, prompting Bardin to leave for a new, online project called the National News Service. It was to be a combination of a news agency and the first electronic archive of news media, launched by the daily newspaper *Kommersant*.

Soldatov had to figure out Relcom's future alone. Then, at a birthday party for Velikhov at the Kurchatov Institute on February 2, 1995, a new and unexpected overture appeared. The fifty-five-year-old director of FAPSI, Alexander Starovoitov, suggested in Velikhov's presence that Soldatov become his adviser, with the specific goal of creating a large new business network. Relcom would use FAPSI encryption equipment as well as hardware and software to protect information so to create a secure channel for business communications in the country. Soldatov immediately accepted the offer.

Yeltsin had signed a decree that declared illegal any encryption software or hardware device that did not bear FAPSI's seal of approval, therefore giving significant control of the market to FAPSI, which also offered its own encryption systems for sale. Such a two-faced approach—a government agency leveraging its power for profit—was hardly unusual in the new Russia at a time when it seemed there were few rules about such behavior and even fewer rules that were enforced. But behind the offer to Soldatov were unseen motives: the agency wanted to create its own network and make big money by using Relcom's expertise.

Soldatov had been a member of the independent-minded group at Kurchatov that had created the first networks and had been somewhat disdainful of the old guard in the last days of the Soviet Union. But now a different government and a different system were rising. He wholeheartedly supported Yeltsin and believed that the new regime legitimately needed security services. As long as FAPSI served Yeltsin loyally, he did not see them as a threat. Moreover, the language used by the generals who ran the security services seemed to have changed with the times—they were suddenly fluent in the vocabulary of contracts and business deals. Besides, Soldatov was confident he could outsmart the security services. He remembered a few years earlier, when they had demanded that he print out everything that came through Relcom's network, he simply said, "Okay, but first, please give me a few hundred printers and huge barracks to keep the stuff." They went away and never returned.

In the first half of the 1990s Bulgak's Ministry of Communications seemed preoccupied with laying cables and replacing phone stations, not with the promise of the Internet. FAPSI was the only government agency interested in the Internet, and that also had a big influence on Soldatov's decision to do business with them. Relcom had found its backer: a government security service.

Anatoly Levenchuk, however, wasn't happy. "I still think it was one of my biggest failures," he said. "I failed to explain to them that money should not come from the state."

In April 1995 Sergei Parkhomenko, a thirty-one-year old reporter for the daily newspaper *Segodnya*, had a very hot story. He was a well-known political journalist who frequently appeared on television. In a biting column that appeared on April 8, he called the lower house of parliament, the State Duma, a circus of clowns, a "crowd of buffoons," and parliament fired back on April 15 with a reprimand, making Parkhomenko even more popular among readers.[10] His career was on the rise. The owner of *Segodnya* was Vladimir Gusinsky, the media tycoon and one of the first Russian oligarchs. Shortly before this, Gusinsky had made an offer to underwrite a new weekly newsmagazine with Parkhomenko as the editor.

A tall, large man with thick dark hair and a beard, Parkhomenko could not be ignored for long anywhere; his loud voice and expressive manner always attracted attention. But he was hardly a muckraker. In April he found himself in a very tricky situation he was not accustomed to: the story he had reported was a startling exposé of the growing influence of the presidential security service led by Yeltsin's sidekick, Korzhakov. The article pulled away the curtain on the ways in which the security service was interfering in political decisions at the highest levels and, when published, would probably cause a stir. Parkhomenko tried to get it printed in *Segodnya*, but the deputy editor, without explanation, delayed publication.

At the time, Yeltsin was enmeshed in the first Chechen war, and Korzhakov had threatened Gusinsky when his television station, NTV, broadcast vivid coverage of the war. After Korzhakov's men raided his offices the previous December, Gusinsky fled to London. With Gusinsky out of the country, the editorial office was now hesitant.

Korzhakov was a dark figure, a general with narrow views but vaulting ambitions. He had started his career as an officer in the KGB's Ninth Department, charged with protecting highly placed Soviet officials, and had been assigned to Yeltsin. He remained loyal to Yeltsin for years and kept guarding him, even after Yeltsin quit the Communist Party and Korzhakov was fired from the KGB. In the days of the August coup in 1991 Korzhakov was among those in Yeltsin's entourage whose phones were tapped by Kalgin's KGB department. In turn, Yeltsin rewarded Korzhakov by naming him chief of the presidential security service. Korzhakov was certain that KGB methods could be applied to everything, from the economy to politics. He wanted to turn his agency into a powerful structure on its own, one that could sway politics, control government ministers, and pressure the new Russian oligarchs. From his Kremlin office Korzhakov had his subordinates interfere in business disputes and had the power to conduct all kinds of surveillance.

Parkhomenko had spent months researching his story, and he didn't want it to die. Frustrated by the silence at *Segodnya*, he went to the newspaper *Izvestia*, a popular democratic daily. "I offered them the story, and they agreed to publish it," Parkhomenko recalled. "They even made the layout of a double-page spread." But Parkhomenko soon realized that *Izvestia* was also holding it up. At home he stashed away two page proofs of his story—one from *Segodnya* and one from *Izvestia*—but he still had nothing in print.

The story was so sensitive and the climate so uncertain that Parkhomenko thought it was time to hide some of his research so the security services could not seize it if they attempted to target him. He was also contributing to Agence France-Press, so one day he went to the Moscow office of AFP with all the documentation and his records. There was a tiny room occupied by the bookkeeping office, and contributors' files were stored there. Parkhomenko said he needed to examine his files and then hid all his records there for safekeeping. "I thought it very unlikely for someone to look for the documentation about the Presidential Security Service in the bookkeeping office of the AFP," Parkhomenko sighed.[11]

In late April 1995 Parkhomenko, increasingly frustrated, decided to approach the newspaper *Moskovskie Novosti*. It was located on Pushkin Square in the center of Moscow, with the newspaper's title proudly emblazoned on the roof. The Russian-language weekly was launched as part of the propaganda effort around the Moscow Olympics in 1980, but during Gorbachev's perestroika period, under editor Yegor Yakovlev, the weekly became an independent and vocal alternative to the official Soviet press. In the late 1980s Muscovites crowded every Wednesday around the stands by the entrance to the offices of *Moskovskie Novosti*, where pages of the weekly were displayed to read and discuss the latest edition. In the mid-1990s its predominance faded, but the paper remained a respected voice, with strong democratic traditions.

Parkhomenko went directly to the second floor, to the office of the editor Viktor Loshak, and brought his story with him.[12] Loshak read the story and at once summoned his deputies.[13] They, in turn, read the story, and the paper didn't hesitate: Parkhomenko's story was made up in pages, now of *Moskovskie Novosti* design, and this time it was published. But because it was huge, the investigation came out as a two-part series, called "Merlin's Tower."[14]

Parkhomenko's investigation exposed—in a way the public had never seen before—the fearsome atmosphere in the offices where power was held in Russia, including the White House, the Kremlin, and Staraya Ploshad, where the presidential adminis- tration was headquartered. In his story Parkhomenko described how presidential advisers conducted sensitive conversations by exchanging notes on scraps of paper, which they quickly burned, fearful that their offices were bugged by the Presidential Security Service. Parkhomenko described how he was forced to keep walk- ing briskly with his highly placed contacts when in these corridors of power because the officials were certain the Korzhakov service could not switch the microphones so quickly. Only a few years since the death of the KGB and the Soviet police state, paranoia was rampant among high-placed bureaucrats. "When one offi- cial showed me to his office he took two pencils and put them in a keyhole of a big safe in the corner. He appeared to be certain there was a video camera inside," Parkhomenko wrote.

The publication of "Merlin's Tower" marked an important turning point, revealing the extent to which Yeltsin had begun to rely on people and organizations of the security services. Memo- ries of the Soviet Union were still fresh, and the idea that surveil- lance and eavesdropping was again being deployed in the new, more democratic environment was deeply unsettling.

Korzhakov met the articles with silence, Parkhomenko went back to the bookkeeping offices of AFP and retrieved his re- search files, and after his reelection triumph in 1996, Yeltsin fired Korzhakov. Although this removed one figure from the palace in- trigues, the jockeying for power never ceased. Yeltsin, struggling with health issues and alcoholism, was still surrounded by fam- ily, staff, oligarchs, and politicians who pulled him in every di- rection. Nonetheless, Yeltsin's 1996 reelection victory seemed to bar a return to the totalitarian Soviet past. A period of optimism prevailed.

These were the months when we first walked through the doors of the newspaper *Segodnya* as reporters. Andrei was twenty years old, Irina twenty-one. We thought it was the best thing that ever happened in our lives. We knew that Gusinsky, the powerful media magnate, owned *Segodnya* and modeled it after the *New York Times*, bringing in very influential political journalists, including Parkhomenko, Mikhail Leontiev, Tatyana Malkina, and Olga Romanova. Romanova, in her late twenties then, amazed everybody with her speed and precision; she rushed in the room, had all stories for the economics page edited in two hours, wrote her own story, made a dozen calls, and then rushed out to meetings.

The newspaper had the best culture department in town. The offices on Leningradsky Highway occupied part of the building of the Moscow Aviation Institute. We saw it as a gateway to the new, modern, and Westernized world. The walls were painted white, and the tables were black with sleek Macintosh computers on them, a striking contrast to Soviet-style offices of other Moscow newspapers, which had faded, wood-paneled walls, slamming metal doors, and pneumatic tubes for delivering typewritten articles. Irina joined the paper three months before Andrei, and by the time Andrei arrived, she had already written critically about municipal policy under Moscow's powerful mayor, Yuri Luzhkov.

Many of the journalists were young like us. The head of Andrei's department was Andrei Grigoriev, who, at twenty-six years old, was considered an experienced journalist. He exposed the vulnerability of prominent banks and was sent for a few months to Europe because the editors thought his life was in danger. Both of us felt the excitement—and a sense that we almost missed the last train—about reading courageous dispatches from the Chechen war by Masha Eismont, who was then twenty-one years old.

Rossiyskaya Gazeta, a newspaper owned by the government, had also approached Andrei. He decided to talk to them. A stiff and officious deputy editor, a woman in her fifties, told him about what kind of future he could expect at there, that after three years he could expect to be given a special press card with the words "Administration of the President" on it, which, she said, would make him very proud. She didn't mention the topic he would be reporting on, saying he would be attached to the city news section. It was such a striking contrast to *Segodnya*, where Andrei immediately was given a topic for reporting—information technology—and told he was to cover it alone. Andrei felt excited: it basically meant he could define the policy of such an influential daily newspaper on this burgeoning subject. (Though his father was not particularly thrilled and told him "to leave his field" after reading a critical article Andrei wrote on FAPSI. After that they didn't talk to each other for a few months.)

Being a journalist in the mid-nineties not only offered the thrill of the work but also changed one's social status. In a few months our monthly salaries reached $600, way higher than Irina's parents' at that time. Young and with no family obligations, journalists filled just-opened bars in Moscow, drinking and talking only about their profession. One day someone brought the Reuters guidelines for journalism to Jack Rabbit Slim's pub—conveniently located next door to the offices of a competing daily *Kommersant*—and provoked all-night talk about Western versus Russian rules of journalism.

In six months Andrei wrote his first lengthy feature. The story was about how Oracle databases were acquired at Lubyanka, the FSB headquarters. Andrei's contacts told him that Oracle technologies, which were subject to export restrictions in the United States (Oracle's CEO, Larry Ellison, once famously said that the Russians would take Oracle only in missile warheads), were sold to the FSB to build a huge database on terrorists. An outraged FSB officer called the newspaper before the publication, trying to kill the story. But nobody paid attention to his threats, and the story made the front page.

One day Irina went to the editor-in-chief and asked to be transferred to the crime department of the paper. The astonished editor tried to talk her out of it: the crime department was not the most prestigious unit in the newspaper. He suggested instead that she move to the political department, but Irina persisted; she thought it was the best place to get journalistic experience. Indeed it was.

On the fifth floor of the offices of *Segodnya* there was a large room with a radio scanner on the windowsill, always turned on to listen to a police frequency. A dozen people hung around day and night, among them a former KGB officer, an ex-policeman, and a pair of sixteen-year-olds. One of them was brought to the newspaper by his father, a policeman, who was troubled by his son's criminal mindset. The boy turned out to have a talent for crime reporting. Parkhomenko's son also landed briefly in the room. Some of the reporters often signed their stories by pseudonyms, and several people shared some of the pseudonyms to make the identification more difficult: the department received calls from angry policemen and "businessmen" with clear criminal connections almost on a daily basis.

In the 1990s these reporters not only wrote about crime but also did the work of the investigative departments: they covered the high-profile assassinations of businessmen and politicians, wrote about secret services, and were sent to the North Caucasus to cover hostage dramas. Within a year Andrei followed Irina to the crime department, where the reporters had developed a camaraderie and helped each other in sometimes very tough circumstances.

In these years journalists had power, and we felt it in our work. But journalism also suffered from a lack of restraint and established ethical standards. The nascent public relations industry often attempted to bribe journalists, promising money for publishing false or sometimes genuinely compromising information about high-placed officials and prominent businessmen. A mix of intercepted phone calls and analytical profiles prepared by the oligarchs' shadowy security branches or the government security services became known as *kompromat*, or compromising materials. What made it all even more confusing was that sometimes journalists willingly acted as mercenaries for various interests or

loyal members of the oligarchic business structures. Russian security services carried out surveillance and intercepted phone calls,
selling their findings as part of kompromat. The resulting articles
effectively influenced the public.

The editorial offices battled frantically with this corrupt journalism. *Kommersant* installed a special department called "rewrite" (in English), tasked to edit heavily—that is, rewrite—every
piece submitted by staff journalists for publication to filter out
any *zakaz,* or information that had been paid for by a special interest. *Segodnya* had a former officer of the Fifth Directorate of
the KGB who in Soviet times was in charge of persecuting dissidents; now he checked suspicious articles after publication. If he
concluded a story was unfair, the journalist was fired.[15]

In the mid-1990s the flow of information in media was free
but could also be confusing for readers. The oligarchs used their
news media outlets as weapons to fight for control of the nation's
vast resources. Around the same time, by 1996, the Russian Internet was undergoing explosive growth. The first search engine,
Rambler.ru, appeared, and the first political party website was established for Yabloko, and Interfax news agency launched its own
website. Internet advertising became a paying business, drawing
real revenue. It was a new, fashionable business that caught the
Russian oligarchs' attention. Boris Berezovsky, one of those who
helped secure Yeltsin's victory in the presidential elections, underwrote a new Internet service provider, Cityline, whose managers
were the first to grasp that people came to the Internet because of
the actual content they could find there. Cityline helped launch a
handful of online media and content projects, ranging from magazines to blogs.

In December a thirty-year-old Internet activist, Anton Nossik,
started a new project, a daily online column called *Vecherny Internet,* or the *Evening Internet,* which was hosted on Cityline.
The project was launched from Israel, as Nossik, born to a prominent Moscow intelligentsia family, had emigrated to Israel in

1990 and became prominent in the Russian and Israeli Internet communities.

Nossik soon realized that the new Internet media could trump the traditional journalism. He believed people would embrace information presented on the Internet, as it would be available sooner, more accessible, and brief. Less concerned about gathering the information, his sought to emphasize the form, not the substance. He wanted to repackage news from traditional print media and deliver it to Internet users quickly. It was an early kernel of what became the news aggregator, and it would define the Russian Internet for the next decade. Riding the wave of the *Evening Internet's* success, Nossik returned to Moscow in March 1997.

The *Evening Internet* became the very first blog in Russia.

In the vast apparatus of the Russian government one group of officials began to pay close attention to this new online activity. The security services were among the first to conclude that it should be controlled.

CHAPTER 4

The Black Box

In 1998 the diminutive Vika Egorova was a twenty-four-year-old editor at an obscure magazine. She had studied at the Moscow Engineering and Physics Institute, a preeminent school for training nuclear scientists, and had an interest in mathematics. After graduating, she worked at a risk management company run by former KGB people, then was hired as an editor at *Mir Kartochek*, or World of Credit Cards. The circulation was tiny, but Egorova's interests ranged beyond credit cards; she began learning about secret codes and developed contacts in the world of cryptology, the science of creating and deciphering clandestine messages.

In June she received a call from one of her contacts, who worked for a small information security company. Egorova sensed the small company was related, somehow, to FAPSI, the Russian electronic intelligence agency modeled after the US National Security Agency.

Egorova knew that FAPSI was fighting the more powerful FSB, the main successor to the KGB. The intelligence services jostled with each other in a competition for power and money and especially fought for control over profitable businesses, such as

encryption technology that the banks were required to buy from
the secret services.

Egorova's contact offered some information about credit card
technology that might interest her magazine, so on June 10 she
went to meet with him. He handed her several pages of documents, but when she scanned them quickly, she saw that the
first page obviously had nothing to do with credit cards. It was
an official document of some kind, a draft with places for signatures—still blank. But at the very top of the draft was the word
soglasovano, or "approved."[1]

The draft document described a government policy that would
require all of Russia's ISPs to install a device on their lines, a
black box, that would connect the Internet provider to the FSB.
It would allow the FSB to silently and effortlessly eavesdrop on
e-mails, which had become the main method of communication
on the Internet by 1998. The device was called SORM, an acronym in Russian for *Systema Operativno-Rozysknikh Meropriatiy*,
or the System of Operative Search Measures. The document said
that SORM was "a system of technical means for providing investigative procedures on electronic networks."

More simply, eavesdropping on the Internet.

"Do what you want with that," her contact said of the papers,
suggesting she might pass them along to her editor at the magazine or give them to an editor at *Computerra*, another computer
weekly popular among Russian programmers. Egorova realized
the documents were a leak—a leak probably from FAPSI, intended to unmask the FSB's plans to monitor all of the Russian
Internet.

As she left the meeting, Egorova was uncertain what to do.
But she knew she had to do something—and quickly. She called
her editor, who was out of town. She called her contact at *Computerra*, who was also out of town. She knew she had been given
the documents in a leak—it was pure politics—but wasn't sure
how to use them. Then she remembered Anatoly Levenchuk. She

had met him only a few months beforehand, and his combative debating style had impressed her. Maybe he would know what to do with the information.

In Russia Levenchuk, then forty years old, had become something of a legend in the early days of the Internet and was a well-respected expert in the Russian stock market. But Levenchuk's real passion was ideas. He had become a devoted follower of libertarianism, and he firmly believed in the smallest possible government intrusion into the economy. He attempted to launch a libertarian political party in 1992, but it flopped and never got on the ballot. The ideas of libertarianism and freedom from government control were not widely or immediately grasped, and Levenchuk felt it needed to be explained to the Russian citizenry. With the arrival of the web, Levenchuk found the answer. In 1994 he established Libertarium.ru, a website that grew into an important source of libertarian ideas, a place for debate about freedom, and a launching pad for various public campaigns for change.[2] He was often invited to speak at conferences, and when he gave a talk, he would immediately stand up, walk onto a stage, and wave his arms for emphasis, with his sentences laden with an evocative Rostov accent, which was much more emotional than Moscow's everyday idiom.

Egorova called Levenchuk at home and said she needed to have a "serious talk" with him. He picked up her worried tone and suggested they meet. There, she showed him the papers. "Look," she said. "It seems I've got a leak, and I don't know what to do with it. But I think you should know what to do with that piece of paper." She had a hard time persuading him at first; Levenchuk's mind was wrapped up in a battle over the rules of the stock market—fighting with FAPSI, which wanted to make all stock market details as secret as possible. Levenchuk insisted that openness was essential in capital markets—it was the pillar of how a free market worked.

When Egorova said, insistently, that it was a leak—*a leak from FAPSI!*—she finally got his attention.

Levenchuk read the document and decided immediately. His experience with the Internet made him particularly sensitive to what appeared to be almost unlimited powers granted to the FSB in the document. Although they would have to get an eavesdropping warrant from the court, the FSB was not obliged to show it to anyone, not even the Internet company they were tapping. The ISPs had no right to demand the FSB show it to them either, as they had no security clearance. Making matters worse, the ISPs would have to pay for the black boxes, the SORM equipment, and the installation, but they would have no access to it.

Pure and simple, the SORM box was a backdoor to Russia's Internet, and the security service was about to open it.

Levenchuk and Egorova walked back to his residence. Libertarium.ru was hosted in his cramped, three-room apartment in southeast Moscow, in the shabby district of Kuzminki. In the kitchen was a personal computer, which had become the server for the website, and a scanner. They scanned the document, and she helped him create hyperlinks. The next day, on June 11, 1998, Levenchuk posted the SORM document online for the first time.[3]

This was probably not what the leakers envisioned. Egorova thought they wanted it passed to an editor, maybe written up as a small magazine item. Perhaps FAPSI intended it as nothing more than a shot across the bow of the FSB, a message that *we know what you are doing.* But the document had come into the hands of the flamboyant and outspoken Levenchuk, who had long been struggling for more openness, and now he had a chance to do something about it. By posting the document, he thought he might force the FSB to at least adhere to their own requirement to seek a warrant before they tapped the Internet. "I always understood these were the security services, and if they say they do it, it's impossible to stop them," he recalled. "I was interested in only one thing, whether they would tell the truth, whether they would comply with the rule about a warrant."[4]

Levenchuk didn't stop there. He launched a public campaign to call attention to the draft and, in a larger sense, to push back against SORM. He called all his contacts in the news media, started collecting signatures in protest, and contacted the major telecom operators, where he had high-level contacts. He collected and posted on his website a list of questions that an ISP could ask the FSB when the security agents came to install the SORM equipment. He also solicited—and received— feedback from some of the ISPs. Levenchuk gleefully posted some of their feedback, maintaining the ISPs' anonymity. The Internet service providers were furious with the FSB less because of the principle of eavesdropping but because they were being asked to pay for it.

"Full, primitive caveman savagery," one service provider wrote. "Give them all, and more. And all at our own expense." The provider added bitterly, "We will soon shoot each other on their orders, and bury—at our own expense."

Levenchuk gave interviews and wrote articles, and the story of the Internet black boxes was reported domestically and internationally. A few service providers used Levenchuk's suggested questions to push back when the FSB agents called to install the black boxes. But Levenchuk encountered something he never expected: the industry, in the end, did not resist. "It ended bitterly," Levenchuk told us. "I won only a year. But it didn't bring happiness to anyone. The providers, instead of resisting, they all gave up."[5] Among those that installed the black boxes were the Internet pioneers Demos and Relcom.

Friends passed to Levenchuk warning messages from the FSB that he should be careful, but the security service never contacted him directly. In public the government and the security services stayed out of the debate about the SORM.

In 1998 there were no social networks in Russia; the Internet was mostly e-mail, some early e-commerce, and websites. But the Internet had already changed the rules for public debate. Unlike traditional media—newspapers, radio, television—it was not a one-directional flow of information. The Internet was filled with chats and discussion boards, and Levenchuk's site posted dozens of comments and questions about the black boxes.

Many years earlier the first generation of SORM had begun when the Soviet KGB had tapped telephones. Then it was known as SORM-1. When it moved to the Internet in the 1990s—capable of intercepting e-mail, Internet traffic, mobile calls and voice-over Internet such as Skype, that was SORM-2. In the end the security services developed a third generation—SORM-3—which encompassed all telecommunications. All Russian operators and ISPs were required to install the black boxes, about the size of an old video tape recorder, which would fit on a rack of equipment, and permit connection to the regional departments of the FSB. The result: the FSB could intercept whenever anyone on Russian soil made a phone call or checked an e-mail.

The surveillance system enhanced the power of the security services, which lacked any kind of oversight. They didn't hesitate to interfere with politics by using the tools of surveillance and interception. Levenchuk grasped this danger almost immediately and realized that the FSB intercepts of phone lines—and then the Internet—would further feed kompromat. It could include all kinds of misdeeds, from a target's supposed connections with criminals to nasty details about bribery or prostitutes. At times kompromat was aimed at business rivals, prominent journalists, and politicians. But now the FSB was harvesting the raw material—intercepts from phone calls and e-mail messages—to manufacture kompromat.

For more than a decade, as investigative reporters for newspapers, we covered the Russian secret services. Andrei wrote his first article about SORM in July 1998. Then in 2000 we set up a website Agentura.ru, which we intended to be a watchdog of the Russian secret services. We've had a section on SORM issues ever since.

We were curious about many aspects of the story that had never been fully explained. First, we wondered why the communications industry, in the years of relative freedom in the 1990s, had been so willing to comply fully with the security services and put the black boxes on their lines? We knew there were open debates in the United States and elsewhere about electronic surveillance, such as the 1994 Communications Assistance for Law Enforcement Act, which required telecommunications providers to make their lines available for law enforcement purposes. Why was it different in Russia? Did SORM signal a return to the Soviet totalitarian practice of surveillance, or was it a legitimate method of law enforcement wiretapping in the digital age?

Second, how did SORM really begin? Was it an outgrowth of the old Soviet police state or something new?

To answer the questions, we first looked at the document leaked to Egorova and posted by Levenchuk. We noticed that it included the identity of a special research institute in charge of the technical aspects of SORM, the Central Research Institute of the Communications Ministry. We found it had a whole section in charge of SORM, and the chief of the section was listed as Vyacheslav Gusev.

When Andrei called him, Gusev was less than helpful. He told Andrei that all work on SORM started in 1994 because that was when Russian communications switched over from analog lines to digital cables. Then he said, "I've been doing SORM for thirty years. I looked at your articles, our views are different, and I do not want to help you write your book." Later the same day he sent an angry e-mail. "There are plenty of problems in this area, and your publication will not solve anything and only cause various squabbles. People who are engaged in SORM do not deserve" this critical attention.[6]

That avenue was obviously a dead end. But he exposed a serious contradiction: Gusev said that all work started in 1994 *and* that he had been working on it for thirty years. If SORM started in 1994, then it was a relatively recent invention, created after the Soviet collapse. But if he had been working on it for thirty years, then perhaps it originated in the KGB.

We searched through documents of the Ministry of Communications under Yeltsin and found that the first time SORM was mentioned was in a decree of November 11, 1994. The decree was about phone eavesdropping and said the SORM system would be established on Russia's communications lines.[7] But the document also contained another clue: not only was the research institute in Moscow working on SORM, but there was mention of a branch in St. Petersburg as well. We knew of a scientist who was one of the most prominent Russian technical experts on SORM, Boris Goldstein, who had provided us with comments and explanations for our investigations in the past, and it turned out he had worked at the St. Petersburg branch for decades. Irina went to see him at the University of Telecommunications on the outskirts of St. Petersburg, where he teaches. When Goldstein opened the door to his study on the fifth floor of the university, she saw a tall, slim, well-mannered professor, sixty-three years old. And he had a very good memory.

Goldstein recalled Soviet times, when KGB officers eavesdropped on the telephone system. They connected wires from the phone exchanges to hidden rooms where the monitoring took place. "Big, old-fashioned tape recorders turned on at the beginning of a conversation and started recording," he recalled. "All of this was done in secret."[8]

Goldstein described a critical difference between the Western and Russian approaches to intercepting communications. In the

West, he said, the phone company or ISP gets an order to begin the interception, receives the identity of the target, and provides access. But in the Russian system the phone company or service provider has no idea who is being tapped. As Goldstein explained it, the Russian security agencies do not trust the operators—they only want the backdoor to the information.

SORM was the backdoor.

Then Goldstein clarified why SORM was carried out in such secrecy. The black box installed at the provider is just one part of the system. The cable connects it to a second part at the office of the FSB, and these second devices are the work of the FSB's own secret research institutes and are manned by the FSB. Goldstein made one thing very clear: it was not all that difficult for the authorities to shift from monitoring telephones, in SORM-1, to monitoring the Internet, in SORM-2. "Technically there was nothing new" in SORM-2, he said. To scoop up the data, "you didn't need anything very special, just to mirror the traffic." In some respects, Goldstein said, monitoring data was even easier than voices. After talking to Goldstein we realized that SORM probably had roots in the long Soviet practice of tapping telephones. When the technology changed, the black boxes simply adjusted.

Still, not all of the pieces of the puzzle were fitting together. To get a better picture of how SORM began, we continued to scrutinize the Ministry of Communications documents in the 1990s, searching for clues in names, organizations, and facilities. Soon we discovered the name Sergei Mishenkov. He was chief of the scientific department in the Ministry of Communications then. In some documents he was identified as the official in charge of supervising SORM research "at the request and with the financial support" of the Russian security services. It seemed he might know a lot about SORM.

Andrei found him one day on the fourth floor of the Ministry of Communications in Moscow. Cheerful, paunchy, and with unruly hair, Mishenkov was a radio enthusiast from his youth—his e-mail address is his radio call sign—who filled his inner office with old radio sets made in Soviet times. He was an engineer who devoted his career to Moscow's radio network and was recruited into the government in the 1990s to bring more discipline to the ministry's research institutes. They were accustomed to years of government subsidies, but now Mishenkov had to press them for real results. They also needed money. Mishenkov needed to find funds, and that is how he got involved with SORM: the FSB paid for the research on the black boxes.

Mishenkov explained to Andrei that the ministry's central research institute in Moscow had traditionally been responsible for intercity phone lines, so naturally they got the assignment to handle the SORM black boxes for those. The St. Petersburg institute historically worked on local phone stations, so of course they were assigned the black boxes for local phones. When cell phones appeared, a third institute was put in charge of intercepting cell phone calls.[9] All of it was to help the FSB snoop on anybody.

After Gusev's hostile reaction, Andrei didn't have high expectations for his conversation with Mishenkov. But he had one small fact in the back of his mind: he had heard from another source that the real history of the SORM system could be traced to a place that Mishenkov had, so far, neglected to mention—the KGB's top-secret research institute at Kuchino.[10]

"Kuchino?" Soldatov asked Mishenkov, almost casually, probing for more information about the black boxes.

Much to his surprise, Mishenkov nodded affirmatively. All the other institutes had done some research, but the birthplace of SORM was behind the walls at Kuchino, about twelve miles east of Moscow. Kuchino was the oldest research facility of the Soviet police state, and it had been in service as far back as 1929 for Stalin's NKVD, a forerunner to the KGB. Kuchino had a storied history of accomplishments, such as figuring out how to intercept a human voice from the vibrations of a window. It was the sharashka—the prison camp—where the talented engineer Lev Kopelev had worked from January to December 1954.

Even today the facility is heavily guarded and the engineers carry the rank of officers in the FSB.[11]

Finding someone in the FSB to explain more about how SORM worked and began was nearly impossible. For years the FSB had been closed and inaccessible to journalists. The press office stopped responding to media requests; they didn't care about public opinion anymore. After all, the rise of President Vladimir Putin had given the FSB a huge lift in power and resources.

We noticed in the documents the signature of Andrei Bykov, who was deputy director of the FSB from 1992 to 1996, holding the rank of colonel-general. Before 1992 he had been head of the KGB Operative-Technical Department, in charge of bugging, interception, and technical surveillance operations. It was Bykov whom the chairman of the KGB ordered on December 5, 1991, to hand over to the United States the documents that confirmed the bugging of the new US Embassy building in Moscow.[12] In the 1990s Bykov's signature was on most of the SORM documents.

When he left the FSB, Bykov followed the path of many former security officers—he went to work at a private company, in this case a communications business.

Andrei tried to call, then sent an e-mail leaving his cell phone number.

That same day Andrei's cell phone rang. He answered it. A few minutes later, looking shocked, he hung up.

"What happened?" asked Irina.

"You know who it was? It was Bykov!" he said. "I've never had a colonel-general of the FSB call me back!"

"What did he say?" Irina asked.

"He offered to meet in person," Andrei replied. "He said the topic of SORM is not a phone conversation."

Bykov offered to meet the next morning at ten o' clock on Lubyanka Square, near the monument to victims of repressions. "There is usually nobody there in the morning, so we won't miss each other," he told Andrei and then hung up the phone. His voice was brusque, and Andrei thought Bykov might refuse to meet in a coffee shop. The next morning it was raining, and Soldatov went early, walked to the nearest café, ordered a cup of coffee and a cup of tea, and carried them to the rendezvous point.

Lubyanka Square is rectangular. On one side is the new luxury St. Regis Nikolskaya Hotel, on another the Detsky Mir department store, and three huge buildings of the FSB stand clockwise nearby; first, the so-called new building constructed in the early 1980s, then the main building—the most famous—headquarters of the central apparatus of the Soviet and Russian secret police, and finally the angular building built in the mid-1980s to house the Computation Center of the KGB, now the Center for Information Security of the FSB.

On the south side of the square there is a small rectangular park lined by trees. To get to it requires walking through an underpass, beneath the busy traffic above. In the part facing the FSB there is a large, raw stone on a small pedestal and a tiny space before it. In October 1990 the stone was brought from the prison camp, Solovki, which was part of the gulag system, to honor victims of Stalin's repressions. The space before the monument is usually empty but fills up every October when Muscovites gather to read aloud the names of victims in a commemoration ceremony. It was there Bykov chose to meet.

When Andrei exited the underpass near the stone, he saw a small, round-shouldered figure in an oversized gray suit that hung loosely on him. Bykov had gray hair combed back, sunken cheeks, and held an umbrella. As Andrei feared, he refused to walk to a coffee shop. Bykov also refused to have the coffee or tea Andrei brought. Andrei didn't know what to do with the two cups, so he put them on the bench facing the monument. Bykov firmly declined the offer to sit down, saying, "We can have a walk around," and the two of them circled the bench as they talked.

"My office was in the new building," said Bykov, pointing to the edifice on the left.

Bykov, an engineer by training, studied at the Moscow State Technical University in Department No. 6, which focused on small arms research. Within three years after graduation he was recruited by the KGB. In 1966 he entered the KGB's Operative-Technical Department and rose up through its ranks to become department chief. The department in earlier years had supervised sharashkas in Marfino and Kuchino. Bykov spent his career developing new kinds of weapons and special equipment, including listening devices.

The Twelfth Department of the KGB, which conducted eavesdropping, was beyond Bykov's reach during the Soviet years. This was because the Twelfth Department had been always directly subordinated to the KGB chairman due to its sensitivity, and the chief of the section had been chosen for loyalty, not professionalism. But after the August coup attempt and the Soviet collapse, Bykov took over the Twelfth Department, incorporating it into his domain, and he became deputy director of the new Russian security service. The arrangement lasted only for a few years, then the Twelfth Department was raised to the level of a directorate inside the FSB. Its emblem proudly displays an owl. And it is this directorate that is in charge of SORM black boxes all over Russia.

Bykov told Andrei that in 1991 his most immediate problem had been to withdraw the KGB's technical equipment and secret documentation from the Baltics to Moscow. The Soviet Union fell apart, and all of the KGB's surveillance and eavesdropping equipment had been manufactured by two factories, Kommutator and Alfa, in Riga, the capital of newly independent Latvia. When he managed to get everything out, he had to respond to criticism of the KGB's eavesdropping practices from dissidents and journalists. Legally the KGB's eavesdropping was regulated by an order, No. 0050, signed by Soviet leader Yuri Andropov in 1979, but it had only one principal rule: it directly banned eavesdropping on party officials.

Bykov came up with the idea of "sanctioned surveillance." The new system required some outside body to approve surveillance in advance—entirely a defensive move to fend off the criticism. Initially the security services toyed with the idea of having sanctions approved by the prosecutor's office, but in 1995 it was decided that a court warrant would be required for advance approval.[13]

But the technical method of full, unrestricted access to all communications, developed at Kuchino in the 1980s, was not altered according to the new requirement. In practice it meant that the Russian secret service would get the court's approval and then do whatever surveillance it wished. Bykov was confident the procedure would not hinder the way the surveillance was technically organized. This was different from in the United States, where the authorities would have to request Internet or phone operators to tap a line after a court-approved warrant is issued. When Andrei asked why they didn't follow the American example, Bykov simply waved the question away. "Ah, they also sniff all information from the servers. It was proved by Assange and the like, and it didn't start yesterday."

As Bykov walked round and round the little park area with Andrei, the real situation became clear. The court-approved warrant—the procedure Bykov had created—didn't mean very much. The Russian legislation requires an FSB officer to get the warrant, but the officer is not allowed to show it to the operator. He can make the interception on his own. In other words, the methods of SORM directly descended from when no one thought of court-approved warrants—from the Soviet system of phone wiretapping.

We searched hard to find someone who had experience back then, in the secret KGB recording chambers, sitting in front of the whirring tape recorders in the earlier days of phone wiretapping, the days when SORM eavesdropping began. The trail eventually led to a café in Moscow, but once again we found the truth hard to ascertain.

It was a woman's job—to sit for long hours, facing metal stands with reel-to-reel tape recorders on the wall, mostly a West German brand, Uher Royal de Luxe, later replaced by eight-channel devices converted from video tape recorders.[14] The women appeared to be similar to phone operators, with headphones ready on the table, and there was indeed a telephone switchboard in the room. But there were also a few officer-technicians in the large room, and the women were not operators but rather "controllers" of the Twelfth Department of the KGB. Their rank was usually an ensign, the lowest possible rank in the KGB, and it was not up to them but to an officer at the switchboard, also a woman, to decide which stand to choose to connect the phone number marked for control. The job of controller was, in this sense, relatively easy—just make sure all reels moved properly and replace the tape when a reel was full. Sometimes the controllers were ordered to conduct "auditory control": when they put on their headphones and grabbed the work notebooks to scribble notes. The women were trained to type and in stenography. They also were trained to remember over fifty voices and to recognize instantly who was calling.[15] For these skills they received a handsome Soviet salary of 300 rubles per month (an engineer or scientist earned around 180 rubles), with the real possibility they might become deaf in fifteen years.[16]

Andrei found one of these controllers. We met at the café Nikolai on Staraya Basmannaya Street, two hundred meters away from her current job, a pro-Kremlin website called Pravda.ru. A small woman in her early fifties, with black hair, black eyes, and wearing a modest business suit, she sat at a table in a corner of the café and looked around nervously. Her first name was Lyubov, and Andrei just showed her the report signed with her name, which we had discovered in a small-circulation book published in 1995.[17] A KGB document about the surveillance of Yeltsin's people during the August coup showed that Lyubov was then a KGB senior lieutenant, an "interpreter of special purpose" of the Twelfth Department.

She confirmed that was indeed a KGB "controller," and in her report she described how, on the evening of August 20, 1991, the second day of the putsch, she eavesdropped on the conversations of Vitaly Urazhtsev, a democratic deputy of the Supreme Soviet and a Yeltsin supporter. Urazhtsev, a lieutenant colonel of the Soviet Army, became well known in 1989 when he was expelled from the Communist Party for his ideas about democratizing the army. In the early morning of the first day of the putsch he was arrested at a bus stop and interrogated by KGB officers who asked him whether he was planning to oppose the putsch. They urged him to support the coup, but he refused. In a few hours he was released. However, the next day he was put under surveillance of the KGB's Twelfth Department.

Silently listening to his conversations was Lyubov. She was a 1984 graduate of the best university in the country, Moscow State University, with a degree in geography. She pursued work as a specialist economic geographer and Portuguese interpreter, but she didn't remain a geographer; the KGB recruited her to join the Twelfth Department as an interpreter. If the KGB needed to eavesdrop on the Portuguese, Brazilians, or Angolans, Lyubov got the job. The rest of the time she listened to whomever was of interest to the KGB.

In the days of the putsch this meant eavesdropping on the parliamentarian Urazhtsev. Now, in January 2015, Lyubov looked worriedly at her report, published in the 1995 book, *How Could It Have Happened?* She looked at the once-secret report lying there, in the open. "It's our internal things," she said. "It should be secret." She clearly didn't know what to say: in the first line of a report written at the time for the investigation, Lyubov acknowledged that on August 20, 1991, she took part in the "anticonstitutional, unlawful operation" to eavesdrop on Yeltsin's people. She wrote that she was ready to take responsibility. She even offered to reorganize the activities of the Twelfth Department to make it lawful. At that time she seemed contrite for what had happened.

"Despite all I wrote here, I'm a patriot!" she said nervously. We both knew in January 2015 her critical words about the way KGB surveillance had been organized had gone out of fashion. Andrei persuaded her to meet him again in the café, hoping to learn more. But she seemed edgy, nervous, and unsettled, only staying long enough to say that the FSB were the best people in the country—and then she was gone.

From other sources we learned somewhat more about the history and scope of SORM. The Twelfth Department had 164 control points arrayed across Moscow.[18] Tape recorders were rolling in district KGB offices, at the central listening point on Varsonofyevsky Lane, and in city telephone stations, where there was room for KGB controllers to hide and do their work. Foreign embassy phone lines were eavesdropped separately. It was called "object control," which meant that each major embassy had its own surveillance team stationed permanently in nearby buildings, with KGB operatives at the ready in case someone of interest made a call to the embassy and would have to be apprehended before reaching the gates. All in all, until the breakup of the Soviet Union, over nine hundred people served in the Twelfth Department of the KGB in Moscow, with four hundred in Leningrad.

Even so, it wasn't always that effective. At most, the department could simultaneously wiretap no more than three hundred people. Twenty-four hours of eavesdropping produced between eight and eleven hours of recordings, but one hour of recording required seven hours of transcribing by controllers. The existence of 164 control points was actually a sign of weakness; the KGB needed so many points to direct the traffic by hand because the quality of phone lines was poor, and phone stations in Moscow were of all different types, some dating back to the 1930s. The underground communication lines were awful; in some cases it was physically impossible to get lines connected to the central listening point.

In our investigation we learned that Moscow had extensively borrowed technology and know-how from the feared secret police in East Germany. The Ministry of State Security, known as the Stasi, started working on a national system of wiretapping in East Germany in 1956, at that time called "Systema-A."[19] By the end of the 1960s Stasi introduced a more efficient, centralized system, known as Centrales Kontrollsystem, or CEKO, which became operational in 1973. It allowed Stasi to eavesdrop simultaneously on four thousand phone numbers, out of a total of 8 million in the country. In the early 1980s the system was updated once again, which became known as CEKO-2, with a very advanced and elaborate system, from the phone lines to tape recorders. CEKO-2 was equipped with tape recorders of the brand "Elektronik," specially designed for the Stasi, the only security service in the Eastern bloc that enjoyed its own tape recorders. All technical hubs of CEKO-2, in 209 territorial departments of Stasi, were connected with fifteen district departments. In Berlin CEKO-2 had eighteen specially built stations. Central Berlin's point of CEKO-2 on Frankfurter Allee had four huge communications racks with eleven hundred control points. Special cables were laid from CEKO-2 stations to the switchboard of the nearest phone station, and Stasi "controllers" could listen to conversations directly. Over 70 percent of connections were done on the main switchboard. Such an achievement was possible because the underground communication system in Berlin, built in Hitler's times, had largely survived the battle for Berlin in 1945.

The KGB learned at the knee of the Stasi officers, envying the technical level of Stasi surveillance. Nikolai Kalyagin, a major-general of the KGB, was in charge of relations with East German secret services for twelve years, first as chief of the KGB station in Bonn and then as chief of the section responsible for cooperation with Stasi. We found his home phone number, and Kalyagin himself answered the call.

Kalyagin told us that there were indeed technical officers of the KGB permanently stationed in Berlin, always interested in German know-how in surveillance. Evidence from our source who served in Germany in the 1980s supported this confirmation.

Kalyagin was helpful, and then Andrei asked him, "Do I understand correctly that the control of phone lines was better organized in Berlin than in Moscow? And that sometimes Germans overtook us in technical means, especially in phone control?"

"Yes, you understand this right," said Kalyagin.

The Stasi possessed what the KGB so badly wanted—a national system of eavesdropping on communications. SORM was designed to fill this gap, to provide the Soviet KGB with a system built in Moscow and then replicated in all Russian regions. At the time the Soviet Union fell apart, the KGB was working on it but had not fulfilled its goal. After a few years the new Russian secret service, the FSB, took over, and this time new digital technologies helped make the system quite sophisticated.

When, on a summer day of 2014, Andrei walked into the tall building on Butlerova Street in Moscow that houses M9, he saw for the first time the mammoth crossroads for traffic moving between the Russian Internet providers. Nearly a decade ago a single Internet exchange point, MSK-IX, had started in a corner of the twelfth floor of this building. Now it expanded to seven floors, filled with hundreds of communications racks.

With the help of some engineers, Andrei got a pass into the restricted building. Every floor has a special door with a separate code requiring a key to get through. Andrei's contacts had a key for the eighth floor. The heavy metal door was opened, and Andrei quietly stepped inside a small room, packed with equipment on

the racks. One of them had a small black box. It was labeled
SORM. It had a few cables and a few lights. Andrei was told that
when the small green lamp was illuminated on the box, the FSB
guys on the eighth floor have something to do.

As he looked down, Andrei saw the small green lamp winking.

In 1998 and 1999 Levenchuk had done much to bring SORM to
public attention, but when none of the big ISPs resisted, he felt
deflated and discouraged. He gave up his involvement in politics.
Levenchuk had lost his battle against SORM, and he lost it to a
new director of the FSB. His name was Vladimir Putin.

CHAPTER 5

The Coming of Putin

In the aftermath of the Russian economic crisis of 1998 President Yeltsin appointed three prime ministers in succession. None were economists, but all were closely tied to the security services. Yevgeny Primakov, who had been head of the foreign intelligence service, served as prime minister from September 11, 1998, to May 12, 1999. He was replaced by Sergei Stepashin, who had been director of the FSB in 1995. Then, on August 9, Yeltsin appointed Vladimir Putin, who had served as director of the FSB from 1998 to 1999.

By the summer of 1999 Russia was slowly and painfully recovering from the economic crisis, and in September Moscow was shaken by two apartment-building bombings that killed 216 people.[1] Chechen terrorists were blamed, and soon a new military offensive was launched in Chechnya in retaliation. But Yeltsin was not afraid of riots or terrorists; he and his entourage only feared his former close allies. A powerful political figure, Moscow Mayor Yuri Luzhkov, made a bid for the Kremlin. He also launched an attack on Yeltsin's family, accusing them of corruption. Yeltsin's team watched anxiously when Primakov joined with Luzhkov, and together they formed a new political party called Fatherland, seeking seats in parliament in the election of December 1999 and, it was assumed, the presidency in the contest set for March 2000. Yeltsin's term was to end in a few months, and his safety and that of his family was under question.

O n Sunday night, May 30, 1999, Yeltsin was stunned as he watched TV in his mansion in Barvikha, a village filled with walled-off mansions of top-level Russian officials, thirteen miles from the Kremlin in the lush green forests outside of Moscow. The influential journalist Yevgeny Kiselev displayed a chart of the president's family, suggesting they had engaged in corruption and had spirited their illicit gains abroad. This appeared on NTV's widely respected show *Itogi*, then the most popular political broadcast in Russia.

Kiselev, then forty-two, the most prominent and respectable political host on television, specifically raised questions about the integrity of Yeltsin's daughter Tatyana; her husband, Valentin Yumashev, both of whom worked in the presidential administration; as well as Alexander Voloshin, the chief of the administration; and billionaire oligarch Roman Abramovich. "The photographs on TV reminded me of wanted posters I used to see at factories, bus stations, or moving theatres in Sverdlovsk," Yeltsin later wrote. "The posters usually depicted the faces of drunks, thieves, murderers and rapists. Now the 'police,' in the person of NTV, was talking about my so-called Family—myself, Tanya, Voloshin, and Yumashev. All of these people were accused of everything under the sun—bribery, corruption, the hoarding of wealth in Swiss bank accounts, and the purchase of villas and castles in Italy and France. The NTV show put me in a state of shock."[2]

Every night the power struggle played out on television. The wealthy oligarch and wheeler-dealer Boris Berezovsky, who was close to Yeltsin's team, controlled the first channel, ORT, with a massive audience across Russia's eleven time zones, a legacy of

Soviet state television. A second force was Gusinsky's NTV, a channel that earned its reputation for professionalism in the first Chechen war. Luzhkov, the Moscow mayor, also had his own television channel, popular only in the capital. All of them—Berezovsky, Gusinsky, and Luzhkov—had supported Yeltsin in the 1996 reelection effort, but now, in the twilight of Yeltsin's second term, they were jockeying for power, anticipating the moment when Yeltsin would leave the scene.

While Yeltsin endured the criticism from Luzhkov's media outlets, he was stunned at the NTV broadside, which he called "a stab in the back from people I had thought were of my mind." Gusinsky's media empire, called Media-Most, consisting of NTV, the newspaper *Segodnya*, and the weekly *Itogi*, had placed their bets on Luzhkov and Primakov in the great power struggle. Like the other oligarchs, Gusinsky wielded power through his media holdings. Investigations of corruption targeting the Kremlin were exposed by NTV, then commented on in *Segodnya*, and then picked up by other printed media.

For the Yeltsin circle it was a very serious and direct personal threat. Following Kiselev's program, Voloshin summoned journalists in the Kremlin pool to a meeting and told them, rather melodramatically, of Gusinsky's Media-Most. "Either we break Most," he said, "or Most breaks the state." Elena Tregubova, a correspondent of *Kommersant*, present at the meeting, was certain that Voloshin meant the Kremlin when he was speaking of the "state."[3] And the Kremlin decided to retaliate. In July the state-owned Vnesheconombank refused to extend a previously agreed-upon loan to Gusinsky's Media-Most, then announced that Media-Most had failed to repay the loan.[4] Later Media-Most's accounts at the bank were seized, journalists who worked in Media-Most outlets were denied access to the Kremlin, and their accreditations for briefings by Voloshin were annulled.[5] Sergei Parkhomenko, the journalist who had earlier exposed reasons to fear the security services in "Merlin's Tower" articles, recalled that one day his chief political correspondent, Dmitry Pinsker, came to him with bad news. "The Kremlin decided to end my access to information," he said. "My sources refuse to talk to me and be quoted, so please understand why in my stories there will be more anonymous sources and commentators." Parkhomenko added, "It happened not only with information from the Kremlin. When the war in Chechnya started in September, our correspondents were not given access to the military nor provided help in getting to the troops. It was a well-defined strategy."[6] In the view of the Kremlin the journalists working for Gusinsky's media were the enemy's soldiers.

Yeltsin and his entourage desperately looked for someone to whom they could entrust their fate after his presidency ended. On August 9 Yeltsin named Putin, then forty-six years old and a protégé of Berezovsky, as the new prime minister. Yeltsin also made clear that he considered Putin his successor. Putin then appeared on television after the appointment and declared, "The main problem—I repeat, I have already spoken about this—what we have is the lack of political stability." It was a remark aimed directly at preserving the status quo.[7]

In 1999 Putin was not a public figure accustomed to journalists and the free exchange of information. In the perestroika years Putin had been stationed in Germany as a KGB officer, and he missed everything that happened, including Gorbachev's campaign of *glasnost*—or openness—when newspapers were competing to expose Stalinist crimes; Soviet apparatchiks argued with dissidents like Andrei Sakharov at Congress of People's Deputies, broadcast in real-time on television; and the pages of democratic *Moskovskie Novosti* were read aloud by Muscovites on Pushkin Square. Putin had little idea of how the West functioned from his posting in East Germany, which was under total control of the secret services. He missed even the fall of the Berlin Wall, because he was serving in Dresden, 125 miles south of Berlin.

Upon his return to St. Petersburg in 1990, Putin was hesitant. He later said he didn't want to remain with the KGB and refused a transfer to the central headquarters in Moscow. "I understood this system had no future," he recalled.[8] But he was afraid to leave it entirely, so he chose instead a "safe" option, asking to be attached to Leningrad University, as a KGB officer, to get a doctorate, which he later abandoned. The following year Putin went to work for Anatoly Sobchak, a prominent democrat who led the Leningrad City Council and became the first post-Soviet mayor of St. Petersburg, the city's imperial name, restored after the Soviet collapse. But Putin formally retired from the KGB on August 20, 1991, when it was crystal clear the coup had failed in Moscow.

In the 1990s Putin hewed to the methods he had been taught at the KGB, especially when he dealt with journalists. He sought to flatter and recruit.

In 1995 a group of journalists from *Moskovskie Novosti* went to St. Petersburg for a meeting with the newspaper's readers. Sobchak was an old admirer of the *Moskovskie Novosti* but was out of town, so he asked his deputy, Putin, to arrange a dinner for the journalists. Mikhail Shevelev and his colleagues found themselves at the table with Putin, who didn't impress them, though he tried his best to entertain them. He saw they were Jewish and carried on about his recent visit to Israel, praising the country, but his attempts to please them fell flat. "That evening I tried to get more drinks to forget him," Shevelev said.[9]

In late December 1998, having come to Moscow and been appointed director of the FSB, Putin took Tregubova, a *Kommersant* correspondent, to dinner. Seemingly out of the blue he asked Tregubova about her father and described to her, in astonishing detail, a conflict between the institute where her father worked and its competitor in St. Petersburg. Tregubova realized it was an attempt to recruit her.[10]

Putin was FSB director only for a year, from July 1998 to August 1999. One of his accomplishments was to turn on SORM monitoring of the Internet.

Putin's formative lessons came from a career in the KGB devoted to protecting the Communist Party's monopoly on power. He joined in 1975, at a time when veterans of Stalin's secret services were still serving. He heard something about Stalin's mass repressions, but "not much," he later said, and he was not supposed to, as the KGB officers were mostly inward-looking officers, and for many of them the service was a source of jobs for members of their family.[11] They strongly believed that access to information and to means of communications should be under control of the state. In the same year Putin joined, Andropov, chairman of the KGB, reported to the Central Committee of the Communist Party about the threat of international phone calls made by Jewish refuseniks, proposing to sharply restrict the use of international communication channels.

Although Putin was trained as a foreign intelligence officer, he was not immediately sent abroad. He spent four and a half years at the Leningrad KGB office in a section recruiting foreigners. He was in the KGB when it crushed dissidents, hunted for samizdat publications, and sought to cut back the international phone lines after the 1980 Olympic Games in Moscow. This was the organization that shaped Putin's view of the world.

Long after he left the KGB and after he was promoted to prime minister, Putin still retained a deep suspicion of journalists, a legacy of his years in the security service. One day at the Helsinki airport, during his second visit as prime minister overseas, Putin stopped to answer questions from Finnish journalists. One reporter asked, reading from a paper slowly in Russian, about the war in Chechnya. Putin responded harshly, "First, we are not on equal terms: You were reading your question prepared beforehand on paper, and I should respond right now."[12] For those trained in Soviet secret services, if a correspondent reads a question, this signaled that someone else had written and prepared the question for the journalist. In fact, however, the Finnish reporter had just wanted to ask the question properly in a foreign language.

The fall of 1999 was full of dramatic events: the apartment bombings in Moscow, the war in Chechnya, and parliamentary elections. The Kremlin's political masters saw every critical piece of reporting by journalists of Gusinsky's media empire—above all, NTV—as yet more signs of a conspiracy against them. In this dramatic battle newspapers were not major players, and the Internet was not taken seriously; television dominated all.

However, one person saw the potential to exploit the Internet for the Kremlin. Gleb Pavlovsky, then forty-eight years old, was a plump, round-faced public relations man with gray hair and brown-framed glasses and always dressed in a sweater. Though self-assured, Pavlovsky harbored memories of his own harrowing experience with the KGB. Born in Odessa, Pavlovsky went to Moscow in 1974, where he continued his involvement with the dissident movement. Under a pseudonym, he wrote a long and critical article about Brezhnev's constitution for the samizdat journal *Poiski*. In April 1982 the KGB went after him. During the investigation he repented and began to cooperate with the authorities. As a result, instead of being sent to prison camps, he received a few years of exile in the Komi Republic, eight hundred miles northeast of Moscow. "Internally, I realized that I crossed the line," Pavlovsky admitted many years later.[13] Although his behavior appalled his former dissident friends, he returned to Moscow in 1985, and soon after perestroika started, he found his way back to democratic circles, with at least some of his former friends accepting him back. In 1989 he founded the very first independent news agency, Postfactum. Pavlovsky saw that sometimes it was possible to cross a line and then to cross back again.

In 1999 Pavlovsky was called on by the Kremlin to help build a new progovernment party, Edinstvo, or Unity, and to devise a smear campaign against the Kremlin's opponents, including Luzhkov, Primakov, and the tycoon Gusinsky and his mass media. "There was a war with Gusinsky then," Pavlovsky said.[14] Pavlovsky's organization, the Foundation for Effective Politics, was a public relations company. It launched a number of websites with kompromat aimed at Luzhkov, a collection of revealing dossiers on various profitable Moscow businesses under the control of the mayor's associates. It also created a false site that pretended to be the official website of the Moscow mayor. Television journalists close to the Kremlin then recycled the kompromat posted on these sites.

One day in 1999 Pavlovsky came to the presidential administration with an idea. At the time it was against the law to publish exit polls on Election Day, but the restriction applied only to traditional media—the law did not cover the Internet. Pavlovsky suggested a way to exploit the gap. On December 16, three days before the parliamentary elections, Pavlovsky's foundation launched a website, elections99.com.

On Election Day the website published real-time exit polls from the Russian regions. Widely quoted by traditional media, including TV channels, its data helped sway voter sentiment in favor of Putin's Unity Party, helping it gather 23.3 percent of the vote, compared to 13.3 percent for Luzhkov's party, translating to 73 seats in the 450-member State Duma, the lower house. This was a victory for Unity, which had not existed before as a party.

At 9:51 a.m. on Election Day, Pavlovsky, excited, sent a message by pager to Yumashev, Yeltsin's son-in-law and a member of the Kremlin's inner circle, saying, "It looks a lot like victory!"[15]

Pavlovsky had been busy in other ways too. Putin, having been appointed prime minister, was actively planning to run for president to succeed Yeltsin. Pavlovsky had been regularly going to Putin campaign meetings, which convened at Alexander House near the Kremlin and often included Putin. Putin's presidential campaign staff was headed by his loyal ally, Dmitry Medvedev. Pavlovsky spoke up to suggest that Putin should meet with Internet entrepreneurs, explaining that the meeting with the Internet

crowd could help shape Putin's image as leader of the new generation. After all, he said, Russia was approaching the twenty-first
century, and the country wanted to rely on new people. Pavlovsky
got a green light to set up the meeting.

In the 1990s Pavlovsky had not been very successful, always
close to many promising projects, but he had never really come
out on top. The Postfactum news agency closed in 1996, and he
had been on the board of *Kommersant*, the most successful Russian
business daily, but somehow was distracted with minor public relations projects throughout the 1990s. Now Putin's campaign offered
him a new route to success. But he knew the rules: you should have
something behind you to be useful, either a reputation—which
Pavlovsky lacked—or a TV channel or a newspaper, like the ty-
coons had; he did not have those either. The one thing he did pay
attention to was the Internet. The meeting between Putin and the
Internet entrepreneurs could prove to the Kremlin that Pavlovsky
was in command of the Internet and, thus, enhance his prestige.

Pavlovsky called Anton Nossik, the then thirty-three-year-old
editor-in-chief of a new online media outlet, Lenta.ru, and invited him to attend the meeting with Putin. Nossik had few illusions about Putin and his KGB past. His family was a part of
rebellious liberal-minded Moscow intelligentsia who didn't like
official Soviet policy regarding art. Nossik was quite certain that
his generation was smarter and had brighter prospects than the
old Yeltsin elite. It didn't help that a week before the scheduled
meeting, on December 20, Putin went to FSB headquarters on
Lubyanka Square to celebrate the Day of Security Organizations
and made a famous remark: "Dear comrades, I can report that the
group of agents you sent to infiltrate the government has accomplished the first part of its mission." This was followed by approv-
ing laughter from FSB officers.[16]

Nossik wasn't surprised by the invitation; his new project was
part of Pavlovsky's collection of online media. "I had known Anton for long, over ten years maybe, and I invited him to launch

Lenta.ru," said Pavlovsky. And Nossik recalled that "all our projects then were with" Pavlovsky. Nossik's office was located in the hulking building of the state-owned news agency RIA Novosti on Zubovsky Boulevard that also housed Pavlovsky's online media.

Pavlovsky asked Nossik and Marina Litvinovich, a young online journalist well connected in Moscow's Internet subculture and working in Pavlovsky's foundation, to select people for the meeting with the prime minister. Nossik selected his young friends, most in their twenties, including colleagues at Pavlovsky's organization, and people who had websites and online media.

But the preparations took time, and word of the meeting filtered over to the offices of the Russian government, the formal structure of ministries and agencies, led by Prime Minister Putin. One of those who heard about it was Oleg Rykov, a veteran adviser to the government on information technology.[17] In the 1980s Rykov was involved in a top-secret, ambitious, and very expensive program, supervised by the KGB, to build a system of managing the Soviet Union during war with underground city bunkers built all over the country as well as powerful computer centers burrowed deep underground. He knew a lot about computers and hated secrecy; he was sure that in most cases it just covered up incompetence. He was also very skeptical of government intrusion into the Internet.

Rykov became alarmed when he heard of a plan drafted by Mikhail Lesin, then minister in charge of the news media, that would effectively hand over the distribution of domain names from the nongovernmental organization based at the Kurchatov Institute to the government. For him, it meant only one thing. "Lesin wanted to take away the entire Internet," Rykov said later.[18] Rykov learned that Lesin would present the plan at the meeting with Putin that, if approved, would effectively put the Russian Internet under direct control of the state, determining who used which domain names.

Rykov immediately called Alexey Soldatov and warned him about Lesin's worrisome plan. Officially the Information Department of the government was tasked to select the meeting's participants, so Rykov lobbied to include his government department, the Department of Science, as one of the official organizers. Finally it was agreed that both departments would jointly select the attendees. Rykov and Soldatov huddled to make choices for their slots, choosing mostly veterans of the Internet of the early 1990s.

Simultaneously Soldatov, seeking to build a united front against Lesin's initiative, called Anatoly Levenchuk and asked him to find Nossik. Levenchuk put all his energy into it and tried for two weeks to locate Nossik, but without success.

When the date of the meeting was announced, Soldatov gathered his group at the offices of Relcom, still next door to the Kurchatov Institute, to establish their strategy. They decided that Soldatov was to speak first and that they would try to kill the Lesin proposal.

On December 28, 1999, two groups of people went separately to the White House. Eight years after Yeltsin and his supporters had barricaded themselves inside and seven years after the violent confrontation with hardliners in 1993, when it was shelled by tanks, there were no visible traces. The building was now renovated and surrounded by high fences and checkpoints, and demonstrations were prohibited near the building.

The two groups, totaling twenty people, saw each other for the first time in the lobby, then took the elevator to the fifth floor, to the so-called central zone of the *Dom Pravitelstva*, or house of government. As they waited outside the conference hall on the fifth floor, they didn't talk much to each other.

They looked as different as they felt. The younger ones were dressed casually, whereas the older generation wore suits. The younger group "was another crowd," recalled Alexey Platonov, a director of the nongovernmental organization that managed domain names and a friend of Soldatov. "We were dealing with the infrastructure," Platonov said. "There are several levels of the Internet, and ours was the low and the middle levels, and then on the top there is the add-on that became known as 'the Internet.' They then considered themselves the elite, and they called us communication people, plumbers."[19]

Finally the participants were shown into the large conference hall with a long horseshoe-shaped table with chairs lined up shoulder to shoulder. They sat as they wished. Putin was at the head of the table, along with a deputy and two ministers—Lesin and Leonid Reiman, who was minister of communications. Soldatov sat to the right of Putin, and Nossik sat opposite him. Pavlovsky, who had thought up the idea of the meeting, did not attend.

Putin made a brief introduction. Soldatov immediately raised a hand.[20] He delivered a lecture, speaking somewhat slowly and clearly, about the history of the Internet in Russia. Then, following a plan agreed beforehand, Soldatov turned to Mikhail Yakushev, a well-known jurist, who explained with equal care how the Internet was regulated.

Putin nodded and then suddenly produced a file. Inside it was a description of the Lesin plan to take over the domain names, agreed upon with Reiman. It had two chapters, titled, "On Ordering the Allocation and Use of Domain Names" and "On the Establishment of a National System of Registration of Domain Names." Taken together, they would deliver control over the domain .ru to a government body and to make all kinds of organizations, from joint-stock companies to media to schools, use these domain names and launch their corporate sites by December 31, 2000.[21]

Putin asked what everyone at the table thought about the proposal. They all pretended to be surprised. Nossik raised his hand. "This is exactly why we are afraid of the government," he said. "Like a magician, you pull out of your sleeve some government regulation, after which everyone can go home!"[22]

A close friend of Nossik, Artemy Lebedev, a young website designer, arrived late to the meeting and took an empty chair, followed by his girlfriend, Litvinovich, who worked for Pavlovsky. He was the son of a famous Russian writer, Tatiana Tolstaya, wore a bandana over his head, and was always carefully unshaven, with the manners of a creative type. Lebedev at once launched into an attack on the nongovernmental organization that was controlling the domain names. The director, Platonov, sat directly opposite Lebedev during the tirade. Lebedev accused the organization of unfairly setting prices too high for domain names.

Platonov, forty-five years old, was a nuclear physicist who had spent his entire career at the Kurchatov Institute. Sitting there, the target for a verbal attack right in front of a prime minister whom he just met for the first time, he was evidently confused. Platonov surmised that Lebedev's angry speech was not accidental. The main topic of the meeting was state regulation and, in particular, the question of what to do with the domain .ru. For Platonov, the idea of state regulation of domain names—what Lesin was proposing—seemed "some sort of a racket: you have something profitable—give it to me." And Lebedev's attack in front of Putin provided the government arguments for why the status quo should be changed. Platonov responded emotionally.[23] The volume of the discussion and the cross talk soon became unmanageable, but it was clear that everyone at the table, both old and young generations, were dead set against the Lesin proposal.

Soldatov raised his hand again. When Putin nodded, he said, "I suggest we should have the project subjected to public discussion."

Putin immediately responded, "Agreed. Let's decide that this project, and all projects in the area of the Internet, will be subject to public debate."

With that, the Lesin proposal was effectively killed off. The meeting had lasted more than an hour and a half.

Arkady Volozh, the founder of Yandex search engine and present at the meeting, though mostly silent, took with him a pencil
from the White House, which his son put up for sale the next day
on the online auction Molotok.ru for 2,500 rubles, with the description, "A pencil stolen from Putin's meeting with the Internet
professionals."[24]

To Nossik, the meeting was pure theater. He was certain that
Putin knew the script and how it would turn out. He concluded
that the real purpose of the meeting was to improve Putin's image as an advanced and liberal-minded leader of Russia. After all,
Putin was, at the time, making parallel efforts to persuade Western businessmen that he accepted the free-market system and
would be committed to Yeltsin's path. Nossik also thought that
the Internet crowd was summoned to show their support, and
they delivered. "Thanks to me, thanks to all of us, Putin got what
he wanted," Nossik recalled. "He was supported by the most advanced part of society."

Nossik never thought the Lesin project had a real chance of
being implemented. But Soldatov thought the project was for
real, and he felt great relief when they secured Putin's promise not
to sign anything without a public debate. For years the Kremlin
kept this promise. "We got what we wanted," Soldatov recalled.

For all of the Internet people who came to the White House
that day, the encounter left the rules as they were. The status quo
remained in place, and that was what they wanted.

Putin took away a different impression. In 1999 Putin was not
very familiar with the brave new world of the Internet. He didn't
have e-mail, and he was given information from the Internet on
printouts. As always, he tried to shape the people he saw into his
understanding of the world, defined by his KGB background and
his tough years in St. Petersburg in the early 1990s. And what he
saw was that the most important figures in this new area were all
closely tied to the Kremlin in one way or another—through his
spin doctors or government agencies, many of them dependent

on government contracts. He also saw, in Lebedev's remarks, that these people could be easily manipulated. They could be divided and subdivided. This was a KGB method, but for now he didn't need to do anything.

Three days later, on New Year's Eve, Yeltsin announced he was resigning and then handed over his powers to Putin.

CHAPTER 6

Internet Rising

President Putin never forgot that Vladimir Gusinsky's media empire had nearly broken the Kremlin. He was determined to seize control of broadcast television, by far the most pervasive and effective news media in Russia. But just as Putin went after television, the news media reached a turning point. People lost faith in traditional news sources and began to rely on digital outlets. A new wave was coming, gradually but with profound consequences, and it all started with a few independent bloggers.

Putin won the presidential elections on March 26, 2000, and took the oath of office on May 7 in a grand ceremony in the gilded and chandeliered Andreev throne hall of the Kremlin Palace. Four days later, on May 11, armed officers of the security services raided the offices of Media-Most on Palashevsky Lane in Moscow. A month later, on June 13, Gusinsky was detained and imprisoned in the Butyrka jail in the center of the city, placed in a tiny cell with six other inmates in the most notorious of Russian prisons. On the morning of his first day in jail, while meeting with his lawyer, Gusinsky wrote on a copy of his arrest warrant, "It is a political intrigue, organized by high-placed officials for whom freedom of speech poses a danger and an obstacle to their plans."[1] Soon he received a message from Mikhail Lesin, the Russian government's press minister. Lesin wanted Gusinsky to sell Media-Most in return for his freedom. After three days in jail, Gusinsky agreed. He was released on June 16, and from the prison he went directly to the Media-Most offices and secretly recorded a video statement saying that he only agreed to sell the company under duress.

Gusinsky was put under house arrest. Over the next three weeks his lawyers hammered out the terms of the sale of Media-Most to the state-owned natural gas monopoly Gazprom. Gusinsky signed the agreement, and it was countersigned by Lesin in his capacity as minister. Then Gusinsky was allowed to leave the country. He fled to London and exile.

Despite the agreement, Gusinsky was reluctant to hand over the company. To pressure him, different law enforcement agencies, under guidance of the General Prosecutor's Office, launched a massive attack on him personally and the media that were part of his empire. To turn up the heat, arrests, criminal cases, accusations, and visits from the FSB and tax police followed. The financial director of Media-Most, Anton Titov, was accused of fraud and sent to jail.

In January 2001 the General Prosecutor's Office summoned Tatiana Mitkova, the top NTV anchor, for interrogation. Now the NTV journalists felt they needed to act on their own. Mitkova's colleague, Svetlana Sorokina, the presenter who had first interviewed Putin a year earlier, addressed Putin during her program on NTV, saying, "Vladimir Vladimirovich, maybe you can find some time to meet us, the journalists of NTV?" The same day she got a call from Putin, and a few days later the president invited eleven journalists from the channel to a meeting at the Kremlin.

At noon on January 29 the NTV journalists gathered at Red Square. They were ushered into the Kremlin through the gates of the Spasskaya Tower and directed to the Kremlin Senate building, an ornate, neoclassical structure with a dome visible from

Red Square. Since the Bolshevik Revolution this stood as the very symbol of the state and the seat of power for Soviet leaders: Lenin lived here, and Stalin had kept a small apartment in the building. The journalists were escorted to the presidential library on the third floor. The round hall housing the library had recently been renovated: the expensive wooden shelves held beautiful volumes, but all of them were stored behind glass, mostly brand-new encyclopedias, books on Russian history, or gifts from foreign leaders.

Suddenly Sorokina was called to a private meeting with Putin while others waited at the library. Putin spoke to Sorokina for forty minutes. Only after that did Putin proceed to the library, accompanied by Vladislav Surkov, a backroom political strategist, and Alexey Gromov, an official from the presidential administration.

Putin walked around the group of journalists, shaking hands.

Viktor Shenderovich, a famous television presenter and political satirist, was in a gloomy mood. "I didn't like the idea of asking the president for help, as if we were his slaves. I didn't believe it would end well," he recalled. He already knew that the Kremlin had quietly hand-carried a proposal to NTV with three demands: stop an anticorruption investigation of Yeltsin's family, stop criticism of the Chechen war, and remove the puppet portraying Putin on Shenderovich's satirical television show known as *Kukly*, or puppets. The show had been poking fun at Russian politicians for five years by creating skits with puppet characters. It was wildly popular and had skewered Yeltsin and other politicians, but Putin disliked being mocked. Shenderovich had recently portrayed Putin as a character from German author E. T. A. Hoffmann's *Klein Zaches*—an ugly dwarf who got magic powers over people.[2]

Shenderovich decided to speak first. He thought that, as a satirist, he had more freedom to speak out about uncomfortable truths. He asked whether Putin was ready to talk honestly, or would they talk on PR terms. "What PR?" asked Putin, "I don't understand a thing about it!" And his blue eyes zeroed in on

Shenderovich. Then Shenderovich asked Putin to make a call to the general prosecutor and ask why Titov, the NTV financial director, was still in prison. Putin said that as president he couldn't interfere with the general prosecutor's activities.

The meeting was a disaster. At the very beginning Sorokina wrote two words on a sheet of paper and handed it over to Shenderovich: "All useless." But Shenderovich kept trying, as did his colleagues. To every question the journalists posed, Putin answered with bland formalities. He said he could not talk to the general prosecutor because the office was an independent institution in Russia. He claimed he did not appoint the general prosecutor because it was the right of the Federation Council, the upper chamber of parliament; the president could only propose. And so it went on. But the journalists knew that Putin's answers were a far stretch from the truth. "What should one do when faced with a bald-faced lie over and over again?" Shenderovich said. "The most silent protest is to get up and leave. Maybe we should have done that, but nobody dared. He was a president, after all. And we had been sitting there for three and a half hours."

For the next three months NTV was left twisting slowly in the wind. Then on the night of April 14 journalists were thrown out of the NTV offices located on the eighth floor of the Ostankino television building. The old NTV was over. Two days later the newspaper *Segodnya* was shut down, and the seventy-four people staffing Parkhomenko's *Itogi* newsweekly were ejected from their offices. The largest media empire independent of the Kremlin was brought to heel.

The journalists of Media-Most fought desperately, and they fought almost alone. Others in Russia's journalistic community did not support them. We then worked at *Izvestia*, and although Irina was able to write critical stories about the government pressure on Media-Most, the newspaper office was filled with a mood of indifference if not quiet pleasure at the downfall of the

Media-Most empire. The NTV journalists were regarded as very professional in news, but they were also seen as arrogant. They were well paid in a field where others were not. Many Russian journalists also rejected the argument offered by NTV that the Kremlin attack was aimed at silencing the only independent television channel in the country; they thought Gusinsky had just made a bid for power and lost. They did not see the attack on Gusinsky as an attack on them or press freedom generally.

What was missing from this picture was the fact that the public began to slowly turn against journalists. During the kompromat battles of the late 1990s and the television wars between the channels, the very idea of investigative journalism was seriously compromised. A number of famous reporters who made their reputation in the early 1990s turned out to be fairly corrupt, ready to publish all kinds of stories if paid properly.[3] The profession of journalism was thrown off the pedestal it had occupied since the perestroika years in the late 1980s. Perhaps even more salient was that to many people in Russian society, journalists and the free press symbolized the liberal values that flooded in after the collapse of the Soviet Union. A large segment of society still felt embittered and betrayed by the West, especially since the Russian economic crisis of 1998, when it seemed that markets and democracy, ideas imported from the West, had produced nothing but chaos. The very ideas of journalism and the free press suffered a loss of credibility.

Journalists in traditional media were losing not just the trust of the public but also their jobs. Over seven years the authors held positions at five publications: the political department at *Izvestia* was dispersed, the editor of *Versiya* weekly was fired, *Moskovskie Novosti* was closed down along with two subsequent attempts of the *Moskovskie Novosti* team to launch a political magazine, and a political website came to nothing. We then joined *Novaya Gazeta*, but after two years it let us go when the management decided to reduce its coverage of the secret services. In the early and mid-2000s

Moscow's newspapers and magazines often changed hands, most of them ending up at the hands of oligarchs loyal to the Kremlin, which helped Putin dampen any hostile reporting. This trend went almost unnoticed by the public. On October 6, 2006, Anna Politkovskaya, the most famous independent investigative journalist in Russia, was killed by hired assassins in the center of Moscow. More people went to the streets to honor her in Paris than in Moscow. Those who ordered this crime were never found.

With television under the control of Putin's government and with the newspaper industry in pro-Kremlin hands, the oligarchs now turned to the Internet. In 1999–2000 they launched the most prominent and potent of the new media in Russia: Gusinsky started NTV.ru (Newsru.com since 2002), and Berezovsky started Grani.ru. The oil tycoon Mikhail Khodorkovsky bought Gazeta .ru from Pavlovsky and relaunched it.

Meanwhile Pavlovsky's Foundation for Effective Politics, still in Putin's corner, enjoyed free reign from the Kremlin and launched a number of ambitious projects, including Lenta.ru and Vesti.ru, both Internet newspapers, and Strana.ru, a Russian national news service, which was presented as a new kind of media combining text, video, and audio. Strana.ru's editor position was given to Marina Litvinovich, Pavlovsky's deputy, who, with Artemy Lebedev, had arrived late to the meeting with Putin in December 1999.[4]

All these new media lacked in-house correspondents, and Lenta .ru and Newsru.com were just news aggregators. Gazeta.ru was the only website with a full-scale editorial office. It was also the only site staffed by print journalists; Gazeta.ru was created by reporters who had previously worked at *Kommersant*. But Gazeta.ru was also the most expensive website to run, while the news aggregators limited themselves to few editors whose task was to rewrite the stories published by wire agencies and newspapers as quickly as possible. Presentation and packaging took over from fact-checking.

But it was clear that a new age was dawning.

On October 23, 2002, a group of armed Chechen terrorists seized a packed theater on Dubrovka Street in Moscow. The Nord-Ost crisis lasted for three days. On Saturday, October 26, FSB special troops stormed the theater, and 130 people were killed, many of them innocent civilians poisoned by a gas containing fentanyl, a narcotic pain reliever, that special forces pumped into the theater in order to subdue the terrorists. During and after the siege the Kremlin found itself for the first time overwhelmed by hundreds of news items and electronic messages critical of the official version of events, circulated on the Internet and promoted by news aggregators.

We worked then for the weekly *Versiya*, and on Sunday, October 27, the day after the storming of the theater, we realized we could not wait a week for our reportage to run in the printed paper. We had a story about what a disaster the storming of the theater had been, and we needed to get it out quickly. We decided to publish it on our website, Agentura.ru, launched two years before to cover the activities of the Russian secret services.[5]

The following Friday, November 1, when *Versiya* was finally going to press with our print story, a group of FSB officers arrived at the editorial offices of the paper and began a search. They hoped to stop the paper from printing but were too late—the pages had already been sent off. A few computers, including the editorial server and Andrei's computer, were seized.[6] The FSB's raid lasted for hours, and our editor, fearing our arrest, told us to stay out of the office. We found a tiny café on Stary Arbat Street near the *Versiya* office. As we sat waiting, a gaggle of reporters we had worked with in the late 1990s at the crime department of *Segodnya* arrived. Hugs and smiles and jokes followed. Immediately they floated dozens of wild ideas on how to organize public support for us, but they were all pure fantasy. We all knew that this time was different. It was clear that the traditional print media our friends worked for were hardly in the mood to support journalists.

The stakes were high. The FSB kept up pressure on *Versiya*. Journalists were summoned for interrogation, including us, and we understood from the questioning that the security service was building a criminal case around a supposed disclosure of state secrets.

What was different this time, however, was the rise of the new media. A few days after the FSB had raided *Versiya* we went to the offices of Newsru.com, a few tiny rooms in the building occupied by Media-Most on Palashevsky Lane. We met with Lena Bereznitskaya-Bruni, an editor of Newsru.com, who had been a friend since the days when we worked at the newspaper *Segodnya*. Lena was outraged by the storming of the theater and promised to help. Newsru.com organized a constant stream of public pressure, reporting every interrogation, and finally succeeded in forcing the FSB to back off bringing any charges.

Meanwhile other traditional media who questioned the special forces' performance at Nord-Ost were put under pressure. The press ministry officially warned the radio station Echo Moskvy that it could be closed down for airing interviews with the Chechen terrorists. The television channel Moskovia's broadcasts were temporarily halted. Putin personally criticized the NTV coverage of the crisis.[7]

But the Kremlin could not catch the new media. The independent digital outlets were better designed, faster, and smarter than anyone else. This time the flow of information turned squarely against the Kremlin. Pavlovsky's pro-Kremlin websites lost the battle for the online audience. In 2002 Pavlovsky had sold two online projects, Vesti.ru and Strana.ru, to the All-Russia State Television and Radio Broadcasting Company, a state-owned corporation that included a major television channel. If this was intended to bolster the Kremlin's defenses with more resources, it faltered. The problem was that these outlets just appeared hapless and vapid at a time of crisis. As an attempt to spin public opinion, it failed. A few years later Strana.ru was quietly relaunched as a guidebook about Russia's regions.

In the mid-2000s more print journalists lost their jobs. For many the Internet was the only place where it was possible to express their opinions. At the same time, online media had no resources to pay for investigative journalism and genuine revelatory reportage. So instead reporters turned into bloggers and opinion columnists, which would be less expensive. The overwhelming number of them were highly critical of Russian domestic policy, despite lacking access to information. Some enjoyed thousands of followers. Many of them also had very popular blogs on Live Journal.com, a blogging platform. Among them, Nossik had been one of the first Russian-speaking users of LiveJournal.com; soon he was the most prominent Russian blogger. In 2006 he was appointed the chief blogging officer at SUP Media, the owner of LiveJournal.com. Within a year he had a new position in the company: "social media evangelist."

The Kremlin was not happy with the explosion of bloggers and turned to means already proven to be effective in dealing with newspapers: having loyal oligarchs buy off the Internet platforms. The first to go was Gazeta.ru—then the only news website with a fully staffed team of reporters—purchased in 2006 by Alisher Usmanov, founder of Metalloinvest and close to the Kremlin. Early the same year Usmanov had acquired Kommersant Publishing House, including its respected business newspaper *Kommersant*, and Gazeta.ru went under its control. In 2008 Usmanov further expanded his media empire: Kommersant agreed to merge Gazeta.ru into SUP Media, the biggest blog service in Russia. The result was that it all ended up in the hands of an oligarch.

In May 2008 Putin turned the presidency of Russia over to
Dmitry Medvedev, and Putin became prime minister. The
mild-mannered Medvedev, then forty-three, who had first worked
with Putin in St. Petersburg, was presented to the public as a
liberal-minded politician with an interest in the Internet and technology. But he was still close to Putin. He was the same Medvedev
who had been chief of Putin's campaign staff in the Alexander
House back in 2000.

One of Medvedev's early moves was to recruit Alexey Soldatov, who had done so much to bring the Internet to Russia at
the Kurchatov Institute, to become deputy minister of communications, responsible for the Internet. Soldatov agreed to take the
post. The joint venture of Relcom, his company, and FAPSI had
come to nothing, and the company had struggled to survive for
years in competition with big telecom holdings that also had their
own landlines, an advantage Relcom never had. In a last desperate
move the teams of Relcom and Demos tried to unite, but the attempt failed, and the national network of Relcom ceased to exist.

Andrei and Alexey Soldatov's relationship was strained again,
and Andrei learned about his father's appointment when he got
a call from a wire service correspondent. At that moment he was
in the parking lot of *Novaya Gazeta* trying to inflate a tire on his
eight-year-old car, an Opel. "Wow, Andrei, leave your old Opel—
your black BMW is surely coming!" was the first mocking reaction of his amused colleagues at *Novaya Gazeta*.

Months after Medvedev took office, in August 2008, war
broke out with Georgia. In six days the Russian army
crushed the Georgian army, but the Kremlin was not happy with
media coverage, especially on the Internet, where the war was frequently criticized.

At the time the biggest and the most popular search engine in the Russian-speaking world was Yandex. Every day the Russian news media struggled to get their stories placed in the top rankings of the search engine. In the late 2000s the middle class in Russia, especially educated people in the cities, lost their newspaper-reading habit in the morning and instead started using the Yandex home page as the starting point of the day and for their daily journey on the Internet. Five top news items on Yandex's home page replaced the front pages of newspapers for millions of Russian Internet users.

In 2008 Yandex became the ninth-largest search engine in the world.[8] The company grew so quickly that the management thought of moving out of the offices on Samokatnaya Street that they had moved into just three years before. This pleasant area of Moscow was built up with red-brick factories in the late nineteenth century and maintains its character to this day. Yandex extensively renovated a three-and-a-half-story building of a former weaving mill down the road, giving it all the hallmarks of a global Internet giant headquarters: a parking lot for bicycles, a large open space inside, a reception desk held up by the letters of the Yandex logo, and an internal museum, with the very first server of the company on display.

In early September 2008, at the end of a working day, two black BMW sedans with flashing lights passed through the gates at Samokatnaya Street, past the life-sized statues of horses that had been brightly painted by children of Yandex employees, and pulled to a stop in front of the former factory.

Out of the cars climbed Surkov, Putin's backroom strategist who was deputy chief of the presidential administration, and Konstantin Kostin, deputy head of the internal politics section of the administration.[9] Surkov and Kostin went to the second floor, to the office of Arkady Volozh, the head of Yandex. In those days Volozh and the Yandex team were preoccupied with the threat of takeover by the oligarch Usmanov. His moves mysteriously coincided with the troubles the company now faced: a new data center had not opened because of a lack of some documentation, a strange criminal case was launched, with Yandex's CEO made defendant, and so on. Volozh was a frequent guest at the presidential administration, and he tried to make friends to counter Usmanov's moves. The Yandex people expected Usmanov to be the main topic of the meeting. For that reason Volozh invited Elena Ivashentseva, a senior partner at Baring-Vostok, a private equity fund and the main Yandex shareholder, to be present.

Lev Gershenzon, the twenty-nine-year-old chief of the Yandex News section, was also tipped off and told to be ready to provide explanations if the visitors were to ask how Yandex used algorithms to select news for the home page of the search engine. Volozh told Gershenzon that when he had gone to see Medvedev a few days before, he had noticed on his table a few screenshots of the Yandex home page, with headlines from Georgian media. Gershenzon recalled, "I had two tasks: to show them that it was a robot, not a human, who chose the news, and for that, to show the internal interface, the mechanism. The second task was to explain the top of the rating, and to show that it was selected by algorithm, not randomly."

Indeed, soon after the meeting started, Gershenzon was summoned to Volozh's office. When he came to the room, he saw Volozh, with two subordinates, along with Ivashentseva, Surkov, and Kostin standing. He was introduced, but Surkov and Kostin did not introduce themselves. They shook hands, and Gershenzon rushed to the table, knocking a glass over the table. It crashed to the floor. He quickly plugged his laptop into a large, flat TV and started showing his slides.

Gershenzon, who spoke slowly and softly, had strong democratic views. In fact, he had participated in all the anti-Putin protest marches. Gershenzon was not a programmer but rather a linguist. He joined Yandex in the fall of 2005 along with a team of friends to work on a special project—to use the search engine to identify the events connected with known persons, like politicians and celebrities, and fashion it into a news stream. Soon Gershenzon became the head of the larger operation of Yandex News. He knew how it worked from the inside, and when he was summoned to the meeting with Surkov and Kostin, he was well aware what was at stake.[10]

Surkov, forty-three, was widely known as the Kremlin's gray cardinal.[11] He had an astonishing career; he had started in the early 1990s as a bodyguard for one of the most prominent Russian oligarchs, Mikhail Khodorkovsky, then made it to the position of his top advertising and then public relations man. In 1999 he landed in the president's administration. Under Putin, he was believed to be behind most of the attempts to transform Russia into what he called a "sovereign democracy," a term coined by Surkov, meaning that democracy in Russia should have different rules from that of the world outside.[12] These projects included creating pro-Kremlin youth organizations who could take to the streets to counter popular demonstrations, the so-called color revolutions such as Rose in Georgia and Orange in Ukraine, both uprisings that had forcibly ejected leaders from office. Surkov also built an effective system to corral the traditional media. He had sat at Putin's right hand during the meeting with NTV journalists seven years earlier. Kostin, thirty-eight and fat and bulky, in the early 1990s had worked briefly at *Kommersant*, had a brief stint in public relations work, and had then gone to Khodorkovsky's Menatep Bank, where he met Surkov. He worked on many pro-Kremlin projects, maintained good relations with Surkov, and in June 2008 was appointed to the president's administration as "the right hand" of Surkov.

"I briefly explained to them how news stories are selected, what factors affect the ranking, what principles are used for annotation and for headlines," recalled Gershenson. "I showed screenshots related to the war in Georgia." Gershenzon tried to explain why it was normal to have a couple of references to Georgian media, out of fifteen altogether.

Surkov interrupted him, pointing his finger to the headline from a liberal media outlet in the Yandex ranking, "This is our enemy," Surkov said. "That's what we do not need!"

Gershenzon soon left the room, and Surkov told Yandex's leadership that the Kremlin needed Russian business success stories. He clearly tried to leave the impression they wanted to be friends, but Kostin requested access to the interface of Yandex News that had Gershenzon explained to them. When the two Kremlin officials finally left, the Yandex people gathered to talk over what had happened. "Everybody was impressed, and clearly shocked," Gershenzon said. He tried to persuade the Yandex management to not cooperate too closely with the Kremlin. "I told them, guys, these are not our terms, we do not need to talk their language, we do not need to talk in terms of enemies and friends."

Surkov and Kostin wanted to control not only traditional media but also what Russia's growing Internet audience was seeing on Yandex. They wanted to define a political agenda every day and every hour. When they pressured Yandex to exclude Georgian sites from the algorithm, they wanted to control not only Russian media, traditional and online, but also the wider Russian-speaking Internet.

Yandex refused to provide access but instead decided to put greater effort into explaining how the news was chosen.

Kostin returned to Yandex once again in spring of 2009. Eventually they came to some sort of agreement. The Yandex operating model was to have relations with all media they had added to Yandex's database of news; the outlets were called partners. They agreed to treat Kostin as a partner. What did he get? Inside Yandex Kostin was given a special name, "interested representative of a newsmaker," and a special phone number to call in case the presidential administration had any questions about the news headlines the Yandex News algorithm selected. Gershenzon recalled, "It was clear, of course, that they were not very interested in algorithms; they were interested in one thing, that they have only what they wanted in Yandex News, and what they do not want will be removed. But we were playing this game very successfully." Kostin called, and Gershenzon sent back explanatory letters. The reaction from Kostin was, "All your explanations are extremely unconvincing."

In most cases these angry calls were caused by the Kremlin's own public relations mistakes. They might present some sort of initiative they wanted to promote and request progovernment media to publish stories about it, but these media just copied the message over and over again. The Yandex algorithm immediately identified the flood of almost identical stories as duplicates and ranked the story very low.

For some time the game satisfied the Kremlin. Yandex withstood the pressure and did not give in.

On September 6, 2008, Medvedev changed the structure of the Interior Ministry, which acts as a national police force. The department dedicated to fighting organized crime and terrorism was disbanded and a new department established, charged with countering extremism. Similar changes were made through all regional departments. With a new global financial crisis hitting Russia, the authorities feared popular uprising. The new department and the FSB launched a massive program to monitor any kind of civil activity, including surveillance of religious organizations, political parties not in parliament, and even informal youth groups. Most of the effort was invested in building huge databases on would-be troublemakers and developing and installing systems to control movements on all kinds of transport. The intention was to have technologies and logistics that could be used to prevent activists from reaching the demonstration. The Interior Ministry, the FSB, and local authorities started to buy advanced surveillance technologies, ranging from drones to closed-circuit

television cameras to face recognition systems, all installed on railway stations and the Moscow Metro.[13]

Simultaneously the Kremlin was desperately searching for new
methods to deal with the ever-growing blogging community and
independent websites. For some years liberal bloggers had complained of trolls. In Internet slang, a troll means a person who
sows discord by posting inflammatory, extraneous, or off-topic
messages in an online community—a newsgroup, forum, chat
room, or blog—with the deliberate intent of provoking readers into an emotional response or otherwise disrupting normal
on-topic discussion. It is possible to post anonymous posts on
LiveJournal.com, an option the Russian "trolls" exploited to the
fullest. Meanwhile liberal media websites suffered a series of attacks known as distributed denial of service, or DDOS, which
were carried out by "hacker patriots," who also attacked government agencies in Estonia, Georgia, and Lithuania. The DDOS is
a sort of attack in which a targeted site receives so many requests
for access that it simply shuts down. It is a simple, cheap, and effective way to disrupt a website, at least temporarily.

But who were these hacker patriots? During the 2000s the
Kremlin had created large pro-Kremlin youth organizations,
which mostly consisted of youth recruited in Russia's regions.
Two of the most important organizations were Nashi ("Ours"),
the oldest movement, built up under direct guidance of Surkov,
and Molodaya Gvardiya ("Young Guard"), the youth wing of the
pro-Kremlin political party United Russia. It was hardly surprising that activists of both movements were caught trolling and
launching DDOS attacks against the Kremlin's opponents.[14] But
for a while the tactics helped maintain a façade of plausible deni-
ability for the Kremlin.

In May 2009 a Kremlin "school of bloggers" was launched,
headed by an associate of Pavlovsky.[15] The school reportedly consisted of eighty people from all over Russia, each working with two
or three activists, and their graduates were supposed to organize

information campaigns online. The Kremlin also tried co-opting some prominent bloggers and promised them access to high-ranking officials.

Then, on August 17, 2009, the Sayano-Shushenskaya Station on the Yenisei River in Siberia, the largest hydroelectric plant in Russia, suffered an accident that caused flooding of the engine and turbine rooms and a transformer explosion, killing seventy-four people. The accident was caused by human error, and the media coverage of the catastrophe worried the Kremlin. In response, they tested new media approach: A journalist from Interfax, a straightforward news agency, was expelled from the area of the Sayano-Shushenskaya Station for his critical reporting. Instead, the popular blogger, Rustem Adagamov, also known as *drugoi*, or "another," who headed the multimedia department of SUP, the company that owned LiveJournal, was invited to report on the relief operation. So he did, reporting favorably for the authorities. In October Adagamov was invited to join the Kremlin press pool, an elite group given special access to the president who are also sympathetic journalists, and he accepted. The new approach showed that the Kremlin could substitute hard-hitting news coverage with friendly bloggers.

Two developments changed the landscape on the Russian Internet in 2010. In April a new cable television channel called TV Dozhd, or Rain, was launched. The channel's owner and main driving force was Natalia Sindeeva. An energetic woman who always greeted people with a big smile, Sindeeva had no television experience. But she had launched a very successful radio entertainment station, Serebryany Dozhd (Silver Rain), in the 1990s. It had taken Sindeeva three years to launch TV Dozhd, and the idea slowly expanded so that by the spring of 2010 she was leading a small media empire, consisting of the news website Slon.ru, launched in May 2009, and a just-acquired city magazine, *Bolshoi*

Gorod, or Big City. All of Moscow's journalists were guessing
who underwrote Sindeeva's projects, though the official version
was that they were funded by her husband, a banker, Alexander
Vinokurov.

Sindeeva, very ambitious, first wanted to rent a space for her
channel in one of the soaring towers of Moscow city, a skyscraper
financial district still developing. The idea was dropped because of
the economic crisis of 2008. She desperately needed to find space
for a headquarters and one day took a call from friends. "They
told me, look, there are premises which could be rented for 100
dollars for a square meter," she recalled. It was the former Red
October chocolate factory, a large red-brick complex built in the
late nineteenth century on an island in the Moscow River, with a
view of the Kremlin. Sindeeva went to look at it; the large space,
still smelling of chocolate, was almost empty. Sindeeva found the
owner, but the talks took months, and then more months were
spent on renovation. When finally TV Dozhd opened on the fifth
floor of the building, Red October had already become a very
fashionable place in Moscow, the epicenter of the hipster movement, with dozens of cafés and art studios occupying other floors
and premises.

At first TV Dozhd was not meant to have much presence on
the Internet or be a political challenge to the authorities. "In the
beginning we didn't think of a news channel," said Sindeeva. "We
thought of television with hosts as authors, we thought of the
channel that should get the audience back to intelligent content.
After all, I knew that a news channel was the most expensive thing
to launch. And personally I was not interested in news."

The full logo of the channel was displayed in English: "TV
Rain: The Optimistic Channel." And indeed, optimistic it was—
the main color was pink, the channel's logo was pink, and the
office of Sindeeva in the corner of the large, open space on the
fifth floor of Red October was full of devices in pink—even her
chair and the refrigerator were pink. What's more, even though

Moscow was full of disenchanted TV journalists who had lost their jobs in the 2000s, Sindeeva didn't want them; her presenters had no prior experience on television. She wanted a fresh, positive perspective.

The channel was officially launched in April 2010, but it was not admitted to the cable television world right away, as she had planned. "When we went on air on April 27," Sindeeva recalled, "we were immediately turned off by cable operators, not because we did something, but as a preventive measure. Surkov simply didn't want an independent channel and, at a meeting with the owners of the two biggest cable operators, he voiced his opinion."[16]

She turned to the website of Slon.ru, a part of her nascent media empire, and on the home page of the site appeared a window, displaying the broadcasts of TV Dozhd. Quickly TV Dozhd became very popular. Intelligent speech and faces were missed so badly on television that all of a sudden Moscow's middle classes tuned in to the new channel. In the summer Sindeeva realized that her audience wanted not only intelligent faces but political news as well.

Now she needed an editor-in-chief for the channel. As a temporary measure, she asked an editor from Slon.ru to sit in and create a news team. In September Dozhd was included in the package of the NTV Plus satellite pay-TV platform. It was a way to let TV Dozhd in Moscow homes and not just on the Internet.

To lead the news team Sindeeva selected a journalist from Russian *Newsweek*, which had just ceased operating. Mikhail Zygar, twenty-nine years old, had spent nearly a decade at the foreign desk of *Kommersant*. "I saw my task very clearly from the beginning," Zygar remembered. "I was there since June, and, well, I found here twenty-three-year-old journalists, and a twenty-five-year-old journalist was considered very experienced."[17] Sindeeva never defined the task for Zygar; they just decided they could work together.

With that, Russia again had a private, independent television channel.

And the digital wave was unfolding ever faster. In 2010 Alexey Navalny, a thirty-four-year-old lawyer, became the most popular Russian blogger with a clear political agenda. Over the previous decade Navalny tried different roads to prominence. He joined the democratic and socialist party Yabloko, from which he was expelled for his xenophobic views.[18] In 2007 he founded a nationalistic movement, Narod, or People. He even took part in the Russian March, an anti-immigrants rally in Moscow, calling for Russia to separate from the North Caucasus. He didn't gain popularity.

He found his magic tool in the spring of 2008 when he bought stocks of the biggest oil and gas companies like Rosneft, Gazprom, and the oil transport monopoly Transneft, all of which were partially owned by the state. He spent over 300,000 rubles, or about $10,000, for all the shares. He gained the right to receive information about the companies' activity and then sue their leadership for corruption. "My goal is to include the question of this investigation into the political agenda of the country," Navalny declared in a blog post about Transneft on November 17, 2010.[19]

That month Navalny posted on his blog his investigation of corruption in Transneft during the construction of a pipeline from Eastern Siberia to the Pacific Ocean. He found that 120 billion rubles had disappeared, and he then posted online scans of documents he had obtained. The next day he woke up the most popular muckraker in Russia. In the country where traditional media were distrusted and investigative journalism was compromised, he soon earned a reputation as a fearless fighter of corruption. "My blog exists only because there is a censorship in media," said Navalny.[20] His popularity among the middle classes in big Russian cities, fed up with corruption, rocketed. TV Dozhd reported his every move.

Meanwhile the authorities were still foundering in the new digital era. Medvedev made a show of being in tune with the age by visiting Silicon Valley in the United States. He opened a

Twitter account—@kremlinrussia—during his visit to Twitter headquarters and ordered government ministries to launch Twitter accounts as well. Even the FSB followed orders and launched an account, but only for a few months. Medvedev also started a high-tech incubator project known as Skolkovo, an attempt to create a Russian version of Silicon Valley. But it was very late to the game, and rather than springing up from innovation, it was directed from the top down.

Medvedev wanted to make Russia technically advanced but not necessarily more democratic. He was eager to follow the authoritarian leader of Singapore, Lee Kuan Yew, who was put on the board of Skolkovo, chaired by Medvedev. When Medvedev visited Singapore in 2009, the bureaucracy's effectiveness impressed him; he registered a company online, and it took just a few minutes. Medvedev cited Singapore as the model Russia must follow.[21]

Navalny was equally fond of Lee Kuan Yew, praised his effectiveness in fighting corruption, and said, "I would forgive many things to Putin, if he were a Russian Lee Kuan Yew."[22]

Authoritarian leaders don't tolerate criticism from outside and zealously protect their national sovereignty. Medvedev shared this approach, and Shchegolev, his minister of communications, began to promote the idea of Russia's "national sovereignty" on the Internet. Soldatov helped acquire for Russia the Cyrillic domain .рф from the Internet Corporation for Assigned Names and Numbers, or ICANN, in charge of managing domain names worldwide. But he left the government in November 2010, unwilling to support other ideas being debated, such as the development of a national computer operating system or a national search engine that would stand apart from the wider world of the Internet, ideas that were being frequently discussed in the corridors of power.

CHAPTER 7

Revolt of the Wired

The mass protests that broke out in the Middle East in early 2011, known as the Arab Spring, struck Moscow as a threat to the Kremlin too. On January 14 the president of Tunisia, Zine El Abidine Ben Ali, fled to Saudi Arabia after twenty-three years in power. On February 11, following waves of huge demonstrations, President Hosni Mubarak of Egypt resigned after twenty-nine years in office. Ten days later, on February 22, the Russian president, Dmitry Medvedev, flew to Vladikavkaz, the capital of North Ossetia, a republic in the North Caucasus. The visit was not announced in advance. At the airport he was met by FSB director Alexander Bortnikov, and they went together to an urgently convened meeting of the National Antiterrorism Committee, which consisted of leaders of the security and law enforcement agencies. In the past Bortnikov had always chaired committee meetings, but this time Medvedev personally took the chair at the head of the table, with Bortnikov on his right. His face was gloomy; he spoke very slowly, emphasizing each word. He started by describing the situation in the North Caucasus and then turned to the Middle East. "Look at the current situation in the Middle East and the Arab world. It is extremely difficult and great problems still lie ahead," he said. "We must face the truth. That scenario was harbored for us, and now attempts to implement it are even more likely. In any case, this plot will not work." He was suggesting that a Western conspiracy was afoot, aimed at instigating protests to overthrow the Russian regime.[1]

Putin, then prime minister, was even more emotional. On March 21 he visited a Russian ballistic missile factory, and one of the workers asked him about Western airstrikes aimed at toppling Libyan President Muammar Gaddafi. Putin retorted that it was just another example of the United States resorting to armed force. He then compared the Western air strikes to a medieval crusade, a comment with deep echoes in Russia's historical memory: one of the early crusades, in the thirteenth century, was directed at Russia. Although it was repelled, the mention of crusades for many Russians evokes fear of being invaded by Western hostile forces.[2]

Putin had long harbored a suspicion that the United States was working on technology that would allow it to topple political regimes on the soil of the former Soviet Union. The "color revolutions" of the early part of the decade in Georgia and Ukraine were seen in the Kremlin as the direct result of an American effort to interfere with regimes closely allied with Moscow. Putin's fear was uncomplicated: a revolution needs crowds, and authoritarian regimes had often successfully suppressed traditional means of mobilizing people, like trade unions and opposition parties. But the new method championed by the United States would bring to the streets youth movements organized from scratch. To counter this threat, the Kremlin attempted to straitjacket any political opposition groups that might use street demonstrations or occupy government buildings in protest. The Kremlin also launched pro-Putin youth movements, whose role was to fill the streets in case of a crisis.

Beyond this, the Kremlin also saw the Arab Spring as another threatening step toward American hegemony. It was not lost on

Putin and his people that the events in Tunisia and Egypt were widely characterized as Facebook and Twitter revolutions. Putin and his entourage became worried that this time the United States had found a truly magic tool that could bring people to the streets without any organizing structure: the Internet. Anxious political masters in Moscow took careful note of a speech by Alec Ross, adviser for innovation to Secretary of State Hillary Clinton, on June 22 in London, in which he declared that the "Che Guevara of the twenty-first century is the network."[3] Two of his points were particularly threatening to the Kremlin: the Internet acted as an accelerant for the Arab Spring, and the Internet facilitated leaderless movements. Ross said that "dictatorships are now more vulnerable than they have ever been before, in part—but not entirely—because of the devolution of power from the nation state to the individual." For people with a KGB mindset, this was a serious warning that the security services could easily miss the right moment and fail to identify the ringleaders, as there were no leaders of protests in the digital revolution and a crisis could break out swiftly. Soon social network technology was made a priority target for the secret services, primarily the FSB. But it was strange new territory they did not fully understand.

Yuri Sinodov, thirty years old, had been a spacecraft engineer by training but made his career in the new world of digital media. He launched a website in 2007 called Roem.ru, specializing in web enterprises and social networks. By 2011 the site became the most insightful source in Russia on social networks and Internet companies. Sinodov was the owner and editor-in-chief of the site.[4]

On April 28, 2011, Sinodov received a phone call from the FSB in which an officer from the FSB's Center for Information Security asked him to disclose the identity of a journalist who worked for him and had written a posting on the popular social media site, Odnoklassniki, or Classmates, about an obscure legal battle involving a private company. The FSB officer said that all he wanted was the name of the journalist, but Sinodov didn't give it up. Instead, he asked the FSB for official confirmation that they had made the request. He soon received it in the form of an e-mail from "cybercrime@fsb.ru" that arrived with the FSB crest and was signed by the head of one of the sections of the Center for Information Security.[5]

Sinodov then contacted the Directorate of Internal Security of the FSB, asking them whether this interest in his journalists was legal. The reply he received came again from the Center for Information Security, which made the original request, this time signed by a first deputy director, establishing that the request was legitimate and was purely for reference. Sinodov still did not reveal the name. He next asked the General Prosecutor's Office, which is separate from the FSB, whether the request was legitimate. Now the response was different: the procedure in question breached a law titled "On Operative-search Activity," the Prosecutor General's Office said, and the Directorate of the Center for Information Security had been informed that it was not permitted to make such requests.

Sinodov immediately published his correspondence with the FSB and the General Prosecutor's Office on his website. "I thought I had no right to publish FSB letters without the response from the Prosecutor's Office, and now I've got it," Sinodov recalled thinking at the time.

Sinodov believed that the FSB's interest in his employee may have been an example of private firms using FSB officers to investigate leaks of confidential business information. This kind of working on the side—essentially corrupt moonlighting—was known to happen. "I think the company referred to in the post was trying to trace leaks of unofficial information about it," Sinodov said. "The FSB itself has no interest in this. It is not a question of any national significance; it's the company's problem."

But Sinodov's story exposed something much more important than moonlighting. The FSB is divided into two large parts. The operations departments consist of counterintelligence, intelligence, counterterrorism, and other activity, whereas the support side of the organization includes such things as creating and providing special technical equipment and meeting other material needs. It was long believed that the Center for Information Security belonged to the second part, but the FSB letters Sinodov published showed that the center was situated in the first, in the operations part, which is the most proactive, involved not only in the technical protection of computer networks but also in active operational surveillance, clandestine activity, and intelligence collection on the Internet. From this discovery it was clear who inside the FSB was working on social networks.

On the corner of Lubyanka Square and Myasnitsky Street is a blockish, looming structure that was once the KGB's Computation Center. The center was initially responsible for protecting computer networks and tracking down hackers, but it had been greatly expanded. The duties now went beyond just protecting the government's networks but also encompassed monitoring the Internet and the media closely. To do this the center used special analytical search software systems developed by Russian programmers.[6] One of the software systems was "Semantic Archive," used by the security services and Ministry of the Interior to monitor open sources and the Internet, including the blogosphere and social networks.

Denis Shatrov, an energetic thirty-five-year-old programmer, was the brain and driver behind Semantic Archive and the company Analytic Business Solutions that created it, which consisted of twenty programmers in a building on the outer edge of Moscow. Shatrov began developing analysis systems in the mid-1990s with his father, the director of a factory in Belgorod that produced automated steering systems for spacecraft. In 2004 Shatrov led the development of Semantic Archive with a very specific customer in mind. "From the beginning we aimed our systems at the private security services. We thought that if we worked with them, then we would also attract our intelligence services," he said.[7] By 2011 Semantic Archive was being used in the FSB, Ministry of Defense, Security Council, and four departments of the Interior Ministry.

In 2011 Shatrov's team developed a special module for forums and blogs. It looked like a simple table on a screen with space to add names of specific blogs. When a user added the names, the system searched a wide swath of sources—not only the Internet but also such things as Russian law enforcement databases, court records, corporate records, blogs, and social networks—producing a report identifying links and connections, such as whether certain people went to the same school or were partners in a project, and sifting other places and events to tie them together.

Ambitious and confident, Shatrov acknowledged there were drawbacks. Only a few dozen officers could use the module at a time. It was not only Semantic Archive that suffered from this problem; a lack of computing capacity crimped the security services from using these systems more widely. The size of the software packages, usually designed to suit a single department of about twenty- to twenty-five people, explains why the FSB and Interior Ministry bought dozens of different systems from different companies. Moreover, Russian programmers had not been able to overcome other problems. First, the monitoring systems were developed for searching structured information, such as databases, and only afterward adapted, some more successfully than others, for semantic analysis of the Internet, in which information can be more free-flowing. Second, the systems were designed to work with open sources and were technically incapable of monitoring closed accounts on Facebook or Twitter, so they could not be used to identify users and authors of posts on Facebook and elsewhere. Yet that was information the security services wanted. For that the FSB had to pick up a phone and call Sinodov.

As the planned presidential election in 2012 drew closer, both Putin and Medvedev were reluctant to say which of them would run. Both hesitated, and hesitated again. Time worked in Medvedev's favor because Putin was losing popularity among bureaucrats and the elites. Sources inside the security services told us that even the FSB's loyalty to Putin begun to waver as a group of generals attempted to contact Medvedev.

The reason was not political but generational. By 2011 the Russian bureaucracy at all levels was chock-full of Putin's people—appointed in the early 2000s—who clogged channels of promotion. Putin's friends and appointees occupied jobs in government, the news media, and state-controlled corporations. There was no upward mobility and no hope for any among a younger generation. The crisis hit even the security services, where all senior positions were occupied by those Putin selected from among people he personally knew from his time in the FSB in the 1990s. Tensions and mistrust between senior and midlevel officers caused a paralysis of leadership, and the friction between the different generations engendered passivity among midranking officers.

Medvedev's inner circle exploited this frustration. In December 2010 Medvedev signed a law that stipulated a retirement age of sixty instead of sixty-five for military and other state jobs. Many in Moscow wanted to believe it was a sign that Medvedev wanted to get rid of the old guard, Putin's generation. In the spring of 2011 every move by Medvedev, every media appearance, was closely examined for signs of whether it meant he would venture to challenge Putin.

In these months Natalia Sindeeva, the owner of TV Dozhd, was desperately trying to get her channel on cable distribution networks. Finally her friends in the television industry told her that the only thing that might help the channel was to put Medvedev on the air.

The opportunity presented itself in mid-April. It was a difficult time for Sindeeva. She had just killed a short, critical poem about Medvedev that had been written for a very popular satire show on the channel Citizen Poet that often wickedly lampooned politicians, just as *Kukly* had in earlier years. Sindeeva had pulled the piece on grounds that it insulted the president personally. The authors of the show left the channel in protest, and Sindeeva came under a storm of criticism from liberal circles for imposing direct censorship.

Then, one day in mid-April, technicians from Digital October, a mix of digital startups, new enterprise incubators, and a conference center, which occupied space at the former chocolate factory on the other side of the wall from TV Dozhd, came to Sindeeva's producers and asked for help. In a week they planned to host a closed meeting of a presidential council on modernization and innovation, to be chaired by Medvedev. Digital October had no cameras to record the event and asked TV Dozhd to lease them some cameras for the meeting. When Sindeeva learned about it, she at once sent an e-mail to Natalia Timakova, a spokeswoman for Medvedev. She had known Timakova for years and addressed her informally. "Natasha, we need Medvedev to come to our channel!" she wrote. Then she listed her arguments: the channel was all about innovation and modernization, the core of Medvedev's political agenda.[8]

Timakova responded the same day. She wrote that Medvedev would come, adding, "You will have ten minutes." In two days the presidential bodyguards sent officers over to check out the premises, a signal to Sindeeva it was for real. It is not entirely clear what prompted Medvedev to accept the offer—the channel's reputation or the flare-up over Sindeeva's decision to kill the piece critical of Medvedev.

On the morning of April 25, the day of Medvedev's planned visit to TV Dozhd, Sindeeva pondered how to dress for it. She had never met Medvedev before and worried she would look much taller than him—Medvedev was quite short—so she abandoned formality and high heels. Instead, she chose blue jeans with holes, a white shirt, and flats.

The door from the Digital October to the premises of TV Dozhd led to the kitchen, then a long corridor, and a large open space, with the brick walls of the old factory exposed under high ceilings. In the kitchen hung a big portrait of Mikhail Khodorkovsky, the Russian oil tycoon who had been imprisoned during Putin's first term. Timakova arrived and walked with Sindeeva along the short route through the kitchen to be taken later by Medvedev. She saw the portrait and turned to Sindeeva, "Is it correct that you want to meet Medvedev in this outfit and you have no intention to remove the portrait of Khodorkovsky?" Sindeeva made no apologies for the jeans and said, "Look, if you want us to remove the portrait, we can do that, but it would be very odd as it has been here for a long time." Timakova said nothing, and the portrait stayed on the wall.

Finally Medvedev walked in, Timakova introduced Sindeeva, and then Medvedev saw the portrait. He smiled and said, "Well, it seems I found myself in the right place." Sindeeva thought it was refreshingly informal. Medvedev charmed Sindeeva, and she showed Medvedev all the offices of the channel, introduced her journalists, and had Medvedev sit at the news anchor desk. At the head of the desk was the editor, Mikhail Zygar, with his co-anchor, four other journalists, and Sindeeva. All the other TV Dozhd personnel gathered behind to listen to the president. Medvedev seemed relaxed and spoke at length of the future of Internet technologies and Internet television. When Zygar asked whether he was going to run for president, Medvedev didn't answer; instead, he laughed and spoke of his plans to teach at the university after his presidential term ended.

Instead of ten minutes, the visit lasted forty-five and was broadcast live.[9] "We were so charmed and inspired by him," Sindeeva recalled. "We all liked him," said Mikhail Zygar.[10]

When he left, TV Dozhd's employees and journalists applauded. "It was clear—he is a normal guy!" said Sindeeva. After the visit she wrote to Timakova, "Could you pass on from us some sort of message—let him believe in himself. Normal people will support him." The visit changed things dramatically for the channel: officials and politicians started accepting invitations to appear on air, and the channel was included in cable television distribution packages, making it available to millions of people across Russia.

Medvedev was presented as a symbol of the new economy, or "modernization"—the economy of computer and information technologies. His most widely known personal initiative was the launching of the Skolkovo technopark eleven miles west of Moscow, a place to foster new start-ups and advanced information technology projects, modeled after Silicon Valley and funded by government contracts. Medvedev had visited Silicon Valley and Stanford University, wearing jeans and using his iPad. The Russian middle classes, especially the urban Internet users, greeted Medvedev's project as a welcome sign that he was committed to a new economy to compete with the old commodities industries, which were permeated by corruption.

Medvedev's time also saw a flowering of initiative and creativity in Moscow, especially in public spaces. Modern art galleries and critics were courted by the Moscow city authorities and invited to realize their dreams in parks and old Soviet factories, which were being turned into modern exhibition centers. City authorities renovated Gorky Park. For twenty years the park looked like an out-of-time symbol of Soviet style, shabby and full of abandoned old attractions, but soon the park was turned into a Russian Hyde Park. People, dressed informally and brightly, crowded into European-style cafés, free WiFi was available throughout the park, and no chaise lounge remained empty. The middle class spread out in Moscow; they rode fancy bicycles, enjoyed the proliferation of free WiFi networks, marveled at modern, Westernized fonts on public signs, and everywhere there were IKEA chairs in parks and public areas.

The people hanging around the former chocolate factory, a new hipster mecca, clearly placed a bet on Medvedev. But his manners and interest in new technologies, so charming for Sindeeva and the journalists of TV Dozhd, didn't make him more of a democrat. If he dared to make a bid for power, as Sindeeva urged in her e-mail to Timakova, it would not produce an open challenge to Putin in a democratic election; rather, it would mean using turf-war methods to outsmart Putin and force him to quit. For a while the Red October generation turned a blind eye to Medvedev's rhetoric about the Arab Spring, his background, his initiatives in fighting extremism that effectively silenced dissent in the country, because he was their "normal guy," the guy who could get rid of Putin.

On August 1 Putin visited a camp on Seliger Lake where his pro-Kremlin youth movement assembled. Inevitably he was asked about his plans for elections, and he didn't respond. Nobody understood why Putin and Medvedev could not decide who would run for president. Both teams tried to push their candidates toward announcing, and Pavlovsky, who had once been a Putin spin doctor, said that "silence of the president and prime minister costs the country dearly."[11]

But still they hesitated.

On Saturday, September 24, 2011, there was a stir in the seats at Luzhniki, Moscow's vast sports arena, which was filled with members of the establishment, the people of Putin's era, as Putin walked to the podium. Spread out in front of him was a sea of government officials and bureaucrats, famous sportsmen and celebrities, all attending the second day of a party congress for United Russia, Putin's party and the dominant force in parliament and the corridors of power. As the foot soldiers in the party of power looked on from the stadium to a stage decorated with a bear and the Russian flag, a question lingered: Would Medvedev run for president again? Or was he just a puppet, a temporary stand-in for Putin? The Kremlin functioned in such an opaque manner that no one was really sure.

Putin took the stage with a swagger of self-confidence. He leaned on the podium, offered a few pleasantries, then declared that he and Medvedev had settled things among themselves years ago. He spoke slowly and seriously. Putin said that people had wanted him to lead the party ticket in the coming elections for parliament and president, but perhaps it was best to leave that to the current president, Medvedev.

Then Medvedev took the stage. After a long, detailed policy speech, he finally came around to what everyone was waiting for: he was in fact endorsing Putin for a return to the presidency, that he was not going to run again.

The applause from the party people was long and enthusiastic. The real power was coming home to the Kremlin—again.

One of Medvedev's close advisers, Arkady Dvorkovich, was watching on television. He let everyone know of his disappointment on Twitter. "Well, nothing to be happy about," he wrote.

The moment was the first tremor in what would become a wave of discontent in Russia. The boisterous democracy of Yeltsin's era had all but died by this point. The Putin party, United Russia, was gray and unremarkable, without any serious ideology other than loyalty, made up of legions of bureaucrats, politicians, and those who depended on them. But unquestionably United Russia was boss. It had no serious competition for power.

On the day of the party congress Zygar, the editor of TV Dozhd, was in the city of Perm attending a theater premiere.[12] When the Moscow office called with the news that Putin was returning, he was sitting with his wife at a café. It was already cold and snowy in Perm in the Ural Mountains, 725 miles east of Moscow. Zygar went out on the street. In shirt-sleeves in the cold, he made round after round of calls on his cell phone to his producers, journalists, technical personnel, then to the anchor and the chief executive of the channel, Sindeeva. It took almost two hours. His first instinct was to react professionally, to cover the news and only later to think about his personal feelings of melancholy.

At 11:21 p.m., broadcasting from Moscow, TV Dozhd launched a special edition of their show *Here and Now*. The show was aired under the heading "The Third Term: The Next Twelve Years with Vladimir Putin," and it opened with the words that the "castling" was over—a chess reference to a special move, allowed only once in a game by each player, in which the king is transferred from his original square to another. The announcer said ominously, "Putin returns to the presidency." The guests on the show talked about illusions they held that Medvedev might have remained and how they lost these illusions. The mood at the studio was gloomy.

Elsewhere in Moscow emotions poured out on social media, a torrent of surprise and disappointment. "Well, the first twelve years went by fast," wrote Yuri Saprykin, editor-in-chief of the magazine *Afisha*. When his friend Svetlana Romanova pointed out that Putin could serve as president until 2024 and she would be Yuri's age by then, he replied, "Svetlana, some spent all their lives under Ivan the Terrible, or under Stalin, twenty-nine years," then added, "those who survived."

Much of the disappointment was about symbols. The sense of loss was not about Medvedev personally—after all, he was part of Putin's machine. But many felt they had lost a chance to exit the past toward something new and promising. There was also a vague feeling of being insulted, that it was wrong in a democracy for two guys to decide who would be in power, to have worked it all out in advance, as Putin had implied. Wasn't it rather condescending of Medvedev and Putin to just declare who would be the next president of Russia? Weren't the voters supposed to have a say?

On the same day Boris Nemtsov, a longtime leader of the opposition to Putin who had earlier been a deputy prime minister under Yeltsin, held a party congress in Moscow. It was a small party of three well-known politicians, and they were all critical of Putin. The congress was convened to decide what line the party should take at the upcoming parliamentary elections. Nemtsov heard of the news of Putin's announcement when he was at the congress, and he was furious. "The form is mocking," he declared of the Putin-Medvedev job swap. "The Russian people were just told that these two—whether Dolce and Gabbana, whether Socrates and Spinoza—thought it would be like that, period. In principle, it's all about the arrogance and humiliation!" He claimed that Putin's decision was the worst scenario for Russia.[13] Nemtsov was under constant pressure, and surveillance. In fact, a video had just recently been posted on YouTube of a meeting he held in a Washington, DC, coffee shop with an American rights activist and a Russian environmentalist. The video had been recorded just a few weeks earlier—and its appearance was an ominous signal that he was being watched, even on US soil.[14]

On September 25 a rally of the still-small political opposition to Putin was scheduled at Pushkin Square in the center of Moscow; it had been approved before Putin and Medvedev's announcement. For five years the authors had attended almost all of these small rallies by the opposition in the city. Once again, on this day it seemed that we already knew all the participants. Only a few hundred people came. The leaders of the opposition sensed the mood of helplessness we all shared. Ilya Yashin, a twenty-nine-year-old opposition activist, declared somewhat desperately to the crowd, "Yes, there are very few of us. But yesterday the last romantics lost their illusions about the thaw, liberalization, or democratization, modernization. . . . Many people today are starting to think about how to leave the country. People are counting how old they will be in twelve years. People don't want to spend their life under Putin. But I ask you, and your relatives and friends, not to leave our country. We should not give it to bastards!"

One of the few individuals who was not afraid to go public with criticism was Alexey Navalny, the blogger who had been trying to expose corruption in Russia and had gained a wide following, not the least for his courage. Navalny was blunt, posting on his blog evidence of all kinds of crooked and dubious deals. He called Putin's party the "party of crooks and thieves." The words went viral.

The scheduled December 4, 2011, parliamentary elections were approaching, and Putin's United Russia Party was poised, once again, to take the lion's share of seats. But something unexpected happened in November as the elections drew near. The progressive, urban intelligentsia, who had studiously kept out of politics for a decade, was angry about Medvedev being dumped and began to express disgust with the party of crooks and thieves. They concluded there was no way the party could win the elections fairly and wanted to do something about it—and do it now, not in March 2012, when the next presidential election would be held. This impulse to do something gave rise rather suddenly to a dozen or so online groups devoted to monitoring the December 4 elections to make sure they were fair and legitimate. These groups included Grazhdanin Nabludatel, or the Citizen Observer; RosVybori, or Russian Elections; Liga Nabludatelei, or League of Observers; and others. In Moscow alone eleven thousand people volunteered to be observers in parliamentary elections.

The loss of Medvedev was a spark, and more sparks followed. In earlier years the middle class had quietly accepted a broad trade-off: Putin brought prosperity, and the public remained passive and didn't participate in politics. This began to shatter. Now the urban middle class was brimming with enthusiasm for political action, and they were angry. However, they lacked experience and coordination; they needed someone to turn their enthusiasm into a national campaign for fair elections.

They found this person in thirty-year-old Grigory Melkonyants, a short, mercurial man who looked as Armenian as his
name. A committed, restless workaholic who spoke a thousand
words a minute, Melkonyants was deputy director of Golos, the
nation's only independent election watchdog organization.

Melkonyants had been waiting for this moment for years. He
had been observing Russian parliamentary elections since 2003,
patiently gathering and analyzing data about voting. He understood how the system worked and how to identify fraud. In the
presidential election of 2004, which Putin won handily, he had arranged a special phone hotline to gather information about fraud
from polling stations across Russia. Then, in the spring and summer of 2011, Golos upgraded the system. Most significantly, he
created an interactive digital map to mark all questionable activity and violations in campaigns and during elections. All the data
would be in one place and could easily be posted by volunteers.
Melkonyants also decided to program a unique web platform to
display and visualize the data rather than use an already-available
commercial product. In the summer of 2011, when the map project was ready to go online, one of the largest websites in Russia,
Gazeta.ru, offered to cooperate and put the map on their website,
where millions of people could see the results. It first went up in
September 2011.

The authorities noticed the map right away, and they were
not happy. Realizing it was a simple tool that could make fraud
at polling stations all too visible, they attempted to create their
own replica of the map, but no one trusted their version. The
pro-Kremlin hacktivists also tried to compromise the Golos map
by feeding it false information. The attempt was rudimentary,
however, taking existing reports of improper activity and just
changing the name of the party and resubmitting it—so crude
that Melkonyants caught it right away. Then, on the eve of the
December 4 election Gazeta.ru came under pressure and took the

map's banner down from its website, but several other news organizations lent a hand to keep it visible, including TV Dozhd. The map remained up for millions of people to see.[15]

But the Kremlin still had a few tricks to play. The night before the parliamentary elections, at twenty minutes past midnight on December 3, Lilia Shibanova, the head of Golos, landed at Moscow's Sheremetyevo airport on her way home from Warsaw. Her mood was grim. The previous day a court charged Golos with violating Article 5.5 of the Administrative Code, which forbids publishing voter polls less than five days before elections. Just a few hours earlier, as she was en route to the Warsaw airport, the NTV television channel, now a pro-Kremlin outlet, aired a program attacking Golos.

She went through passport control, and everything seemed normal. At Customs she selected the green corridor, with nothing to declare, and suddenly customs officials waved her into their room. They thoroughly searched her luggage and then announced that her laptop was to be confiscated for a search because there could be some sort of illegal software. Outraged, Shibanova started to make calls, and customs officials changed their explanation, telling her they were seizing her laptop "for collection of operative information." Shibanova refused to give up the laptop without her lawyer present and spent the night in Sheremetyevo. The reason for this spectacle was clear to her and her people. Her deputy Grigory Melkonyants posted on his Facebook page:

> I really hope that everything will be ok with Lilia Shibanova, she is at the airport (Sheremetyevo, F). Personal inspection, seizure of computer stuff. The task is clear, to divert attention from December 4.

Shibanova was able to leave the airport around midday the next day and was forced to leave her laptop with Customs.

Despite a cyber attack on December 4 intended to disrupt the project, the Golos map displayed massive fraud in the parliamentary election.

Ilya Azar saw it at firsthand. Working as a correspondent for the news website, Lenta.ru, he decided to go undercover in hopes of exposing the people engaging in election fraud by a method known as "the carousel": the fraudsters would venture from polling station to polling station, stuffing the boxes for United Russia, Putin's party. Forty people in Azar's group were each given 10 ballots, already marked for United Russia, for each polling station, as well as a false identity document giving them the right to vote. They would then visit polling stations, show a simple tram ticket at each, which was enough to be given one ballot paper, fill that out, and then add the ten additional papers they had brought, stuffing about 3,080 ballots for United Russia by evening. Azar gained access to the group by a source he knew who was a courier in a small Moscow company. Azar was promised 1,000 rubles, or about $30, to take part.

When he witnessed the fraud at the first polling station, Azar blew the whistle, and police detained the fraudsters. He then posted a story to his website entitled "Carousel Is Broken," and the whole scam fell apart.[16]

Azar's story immediately went viral in Russia and caused a sensation. The revelation of such blatant fraud incensed the thousands of election observers who had volunteered, galvanized by their disgust over the dumping of Medvedev. Now they were really furious. At the same time, reports of fraud in the election poured in from most of the regions. Golos published seven thousand reports of infringements at polling stations across the country. The anger reached a crescendo when Russia 24, a state television channel, aired election results from the Rostov region in southern Russia. As expected, United Russia was in first place with 58.99 percent of the vote. The Russian Communists, who were quiet allies of Putin, got 32.96 percent. Then each of the other parties picked up a small piece of the pie as well, and when all the votes were tallied up, the sum was astonishing: 146 percent!

The day after the elections, December 5, anger boiled over into the streets. People were upset by the brazen stealing of the election and gathered at Chistie Prudi, a tree-lined boulevard in the center of the city. Thousands showed up, without any serious organizing. Lev Gershenzon, an editor of Yandex News, brought five colleagues from Yandex. They had all been election observers and spent hours and hours at the polling stations. They felt angry and cheated by the election. When they looked around at the crowds, they were surprised to see so many people in the same mood of fury and despair. "The mood was very depressed, this feeling of desperation," Gershenzon said. "We did not expect that there would be so many people."[17]

The police responded with arrests. More than three hundred people were detained, including the blogger Alexey Navalny and the political activist Ilya Yashin.

Navalny at once tweeted from the police van. "I'm seated with folks in an OMON bus," he said cheerfully, referring to the riot police, notorious for their brutality. Navalny had been on Twitter for two years and had tens of thousands of followers.

Police kept detaining protesters and took them away to stations all over the city. Grigory Okhotin, a thirty-one-year-old journalist who witnessed the arrests, was stunned by the numbers of people hauled away, many of them friends who were completely unprepared for such an experience. He then went with his brother to a club nearby where there was free WiFi.[18] His detained friends began posting on Facebook about whom was arrested and where they were being held. Then Okhotin and his brother decided to drive around the city to see whom he could get released. He started posting what he learned on his own Facebook page, using the hashtag OVD, meaning, in Russian, the police station.

Soon, it looked like this:

#OVD-news: OVD Fili-Davydkovo: nineteen people

#OVD-news: OVD Yakimanka: eight people

#OVD-news: in OVD Dorogomilovo there are twenty-five people. Names of some of detainees: Bulgakov Anatoly, Bulgakov Dmitry, Shipachev Dmitry, Chernenko Artur . . . Ermilov Egor, Balabanov Victor, Lozovoi Dmitry, Polyansky Timur, Balabanov Igor, Yudin Sergei, Kapshivy Dmitry

Okhotin and his brother posted their first report on who had been detained that night on the website of the magazine *Bolshoi Gorod*. From that moment everyone concluded that Okhotin was in charge of detentions all over the city. "I started getting calls from complete strangers and was sent messages, 'We are detained, we are here and there.' And it occurred to me that all this information could be centralized," he told us. Over the next two days the Okhotin brothers launched the website OVD-info, which became a public forum for sharing information about Russian citizens detained during protests.

The next day, December 6, the court sentenced Navalny and Yashin to fifteen days in jail. Muscovites went to the streets again, this time gathering at the Mayakovskaya Metro, on Triumfalnaya Square.

In the crowd was a slim, tall, twenty-four-year-old man with light-brown hair and gray eyes. He was already well known and popular: Ilya Klishin. He had come to Moscow from the provincial city of Tambov to study foreign policy at the prestigious Moscow State Institute of International Relations. However, he was soon deeply involved in social media and marketing.

In 2010 Klishin took offense at an article by a pro-Kremlin publicist attacking his generation for being idle "hipsters"— young people who were incapable of thinking about anything other than their iPhones, bicycles, and stylish sneakers. Klishin wrote an article in reply, "Hipsters Strike Back," claiming that his generation was indeed interested in politics. Then he and a friend launched a small website, Epic Hero, concerned with politics but cast in terms of the hipster subculture, which they both embraced. Epic Hero became very popular and gained such wide notice that even Medvedev's staff had invited them to work on the effort to build a Russian Silicon Valley. In November 2011, just before the parliamentary election, Klishin and his friend sold Epic Hero to the liberal website OpenSpace.ru, and he then joined the project as staff editor. On December 6 he went to the square to write about the new face of political protest. Among those in the crowd there was a rumor that the next big demonstration would be in four days and held at Revolution Square, very close to the Kremlin.

Very late that night Klishin got home and opened his laptop. He started searching for anything he could find about the next rally at Revolution Square. He found only a short news piece on another website that permission had been granted for a demonstration of three hundred people on December 10, but that was all.

Klishin went to Twitter and posted a question: "Is there any event on Facebook for December 10?"

A reader of Epic Hero wrote back, "No. Let's start the event."

Klishin knew that Facebook could be used to organize an event, such as a birthday party, so he launched his event—for a rally at Revolution Square—on Facebook, sending the link to his friends and journalists. Finally, exhausted, he went to sleep.[19]

The next morning, December 7, when he opened the computer, Klishin found that more than ten thousand people had RSVPed yes for the event.

At the same time, several other journalists and activists were also using Facebook to trade ideas about what should come next in the protest movement. Among them were Yuri Saprykin, the editor of *Afisha*, and Sergei Parkhomenko, at this point a host

on Echo Moskvy, the popular liberal radio station. In the 2000s
Parkhomenko felt restless, as did many journalists of his generation. He had only his weekly Friday program on Echo Moskvy to
run, and it was not enough for his energetic character.

He was among those who sat down on the evening of December 8 at a restaurant, Jean-Jacques, popular among the Moscow
intelligentsia. Some opposition politicians were there as well as
journalists and activists. All the discussion revolved around how
to persuade the Moscow government to give a permit for a larger
demonstration. Late in the evening they got a phone call from
Nemtsov, the opposition leader, who said the Moscow authorities were ready to talk—and someone should go to City Hall
immediately.

Parkhomenko was the only one with a car, so he volunteered.[20]
He brought with him Vladimir Ryzhkov, a former member of
parliament who was also in the opposition, and two activists, who
were formal applicants for the meeting. Parkhomenko brought
with him his iPad so he could be in contact with the other group
members, who were dispersed over the town, with some, like
Saprykin, sitting in the office of Lenta.ru.

Parkhomenko and Ryzhkov were met at the lobby of City Hall
and were shown to the fourth floor to a large office where they
saw a tall man in a suit with his face strikingly reminiscent of a
young Leonid Brezhnev—it was deputy mayor Alexander Gor-
benko, in charge of information policy. The talks dragged on for
hours. Parkhomenko was carrying an iPad and constantly posted
updates on Facebook in a closed chat with his group. "My page on
Facebook was my major instrument in the talks," Parkhomenko
recalled.

He showed the city officials that thousands more people
wanted to attend the rally and demanded permission for them
to attend. When a young woman, a club manager, wrote on
Facebook that she was scared but would nevertheless go to the
protests, her posting was rapidly "liked" by thousands of people.

Parkhomenko showed it to the city officials. He told them he was not a leader of the movement, just a messenger. His only role was to show everyone what was going on—social networks made the world horizontal. The people in Moscow who had become so agitated didn't need a leader or organization to tell them what to do or where to go; they got it all from social networks, which were filled with information. When, during the meeting, he saw that the number of people RSVPed to the event had hit twenty thousand, Parkhomenko showed the iPad to city officials.

Eventually they agreed to give a permit for thirty thousand for December 10 but insisted that the protest site be moved away from the Kremlin—it could not be as close as Revolution Square—and they offered Bolotnaya Square, not far away, but separated by the Moscow River from the Kremlin. Everybody agreed, and Parkhomenko took a photo of the document and posted it on his Facebook page around 10 p.m. on December 8.

Klishin immediately changed the location for the protest on Facebook.

In the months to come this decision was to be the constant source of confusion and mutual accusations. The most radical protesters argued that such a big demonstration didn't need official approval, causing the protest to lose momentum when the leaders agreed to move the event to Bolotnaya, which was not so close to the Kremlin. The more moderate protesters were convinced that Muscovites were not ready for violent clashes with the police.

Bolotnaya Square is on an island. The Moscow River runs on one side, and a small canal on the other. The Kremlin is located across the river. On Saturday, December 10, more than fifty thousand people crowded onto the island. Nothing so large had been seen in Moscow since the dying days of the Soviet Union. Those who could not make it watched it live on TV Dozhd.

The protesters were the heart of the new Russian middle class, people who usually were found in the restaurants and cafés of Moscow but were now on the island with placards and slogans. The crowd was also sprinkled with the usual assortment of radical anarchists, journalists, and human rights campaigners who had attended demonstrations and marches over the years. But this time they were swallowed up in the mass of completely new faces, most of whom were attending a protest for the first time in their lives. Many of them held placards such as "You are not representing us" and "Putin must go."

Lev Gershenzon, the head of Yandex News who had earlier stood up to Kremlin efforts and who brought his colleagues to the first protest after the fraudulent vote, took with him his seventeen-year-old daughter, Liza, who had with her a placard with big red words on a white sheet: "Give us back our voices," it demanded.

The protest on Bolotnaya Square marked something completely new in Russian society. It was not political parties, trade unions, or charismatic leaders that drove Muscovites to demonstrate by the tens of thousands; those who went to Bolotnaya were not ready to support any political group or party. The crowd responded enthusiastically to popular thriller writer Boris Akunin who, in a speech, called only for the restitution of Muscovites' right to elect their mayor and a rerun of the election in the capital.

The protesters were galvanized by anger over the election fraud, which had been exposed by new technologies on the web, and they were mobilized through social networks. In a country that was for centuries defined by hierarchical order, by a power vertical, it was remarkable to see citizens united so thoroughly by horizontal methods.

The protesters had also enthusiastically embraced a symbol: the white ribbon. It was originally proposed by a user on Live-Journal, Russia's top blogging platform, and it went viral, with thousands taking it up—white ribbons appeared on user pics on users' blogs and social media. Soon people took the white ribbon offline and began displaying them on their cars too.

This new experience also led to something very unusual for Russia: the protesters demanded transparency, which the Internet made possible. The activists posted the results of their talks with city officials immediately, and the organizing committee of the protests, formed after Bolotnaya, broadcasted its discussions online. The leaders reported all their moves—from choosing the new place for the next protest to collecting money—openly online. Navalny and Yashin were not at Bolotnaya because they were still sitting in jail, but crowds of people visited them every day, singing songs outside the police stations. Navalny's charisma and optimism changed people's attitudes to such detentions; it became almost fashionable among hipsters to be detained.

For Putin and Medvedev, the rally at Bolotnaya Square was just what they had feared—a mass protest just outside the walls of the Kremlin. And it was facilitated by Facebook and Twitter, technology made in the West.

Many protesters on Bolotnaya Square were puzzled by the sight of an unfamiliar aerial vehicle with propellers circling overhead—some even thought it might be a UFO. The mysterious device was a radio-controlled aircraft, manned by Stanislav Sedov, a thirty-five-year-old drone enthusiast and highway engineer by training. A few days before the protest he had suggested to a friend, Ilya Varlamov, a well-known blogger who founded an agency for citizen journalism called Ridus, that they try to film the crowd from a drone. They got unofficial permission to launch the drone with a camera.[21] How they secured this permission is not clear, but it was widely reported that Ridus was itself set up with the approval of the presidential administration. Perhaps the Kremlin wanted to get evidence of how few people went to protests.

On Bolotnaya, Sedov launched the little device from a protected police site. The police even chased away curious observers so they didn't get in the way of the launch. When Sedov had his drone in the air, it became clear immediately that many more people had come to the demonstration than expected. The photographs became the very best evidence of the enormity of the crowd.

Almost immediately the pictures from the drone were posted online by the Ridus agency itself. The revolt of the wired was under way.

CHAPTER 8

Putin Strikes Back

The first attack came surging through the Internet on the evening of December 3, 2011, just before the parliamentary election. The target was LiveJournal, Russia's top blogging platform. Along with Facebook, LiveJournal was the favorite place for protesters to find political news and discussion. With an austere and simple design, LiveJournal had been used widely by Russian bloggers and journalists, and it featured well-established figures with thousands of followers. When the attack came, Anton Nossik, who was media director at SUP Media and owned LiveJournal, was in Moscow, monitoring the servers, which were based in Nevada. They were hit with a distributed denial-of-service attack, or DDOS, in which a server is so overwhelmed by requests for access that it simply shuts down. The method is crude, like jamming a radio broadcast, but can be effective. At 8:12 p.m. Nossik wrote on his blog, "The pre-election DDOS-attack on LiveJournal continues. At this minute our servers are bombarded by dump requests with the speed of 12–15 Gbits per sec. The goal of the attacking is clear. It's banal Soviet jamming, and it has the same task: to prevent the uncontrollable exchange of information."[1]

The next morning, on Sunday, December 4, beginning shortly after 6:30, the onslaught expanded to fourteen independent Russian news media outlets. Hackers went after websites of the radio station Echo Moskvy, the newspaper *Kommersant*, the news website Slon.ru, TV Dozhd, and, inevitably, Golos, the election monitor. The radio station's servers remained offline for the entire day.[2]

The attack on Slon.ru, the website of Natalia Sindeeva's media empire, began at about 7:30 on Sunday morning, but it was not until 9 a.m. before the website's programmers reacted to it.[3] At first they tried to solve the problem themselves by asking the hosting provider to cut off foreign Internet addresses trying to access the site. This fixed the problem for a short time, but then the volume of traffic increased and the attackers changed tactics, and the server went down again. The Slon.ru programmers then turned to a protective system, known as Qrator, designed to mitigate such DDOS attacks by monitoring traffic and filtering it.

The Kremlin had tried to pressure Golos and others, repeatedly, not to report election violations to the public. Once they did so, a wave of cyber attacks began, apparently intended to stop the information from spreading. The attacked sites responded by quickly migrating elsewhere. Slon.ru, *Bolshoi Gorod*, TV Dozhd, Echo Moskvy, and Golos all switched to Qrator's servers, where they were shielded somewhat from the DDOS attacks. Still, the active attack phase continued into the evening of December 4, and Slon.ru alone was bombarded by 200,000 to 250,000 bots: an attacker would use a botnet, a network of zombie computers, to send a high volume of fake requests to the targeted sites with the aim of producing a server overload, which would then cause the site to crash.[4]

On December 5 the initial wave of attacks subsided. But Echo Moskvy was still bedeviled by the hackers, who shifted to a different tactic, poised to strike again. The attackers aimed to seize the moment when the site would start to fail and possibly emerge from its protected state. About one hundred bots attempted to send difficult requests to the Echo Moskvy site, still under protection at Qrator. Under constant bombardment, Echo Moskvy and Golos distributed their news and other content on LiveJournal .com. But at the same time, LiveJournal remained under attack too, and Melkoniants, the brains behind Golos, switched to Google Docs to publish the Golos data on electoral violations.

On December 6 Ilya Klishin's Epic Hero was attacked, apparently for announcing the demonstration at Chistie Prudi Boulevard. On December 7 a DDOS attack then shut down our website, Agentura.ru. Our technical staff were forced to reset the site's server every fifteen minutes, but it didn't help: we were down for the most of the day. On December 8 an attack temporarily crippled the website of the newspaper *Novaya Gazeta*. The assaults on Epic Hero, Agentura.ru, and *Novaya Gazeta* were part of a second wave. This phase had a different objective than the first: instead of suppressing information about election fraud, the goal was to eliminate reporting about street protests.

Who was behind the take-downs? The phenomenon of crude DDOS attacks was not new; it first appeared in Russia in January 2002, when hackers paralyzed, for a day, Kavkaz.org, the website of Chechen separatist fighters. In that case the perpetrators were students in Tomsk, a medium-sized city in Siberia. Evidently the local FSB branch was fully aware of the attack, putting out a press release that defended the students' actions as a legitimate "expression of their position as citizens, one worthy of respect."[5] Since then Russian "hacker patriots," as they are called in the press, have launched similar attacks aimed at the websites of independent media in Russia as well as at government agencies in Estonia, Georgia, and Lithuania. Russian government officials always deny responsibility for these attacks, but in December 2011 Konstantin Goloskokov, one of the "commissars" of the pro-Kremlin Nashi youth movement, admitted to the *Financial Times* that he and some of his associates had launched cyberstrikes on Estonia in 2007 after Estonia had angered the Kremlin with a decision to move a Soviet war memorial out of the center of Tallinn.[6] It seems entirely plausible that DDOS attacks aimed at Putin's adversaries were organized not by the security services directly but by youth movements encouraged by the Kremlin.

The most prominent Russian expert on cybersecurity, Eugene Kaspersky, might have been expected to lend a hand to find out who carried out the attacks, but at the outset he didn't seem interested. In fact, he denied that attacks on the media the day of the elections had ever occurred. On December 5 Kaspersky wrote a blog post suggesting that some of the websites could have been "victims of their popularity" and had failed to cope with tens of thousands of simultaneous requests from people who are interested in politics. He repeated the same point a day later. But then, on December 16, he disclosed that he had been given log files from *New Times* magazine, one of the targets. Looking at these, he finally acknowledged the fact of the massive DDOS attack but claimed, rather ambiguously, "Something tells me that neither the opposition nor the Kremlin-Lubyanka are interested in such attacks."[7]

Kaspersky has never denied his KGB background, and the picture of him as a young officer in uniform is available on the Internet. He grew up in the small town of Dolgoprudny, north of Moscow, where he excelled in math and physics at school. Instead of entering the prestigious Moscow Institute of Physics and Technology, located in his hometown, he joined the High School of the KGB to study cryptology. After leaving the KGB, he built his company, Kaspersky Lab, from scratch, and has constantly cooperated with the FSB in investigating computer crimes. When thugs kidnapped his nineteen-year-old son in 2011, it was the FSB that helped release the young man in five days without harm.

The early December cyber attacks were ferocious—but ultimately proved futile. Alternative pages for posting information about the electoral violations were quickly established on social networks. When LiveJournal, the most popular blog platform in Russia, suffered an unrelenting assault, users turned to Facebook, which became a central clearinghouse for collecting information related to the protests.

As a tool for spreading news about the protests, Facebook was more popular than the local social network, VKontakte, a Russian replica of Facebook. For the protest on Bolotnaya Square on December 10, Facebook got more than thirty-five thousand people signed up, compared to some sixteen thousand who signed up on VKontakte. Facebook was simply the first network the Russian intellectual elite, experts, and journalists joined to be in contact with their friends and colleagues abroad. VKontakte, though enjoying great popularity, lacked this elite appeal.

But VKontakte did not escape the authorities' attention. Alexey Navalny, the popular anticorruption blogger, led a user group of protesters on VKontakte, and on December 7 Edward Kot, a moderator of the group, discovered that their group seemed to be blocked, with no new posts allowed. When he complained to VKontakte, he got a reply an hour later from Pavel Durov, the somewhat mysterious founder of VKontakte. Durov, then twenty-seven, explained to Kot that Navalny's group had reached a set limit of 1,634 posts in a single day, then added that VKontakte's technical team was, at that moment, changing algorithms for them.

Twenty minutes later the group was unblocked. Kot was so impressed that he posted a thanks to Durov. Durov replied, "Ah, all's fine. In the last days the FSB has been asking us to block protest groups, including yours. We didn't comply. I don't know how it will all end for us, but we are up and running."[8]

When Kot asked whether he could post this, Durov agreed. Kot published a post on his page on LiveJournal. The next day, December 8, Durov published a scan of the original written FSB request. In the document a general, chief of the FSB branch in St. Petersburg, asked Durov to "cease the activity" of seven online groups related to the protests. The day after revealing the document, Durov was summoned to the St. Petersburg Prosecutor's Office. He refused to come, posted information about the summons to the prosecutor's office, and again refused to close down the groups.

Next, the 1990s technique of kompromat was tried against the protest movement. On December 19 audio files of nine tapped phone calls of Boris Nemtsov, a prominent opposition leader, were posted on the pro-Kremlin website Lifenews.ru. The tapped conversations were very candid assessments of the other opposition leaders, and they were embarrassing. Nemtsov told us that the conversations had taken place in the run-up to the December protest rallies. "Their goal was simple," he recalled. "They wanted to divide us in the run-up to the rally, but the opposition didn't fall for it."[9] The episode didn't have any lasting impact on Nemtsov's standing inside the opposition.

All these gambits—the first Kremlin counteroffensive—largely flopped. The combination of intimidation and direct pressure from the security services, deployment of the Kremlin's youth movements, DDOS attacks, phone tapping, and everything else simply didn't work in the new circumstances of tens of thousands of angry citizens linked together by social media.

Five days after the demonstration on Bolotnaya Square, on December 15, Putin held his annual television call-in show, called the *Direct Line*, broadcast live by three Russian television channels and by *Russia Today* in English as well as by three major radio stations. The call-in show was aimed to demonstrate Putin's confidence that he would win the upcoming presidential election. He answered questions for an unprecedented four and a half hours, displaying a relaxed, self-confident mood. He smiled and laughed a lot during the long hours of the broadcast. He was on stage in a large hall; the audience was stacked with his supporters, members of his United Russia party, and the like.

When he was repeatedly asked about the protests, Putin seemed a little annoyed, but he never lost his cool. He came to the show prepared. Rather than take any personal responsibility for what had inspired the protests, he blamed them on self-centered political jockeying for the upcoming presidential elections. Then he offered to install real-time online video cameras at all polling stations to deter violations in the future. Both answers were intended to tamp down the protesters' fervor. But Putin showed that he completely misunderstood why the people were protesting. "You know the thing about the fraud, about the fact that the opposition is dissatisfied with the election results, here there is no novelty," he declared. "The opposition exists for that purpose. It struggles for power!" In other words, all the complaints about fraud were just critics whining and pursuing their own interests.

Alexey Venediktov, the editor-in-chief of Echo Moskvy, who had been at Bolotnaya Square, fired back, "You are speaking about the opposition, but, believe me, there was not only the opposition on Bolotnaya. You are replying to the opposition in your answer, but what could you tell to these newly outraged people, angry with the unfairness—they believe their voices got stolen?"[10]

Putin didn't understand what Venediktov had told him. His mindset, formed in the Soviet KGB, led him to think that political dissent can only exist because of an organization, and an organization requires ringleaders and money. Putin said that according to his information, the protesters were students who had been paid to attend, and then he blamed the West for sending them and recalled the popular uprisings elsewhere, the dreaded color revolutions. "We know the events of the Orange revolution in Ukraine," he said. "By the way, some of our opposition leaders at that time were in Ukraine and officially worked as advisers to the then-President Yushchenko. They are transferring this

practice to Russian soil." Again Putin sought to portray the opposition as some kind of external, self-interested conspiracy. What
he failed to see was that the demonstrations were not driven by a
plot but were the result of a spontaneous, independent, popular
movement.

Finally Putin made a striking comment on the symbol of the
protests, the white ribbon. "Frankly, when I looked at the television screen and saw something hanging from someone's chest,
honestly, it's indecent, but I decided that it was propaganda to
fight AIDS—that they had hung, pardon me, a condom up."

If he thought that would discourage the protesters, Putin
clearly miscalculated.

What happened at Bolotnaya Square injected enthusiasm
and drive into the protest movement, which then solidified and gained new leadership. Activists, journalists, and opposition politicians formed an organizing committee. There would be
more protests. One of the leaders was Olga Romanova, forty-five,
who had worked as a journalist for twenty years. Romanova, an
attractive blonde, was remarkably versatile, able to talk equally to
an intelligent Muscovite professor or an ordinary, everyday person from a nearby shop. She was prominent in the 1990s when
she had covered the Russian economy in the newspaper *Segodnya*. Since then, her career had risen, and in 2004 she won the
Taffy, the most prestigious television award in Russia, for her
work as a presenter. Romanova's fortunes changed in 2007 when
her husband, Alexey Kozlov, a businessman, was prosecuted on
a fraud charge that he and his wife described as a vendetta by a
well-connected former business partner. Olga tried desperately to
win her husband's release, forming the organization Rus Sidya-
shaya, or Russia Behind Bars, which joined together relatives of
businessmen in jail. She spent her time visiting prisons all over
the country and wrote a blog named after the Butyrka prison in

Moscow, detailing harsh conditions in Russia's prisons. She became the Federal Penitentiary Service's worst nightmare.

Now she volunteered to open an account in her name at Yandex Money, the largest online payment service in Russia, in order to collect donations to support the protests. The organizing committee agreed. With Romanova in charge, it meant that nobody would question where the money went, given her unblemished reputation for integrity. The money would be safe from government pressure too; any attempt to intimidate Romanova would clearly be futile. The account at Yandex Money became known as Romanova's Purse.[11]

On December 20 Yandex published on Facebook a new application that facilitated crowdfunding through Facebook for Yandex Money. Previously Yandex Money had become a common way for Moscow's middle class to carry out e-commerce online; people trusted Yandex with their credit cards and used it to make purchases. Now the crowdsourcing application took it to a new level. Protesters were quickly able to utilize a transparent way to collect money for the demonstrations, and it was all done thanks to Internet technology. Romanova was a fearless overseer. Yandex said it was pure coincidence that the new crowdsourcing app was rolled out at the same time that protesters were raising money for the next rally.

The next big protest rally was scheduled for December 24 on Prospect Sakharova. Ilya Klishin renamed the main protest event page on Facebook, with the cover photo depicting a wide image of the Bolotnaya crowd and the slogan, "We Were on Bolotnaya and We Are Coming Back," and on the side carried a picture with the words, "We Are for Fair Elections." Organizers announced they needed 3 million rubles, about $100,000. Romanova soon collected more than 4 million rubles online and immediately posted a detailed report of how the money would be spent.

Meanwhile Grigory Okhotin's OVD-Info, the project to track detentions, got its own website, two hotline phones, and help from the opposition movement Solidarity and the oldest Russian human rights group, Memorial, which provided lawyers to visit police stations, provide legal support, and collect information. "In two days, I along with my friends made a simple website to gather all information about the detainees and their whereabouts. We also found ten volunteers to monitor the situation," Okhotin said.[12]

Now if a protester was detained, he knew where to call to get legal help and support.

Prospect Sakharova is an eight-lane urban thoroughfare in the center of Moscow, originally built for the 1980 Olympics, with unusually wide sidewalks. In later years stark Soviet-style office buildings were erected along the thoroughfare, dominated by the sixteen-story semicircular complex of Vnesheconombank, with cold, white walls and brown-tinted windows. There, on December 24, the air was frigid, but the wide street was jam-packed with demonstrators, over one hundred thousand people, shoulder to shoulder. Just as with Bolotnaya, the crowd was made up of the intelligentsia and urban middle class. This time many carried stylish placards and posters that had been printed for the occasion. Some bore posters depicting Cheburashka, a beloved, furry Russian cartoon figure who in these posters was in demonstration mode. Other posters featured the reviled head of the Central Election Commission in a wizard costume, manipulating ballot papers. There were also new protesters, middle-aged men in dark jackets and knit caps protecting them against the cold, suggesting that the demonstrations' audience was growing.

A leader of the protest was novelist Boris Akunin, author of popular nineteenth-century detective stories. "Do you want Vladimir Putin to become president once again?" he asked the crowd. "No!" they roared back. Sergei Parkhomenko, the journalist who had paved the way for the first demonstration in the negotiations with City Hall, was also on the stage, taking photographs. He was particularly impressed by a surprise arrival, Alexey Kudrin, a former finance minister and deputy prime minister, who had resigned only in September but remained close to Putin. Parkhomenko posted on his Facebook page that Kudrin had stood on the stage for three hours in the bitter cold to have a chance to address the crowd. He spoke out against the election fraud, and for a moment the protesters seemed to glimpse their first defector from the Kremlin team.

The crowd eagerly waited for Alexey Navalny, who had been released from jail three days before. Widely known for his blog, few were familiar with him as a public speaker. In a black trench coat and a gray scarf, he at first held back on the large stage, standing under the broad banner declaring, "Russia Will Be Free." Finally, Romanova announced Navalny. Navalny was excited by the numbers of people who came, but he was also very angry. He went to the edge of the stage and grabbed the microphone in the manner of a rock star. His face was projected on the large screen on the right of the stage.[13]

In his remarks, Navalny savagely attacked Putin as a "small, cowardly jackal." His voice rising to a howl, he said, "I can see that there are enough people here to seize the Kremlin. We are a peaceful force and will not do it now. But if these crooks and thieves try to go on cheating us, if they continue telling lies and stealing from us, we will take what belongs to us with our own hands." He led a chant: "We are the power!"

The crowd had been curious about Navalny, but they were taken aback by his aggressive rant. Faces were creased by confusion. The crowd had been full of anticipation before he spoke, but his blasts left them uncertain. They may have agreed with the substance of his criticism, but his tone was unexpectedly harsh, puzzling more than a few in the audience.

Navalny didn't notice. He had never seen such big crowds before; he had missed Bolotnaya Square because he had been in jail.

He was, primarily, a creation of the Internet and his sharp skills as a blogger. His only real experience speaking to rallies up to this point had been the annual Russian nationalist marches, to five or six thousand people at most, and it was there he had developed his shrill voice. He shouted into the microphone, "Watching Bolotnaya on TV in jail, we feared that you would never come again. But you have come! You've come! And next time there will be a million!"

On December 27 Vladislav Surkov, Putin's gray cardinal and first deputy chief of the presidential administration, was ousted and replaced by Vyacheslav Volodin. For years Surkov had been in charge of dealing with the opposition, either through the informal pact with the middle classes, micromanagement of media, and pressure on Internet companies, or through funding of pro-Kremlin youth movements. Surkov's strategy had failed to stop the protests.

Volodin, forty-seven, stocky and tense, with high cheekbones and a scowl that rarely turned to a smile, was different from the smooth gray cardinal. Unlike Surkov, he was not trained by the oligarchs, and he didn't pretend to play the game of politics. Surkov loved to present himself as a skillful, worldly master of intrigue who in his spare time wrote songs for rock bands and a book under a pseudonym and then made sure everybody knew the real author. By contrast, Volodin built his career on the rules of the Soviet bureaucracy. He was active in the Saratov Institute of Mechanization of Agriculture in the 1980s, joined the Communist Party, and married the daughter of the former first secretary of the local party committee. In the 1990s he quickly rose through the ranks of Saratov's administration to the position of deputy governor and then moved to Moscow. In 2003 he was made vice speaker of the State Duma from the Kremlin party United Russia. He was known to be tough and ruthless.

On December 31 the protest organizers announced plans for the next big rally, to be held on February 4, 2012. The FSB once again tried its old methods. On January 4 an FSB officer called Ilya Klishin's mother in Tambov and summoned her to an interrogation. The same day his father got a call from the local branch of the Interior Ministry's department for countering extremism. Klishin urged his mother not to go to the interrogation and posted information about the summons online. His father had received a written request, so he went to talk to the Interior Ministry, meeting a police colonel there who told him that his son could face criminal charges of inciting ethnic hatred because, a week earlier, he had been in Kazan, the capital of the republic of Tatarstan, where Klishin met with local activists. "In a way my parents were, if not depressed, but shocked by all that, and their first reaction was to advise me to keep away from all political affairs. But I tried to explain to them that it was meaningless, and all I did was absolutely legal, so I had nothing to fear," recalled Klishin.[14] After that, the security services never called Klishin and his parents again.

The presidential elections were set for March 4, 2012. The opposition called for demonstrations, and although some were held, they seemed to be losing momentum. The opposition had no candidate for the presidential elections, but this was only part of the problem. However much the United Russia party was unpopular and fraud was used on its behalf during the parliamentary elections, Putin personally was popular—the most popular politician in the country. The Kremlin wanted and expected to be able to secure a fair victory, so there was no point in mobilizing protesters to join as election observers, as was the case in December. The video cameras Putin had promised were duly installed at polling stations all over the country.

On the night of elections Navalny was based at a club, Masterskaya, the same place where, four months earlier, Grigory Okhotin had launched the OVD-Info website.[15] When we arrived that

evening it was already dark outside. Putin had won election to a
third term on the first ballot by 63.6 percent. On our way to the
club we passed by groups of drunk strangers clearly unfamiliar
with Moscow's streets, probably heading to Putin's victory rally
near the Kremlin. It was known that pro-Kremlin movements
bussed people from the regions to the city to cheer their winner.

At the first floor of Masterskaya two muscled and forbidding
guards dressed in black stood, crossing their arms across their
chests. When we said we were journalists from Agentura.ru, they
waved us in, to the second floor. Masterskaya occupied a building
of the former Soviet public baths and had two large rooms with
high ceilings on the second floor, previously the baths for women
and men, respectively. On this night one of the rooms was for
Navalny's personal use, and the second was filled with journalists and activists; nearby a small theater hall had been turned into
a makeshift television studio. The mood was downbeat. Navalny
avoided answering questions from journalists that evening and
just issued brief statements.

Barely two hundred meters from the club Putin took to the
outdoor stage near the Kremlin to savor his triumph. He started
thanking the cheering crowds for support, and a tear appeared in
his eye.

The next morning came a new type of cyber attack. According
to the Internet security firm Symantec, experts suddenly identified a surge of spam e-mails, widely disseminated. The messages
seemed to be promoting a rally against Putin, but they were also
carrying malware, disguised as an attachment. The body of the
e-mail had just one sentence, indicating the attached document:
"Instructions for your actions in the rally against Putin."

Symantec detected the malicious document as a Trojan, a disguised weapon. In this case the attachment contained malicious
macros that dropped onto the user's computer and loaded a hidden piece of software, called Trojan.Gen. It then would overwrite
any files with the common extensions of .doc or .exe or .zip. Once

it destroyed all such files, the software would run code to cause the computer to crash.

The attack, however, was far from successful. The e-mail looked odd to many recipients, so they didn't open it. And they knew that real news about the protest movement was spread on Facebook, not by a randomly arriving e-mail.

Two weeks later the first deputy director of the FSB, Sergei Smirnov, admitted that the authorities had not yet found a means to deal with protest activity organized through social networks. At a meeting of the regional antiterrorist group operating within the Shanghai Cooperation Organization, which includes Russia, China, and other nations in Central Asia, Smirnov referred directly to the challenge: "New technologies [are being] used by Western special services to create and maintain a level of continual tension in society with serious intentions extending even to regime change. . . . Our elections, especially the presidential election and the situation in the preceding period, revealed the potential of the blogosphere." Smirnov stated that they needed to develop ways to react to such technologies and confessed that "this has not yet happened."[16]

Putin's victory left the protesters feeling depressed. Their leaders decided to go to the streets the day before Putin's inauguration, May 7. The protest was called the "March of Millions," reflecting the organizers' ambition and desperation. Some protest leaders went to Russia's regions, seeking to recruit as many people as possible for the march. But this was different from previous protests: the organizing committee was disbanded, Akunin and Parkhomenko were not among organizers, and Romanova did not collect money for the march.

Nevertheless, on May 6, thousands turned up and marched down Yakimanka Street to Bolotnaya Square. But then it turned ugly. To get to Bolotnaya Island from Yakimanka Street requires a right turn. The rally was sanctioned by the authorities, which meant that the crowd was required to pass through security gates manned by policemen, always a bottleneck for every Moscow demonstration, but this time it was worse because the number of security gates was unusually small. The way forward was limited by a line of heavy trucks across Yakimanka Street, and there was no way out; the only option was to wait in long lines for the security check. Soon the protesters found themselves clamped between the police trucks, the line of security gates, and the Moscow River, pressed from the rear with nowhere to go. Muscovites loved to bring children to the protest rallies as a way to show it was all peaceful, and May 6 was no exception. Sergei Lukashevsky, the director of the Sakharov Center, took his three children, daughters of eight and thirteen years old and his fifteen-year-old son along with two of his son's classmates.

The organizers tried to talk the police into relieving the congestion, to widen the passage ways, but to no avail. We stood on Bolotnaya Square, close to the stage, when someone started shouting, "Sit down, sit down, it's a sit-down strike!" It was a desperate move by the organizers. Navalny sat, along with Nemtsov, his friends, and supporters. The police considered it a provocation. Soon we saw some people move around the security gates. Fighting started, and the crowd poured through yellow portable toilets next to the gates. Lukashevsky saw that it was clearly not the place to be with children and hastily retreated to a bridge nearby. We took to another bridge, where we met our friend, journalist Mikhail Shevelev, who in 1995 had helped publish Parkhomenko's story in *Moskovskie Novosti*. Usually an easygoing fellow with a sense of irony about any trouble, now he was deadly serious and afraid—he had brought with him his thirteen-year-old son.

Finally Navalny broke through security gates and made it to Bolotnaya Square and then to the stairs leading to the stage. From the stage Sergei Udaltsov, another protest leader, chanted "We won't leave, we won't leave!" Policemen went after him and grabbed him almost immediately. Navalny saw it and asked for a megaphone. Someone handed him one, and Navalny started to check it. Two policemen approached him, declaring, "We are taking you." Navalny shouted, "What? Why take me? I didn't do anything! Just a second!" He tried to climb the stairs to the stage, and at once the policemen grabbed him. "Why are you taking me?" he asked, then he turned to the crowd and shouted, "Don't disperse! All stay here!"

As it happened, Navalny was wearing a microphone and being shadowed by a camera crew for a possible television documentary. When he was detained, the microphone was transmitting and caught his words with the police. The conversation was tense. The policemen twisted his arms behind his back and raised them high and hard to make him bend over, the way dangerous criminals are transported within Russian prisons. Navalny told them it was extremely painful and in a quiet voice said, "You are breaking my arm!" The policeman agreed that he was indeed going to break Navalny's arm, and Navalny said, through clenched teeth, "I'll send you to jail then." Navalny was then forced into a paddy wagon.

The whole thing was transmitted from the microphone he was wearing and soon posted on YouTube, which inflamed the public.

The Kremlin responded forcefully to the protest. Twenty-seven people were arrested and accused, more than two hundred investigators were deployed. The police searched the protest leaders' apartments—Navalny, Udaltsov, Kseniya Sobchak, Boris Nemtsov, Ilya Yashin, and Pyotr Verzilov.

Putin was inaugurated as planned on May 7 in a grand ceremony at the Kremlin. For the protesters, the clashes the day before proved a disaster. Mutual accusations and arguing followed. The Kremlin blamed the opposition for inciting violence on Moscow's streets. The protesters did try other options: the famous Russian writers—among them Akunin, Ludmila Ulitskaya, Dmitry Bykov, and Lev Rubinstein—invited Muscovites to "a walk with writers" on Moscow's boulevards, and thousands joined them, protesting how the Kremlin had responded on May 6. Navalny launched the Russian version of the Occupy movement idea— he took his supporters to Chistie Prudi, and they occupied space near a monument to the Kazakh poet Abay. They lasted only five days: on May 15 police pushed out dozens of the most committed activists. By then the protests gathered no more than a few thousand supporters.

A month after Putin took office as president for a third term, the Kremlin finally found a way to crack down on social media. On June 7, 2012, four members of the State Duma, the lower house of parliament, introduced legislation to begin a nationwide system of filtering on the Internet. The pretext was to protect children. It included a single register of banned sites, which was really, in simple terms, a blacklist.

The principle of Internet censorship was hardly a new one for the Russian authorities. For five years regional prosecutors had been busy implementing regional court decisions requiring providers to block access to banned sites. But this had not been done in a systematic, nationwide way. Websites blocked in one region remained accessible in others. The arrival of a single register made it possible to close down sites across all of Russia, all at once.[17]

Irina Levova worked as an expert for the Russian Association for Electronic Communications, the only organization the Ministry of Communications and Internet companies trusted as a negotiator. She had fought vigorously against the blacklist. When the law passed a second hearing in the Duma, on July 10, she urged Stas Kozlovsky, a chairman of Russian Wikipedia, to stage an online protest. Kozlovsky conducted surveys with the Russian Wiki community, and when he polled, 80 percent of them voted for the protest. For the whole day the work of the Russian Wikipedia was suspended, its pages went blank, and the main page of the site carried a banner with the claim that if the law is approved, it "could become the basis for real censorship on the Internet."

Unfortunately the protest had no impact. The legislation was quickly passed, and Putin signed it into law July 28, to take effect November 1.

The new blacklist panicked Internet companies, and on August 2 they got an invitation to meet with the presidential administration. Among those who came were three high-ranking managers of Yandex, including the CEO, Arkady Volozh, and Marina Zhunich, a government relations director for Google Russia, along with Levova. They walked into the complex of the buildings on Staraya Ploshad, to a building right on the square, a big six-story neoclassical edifice with giant windows, the same building Velikhov had visited in 1982 to talk to Yuri Andropov about the personal computers. It had housed the Central Committee of the Communist Party in Soviet times and now was occupied by the presidential administration, a powerful bureaucracy.

They were shown to the fifth floor. The building had been expensively renovated, but the Soviet grand style was carefully preserved, with carpets in the corridors, wooden panels on the walls, and Soviet-style white telephones in the elevators. The Internet-industry representatives were brought into a large room with four monumental chandeliers. The curtains had been carefully drawn across the windows. Vyacheslav Volodin, the gruff-talking first deputy chief of the administration, personally greeted the gathering, along with officials from the State Duma and the Council of Federation.

The Internet companies had rushed to the meeting because of the technicalities of the new law, which stipulated that websites must be blocked at the level of an Internet protocol address. As thousands of sites can use the same Internet protocol address, the companies wanted to explain to the authorities that this idea was not wise. Volodin declared at the start of the meeting, "In present circumstances the filtration is necessary and inevitable, but we should work on details with the industry." He made sure from the beginning of the meeting that the question of filtering was not open to question or debate.

It didn't take long for the Internet companies to abandon the uncensored Internet and cross the line into accepting a censored Internet in Russia. Facing a fait accompli, they focused on specifics. Zhunich had a good reason to be worried: blocking an IP address meant that any video found inappropriate on YouTube, for example, could lead to blocking the entire service. Soon the talk turned to technologies that allow blocking of particular pages, not sites, and Volodin suggested forming a working group to talk technicalities. The Internet companies were passive, just as they had been when SORM was introduced more than a decade earlier.[18]

After the meeting Levova hastened back to her office and immediately started to search for technologies that could block pages instead of sites. The answer she found enraged her. The only choice, it appeared, was "deep packet inspection," a very intrusive technology, which allows an outsider to filter Internet traffic but also gives that outsider a way to penetrate into the content and effectively conduct surveillance.

Most digital inspection tools only look at the "headers" on a packet of data—where it's going and where it came from. Deep packet inspection, or DPI, allows network providers to peer into the digital packets' message or transmission over a network. "You open the envelope, not just read the address on a letter," said an engineer dealing with DPI. It allows ISPs not only to monitor the traffic but also to filter it, suppressing particular services or content.

In late August 2012 the Russian government's Ministry of Communications, along with some of the Russian Internet companies, concluded that the only way to implement the blacklist was through DPI. "As an example, they spoke of YouTube, to be sure that the particular video could be blocked, instead of the entire YouTube service. And they agreed on this mechanism. It was DPI," Ilya Ponomarev, a member of the State Duma who enthusiastically supported the introduction of the blacklist, told us.[19]

DPI drew concern from leading privacy groups over how governments would use this highly intrusive technology. Eric King, head of research at Privacy International, the leading British non-governmental organization in the area of privacy, declared, "DPI allows the state to peer into everyone's internet traffic and read, copy or even modify e-mails and web pages: We now know that such techniques were deployed in pre-revolutionary Tunisia. It can also compromise critical circumvention tools, tools that help citizens evade authoritarian internet controls in countries like Iran and China."[20]

The system in Russia was tested in September, even before its official launch in November. Several prosecutors requested that access to a controversial video, "Innocence of Muslims," be blocked in different Russian regions.[21] On September 27 the three largest mobile and Internet service providers—MTS, VimpelCom, and MegaFon—restricted access to the inflammatory video. VimpelCom blocked access to websites that posted the video, which made YouTube as a whole inaccessible in seven Russian regions.[22] But MTS and MegaFon succeeded in blocking access just to the video itself thanks to DPI that had been already installed on their systems.

For a number of years the ground had been carefully prepared to reach this point. For commercial reasons, DPI technology had been introduced in Russia in the mid-2000s. It was needed then to control torrents—streams of data often used by pirate file-sharing—which can hog all available bandwidth. DPI technology helped mobile operators in Russia resist those users who would take up so much bandwidth. In a few years all the biggest DPI technology vendors had a presence in Russia: Canada's Sandvine, Israel's Allot, America's Cisco and Procera, and China's Huawei. By the summer of 2012 all three national mobile operators in

Russia had DPI at their disposal: Procera was installed by Vimpel-Com, Huawei's DPI solutions are in use in MegaFon, and MTS bought Cisco technology.[23]

At the same time, the Russian authorities didn't miss the remarkable capabilities DPI would open up for surveillance. On September 27 Russia's largest information security conference, held at the international exhibition center Krokus Expo, featured a panel on "SORM in the Environment of Convergence." The talk was intended for professionals, and the room was filled with the chiefs of SORM departments at mobile operators and the Moscow city phone network as well as representatives from surveillance equipment manufacturers. The most honored guest was Alexander Pershov, deputy director of the Department of State Policy at the Ministry of Communications. DPI quickly emerged as one of the hottest topics of the discussion. Many in the room seemed certain that the only way to guarantee legal interception in the new era of cloud computing and communications was DPI technology.

However, there was a legal issue. DPI devices are manned by the employees of the Internet providers or mobile operators—private companies. But the SORM boxes are at the full disposal of the FSB. Still, the idea of connecting SORM with the operators' DPI seemed not to bother anybody in the room. Alexander Pershov outlined the Ministry's general way of thinking: "The requirements for building networks need to be coordinated with the FSB to ensure that everything is done properly in terms of SORM."[24]

Television remained a battleground over the protests. The government's channels bombarded audiences with special programs attacking the opposition. Several of them were titled, in serial, "Anatomy of the Protest." One, aired in October 2012, accused one of the leaders of the opposition from the left, Sergei

Udaltsov, of preparing a coup d'état. Udaltsov's apartment was searched, and a criminal prosecution was launched against him.

But television brought a new approach to the opposition as well. Back in June the protests' organizers had promised to create a council of the opposition that would represent all political forces opposed to Putin and would be a vehicle for carrying out discussions with the Kremlin. On September 21 Leonid Volkov, Navalny's chief lieutenant, and Yuri Saprykin, editor of Afisha .ru, both deeply involved in the protest activities, paid a visit to Mikhail Zygar, the editor of TV Dozhd. The council was to be selected by democratic means—an election—on October 20–22. Volkov and Saprykin suggested organizing a series of debates on TV Dozhd—online and uncensored.

Zygar was struck by the idea. "We didn't have then the feeling of danger, we thought we need to respond to the expectations of people," he recalled. He worried whether it would at all compromise the television channel's principles and whether it would be seen as propaganda for a political force. But he answered his own questions by saying there were so many different people from so many different forces that it would be impossible to be captured by any one of them. The opposition ran from liberals to nationalists. Zygar decided they would broadcast the debate at midnight, far from prime time, so only really committed people would watch it. The debate project came together very quickly—in a day or two.[25]

The debates on TV Dozhd started on October 1 and lasted for almost three weeks. It proved to be a huge success for the channel. "Our evening news traditionally got the highest rating. And now we saw, wow, our rating rise higher at midnight," said Zygar. Saprykin, who was a cohost on air, recalled that there was a chance that all hell would break loose with so many different views. But contrary to that fear, the opposition was allowed a voice on television, "and nothing awful happened," he said.[26] Russians got their first political debate since the 1990s.

The Kremlin seemed to ignore both the shows and the opposition council.

Then, on November 1, the Ministry of Communications launched the single register of banned websites—the feared blacklist. And then even more pressure was put on the activists. Nossik was summoned for an interrogation on November 16 because he had helped launch the website of the opposition council's elections; in response, in November he left LiveJournal. The same month Lev Gershenzon left Yandex.ru, explaining that he was in charge of Yandex News and for years tried to improve the algorithms of selecting the news while also fighting the pressure from the authorities. But by the end of 2012 he realized that algorithms, however sophisticated and clever, could not resolve a new problem—that it had become increasingly difficult to see differences among the various reports of various media, most of which had started to present a uniform and identical picture. Here the technology was helpless.

The protests convinced the Kremlin that the approach to the Internet developed in the 2000s, a combination of DDOS attacks and trolls, didn't work when tens of thousands of people went to the streets. So the Kremlin decided to put the Internet under control by technical means, through filtering. It was essentially a nationwide censorship, but the Kremlin didn't copy the Soviet example, when censorship was conducted by a government body, Glavlit, with representatives in every Soviet publication.

The actual day-to-day business of Internet filtering was not assigned to FSB officers nor to the officials of Roskomnadzor, a relatively small government agency with no more than a few dozen personnel tasked to deal with the Internet. Roskomnadzor selected what should be censored, but it fell to ISPs and telecom operators to implement the blacklists. To make the system work across the country, the filtering system required a lot of people, and there are thousands of ISPs in Russia. The specialists needed technical training, had to comply with orders, no questions asked, and they had to protect the secrecy of operations because Roskomnadzor deemed the blacklists of banned websites secret.

Russia had plenty of such specialists.

CHAPTER 9

"We Just Come Up with the Hardware"

On the evening of May 27, 2011, a soccer match was about to be held in Moscow between Anzhi, a visiting team from Dagestan, and Lokomotiv, a popular Moscow team. The game was set for early evening so fans could come after work to the modern Lokomotiv home stadium that accommodates twenty-eight thousand in the east of the city. The visiting team, Anzhi, was generously funded by a wealthy oligarch and enjoyed crowds of enthusiastic fans. More than fifteen hundred of them arrived at Lokomotiv stadium that evening from Dagestan to see their team play. They were almost entirely men in their twenties and thirties who wanted to sit together, and they were required to use a separate entrance with high security. They arrived at the gate, holding tickets, and approached what looked to be a rather unremarkable metal detector and some city police. The visitors were from the North Caucasus, where Russia had fought two wars against rebels in Chechnya, so their arrival in Moscow was met with a apprehension and scrutiny. The police routinely patted them down, looking for weapons.

The fans coming through paid little attention to a camera sitting on a tripod aimed at each of them as they stepped up to the metal detector. The lens was aimed at their faces. The camera rapidly attempted to capture each face into a green digital frame and then identified different characteristics of the face, including such distinctive features as distance between the eyes. Then the camera went to work, snapping several photographs of each face. A computer connected to the camera then evaluated each person based on a complex algorithm, and within seconds the person's name was established and they were given a unique number. They may have all come to see a soccer match, but they had also just walked into a modern and potentially powerful system of face recognition. Originally invented to help spot criminals, face recognition had expanded in the hands of security services to be a tool for surveillance of all kinds of people at any kind of public event and in public places.

Near the metal detectors sat an operator with a laptop who worked for a company called Ladakom-Service, and he monitored every face closely. One window on his screen showed the live camera acquiring the face images, another part of the screen showed the captured images, and a program was constantly running to match the captured images with people in a government passport database, one of the biggest in the country. When the match was successful, a photograph just taken appeared along the bottom of the screen with the person's full identity. The government had obtained a current picture and identification of thousands of people that could be used for almost any purpose in the future.

It happened not only at sports events. The same company in 2011 had installed this technology in the entrance hall of one of the busiest metro stations in the city. The station, Okhotny Ryad, is located a stone's throw from the Kremlin and around the corner from the Russian lower house of parliament, next to one of the most heavily traveled streets in Moscow. As people stepped on the subway escalator, their faces entered a frame and were captured by video cameras. The images were rapidly linked to their identity in security service databases. There was no notification to anyone that they were being recorded.

Alexander Abashin, chief executive of Ladakom-Service, the company that developed the system, was a veteran of military intelligence. For twelve years he had been developing and installing facial recognition systems at airports, railway stations, and stadiums across Russia. He became something of a zealot for using facial recognition everywhere as a law enforcement tool—even in schools and apartment building entrances. His enthusiasm came in part from his own experience; when burglars struck his home, he grabbed facial images from surveillance video and used them with government databases to eventually apprehend the thieves. He told us that his system was so advanced that a scan of 10 million images would take no more than seven seconds. "To put it simply," he explained, "the face on the photograph is measured using thirty identifiers, and the resulting mathematical matrix is very difficult to fool."[1] The facial images and video are sent to the Metro system's situation room, the Interior and Emergencies Ministries, and to the FSB.

The facial recognition system is a glimpse into a large and mostly hidden phenomenon that was a profound legacy of the Soviet experience: the use of engineering to build systems for the security services to control information and populations. These systems were invented and developed by engineers who knew what the systems could do but rarely if ever questioned the purpose of control for which they were used.

The Soviet Communist Party held a monopoly on power and did not want competition. It imposed rigid conditions on all kinds of people; for engineers, there was pressure to conform to the goals of the party-state and to fulfill its technical needs. To succeed meant to work on projects without questioning the big picture. For many decades Soviet engineers were schooled intensively in technical subjects but rarely if ever had exposure to the humanities; the breadth of their education was exceedingly narrow.

Unlike medical doctors who were trained in ethics, engineers were not. They were taught to be technical servants of the state. As a result, generations of engineers were trained and worked their entire lives with little understanding of politics or trust of politicians and were suspicious of public activity as a whole. These engineers were focused on the immense technical needs of the Soviet Union and were comfortable with the concept of strict order because it suited their understanding of the mechanical world better than the often-unruly reality of freedom. Events that followed the Soviet collapse only solidified their views. Many engineers who had worked in the sprawling military-industrial complex were left high and dry. They suffered greatly from the deep cuts in military spending and were resentful. Frustrated, they became fertile ground for anti-Western sentiment.

Sergei Koval was just such an engineer. In 1973 he graduated from the physics department of the University of Leningrad and went to work at a research center on acoustics, his specialty. Every day he entered a secret military institute in Leningrad that was developing communications and went to work for an even more concealed secret laboratory to create speech recognition technology that would allow the KGB to identify a person on the telephone from the sound of his voice. After the collapse of the Soviet Union, Koval and his colleagues effectively privatized their expertise, and their business thrived in the 1990s. The main customer remained the security services—primarily the FSB. He never questioned his work for the secret police, in Soviet times or afterward.

Andrei asked Koval what he thought about the ethics of his work and the fact that regimes around the world were using his technology to suppress dissidents. He replied emotionally and with certitude and self-confidence. "All this talk about technology catching dissidents is just bullshit," he insisted. "It's typical of the kind of psychological warfare the Americans use against their opponents. I think all these arguments about human rights are completely hypocritical." Koval proudly listed countries where his company's speech recognition technology was already in use: Kazakhstan, Kyrgyzstan, Uzbekistan, and Belarus—all repressive authoritarian regimes in the former Soviet Union—as well as Saudi Arabia, Algeria, Yemen, and Turkey. He expressed no reservations about whether his technology was being used against journalists, dissidents, and human rights campaigners. "What can we do about it?" he said. "We just come up with the hardware. It's just technology that is developed with law enforcement in mind. Sure, you can use it against the good guys just as easily as you can use it against the bad guys. One way or another, these governments will be able to use surveillance technology, whether we supply it or not. Take, for example, face recognition technology: you can film a demonstration, and with that film you can identify the journalists, the drug addicts, the recently released prisoners or the nationalists. It's all the same technology. I can't think what can be done about that! If governments listen in on people's conversations, it's not the microphone's fault!"

These exact words have been repeated over and over again by engineers who willingly served the Soviet state and then did the same thing in Russia. They believed it was not their fault.

When Stalin's security services in the 1930s and 1940s needed to conduct secret research in particular areas, they arrested scientists and engineers and sent them to special installations, the sharashkas, which were closed off from the outside and heavily guarded. The scientists and engineers were motivated to produce quick results under the threat of being sent to labor camps if they failed. But in the years after Stalin's death in 1953 this system evolved into a far-reaching system of research institutes, not all of them closed. A result was that many thousands of Soviet engineers were working in security or military research.

The sharashka in Marfino, east of Moscow, was especially important, and by 1948–1949 it had become a relatively large research effort, with 490 personnel, of which 280 were prisoners, divided into twelve research groups, including the acoustic laboratory of Major Abram Trakhtman.[2]

Marfino's main task was to develop a special kind of secure telephone system that would allow Stalin to speak on the phone without interception. To accomplish that, the voice on the phone would have to be split into pieces, coded, and then reassembled. The problem was not only how to code the pieces but also how to repair the speech in a way so that the speech and speaker would be instantly recognizable. For months Marfino's acoustic laboratory tried to make the decoded speech recognizable. The effort required the focus of both inmates and their superiors. They worked under the guidance of Trakhtman, but the real brain behind the research effort was Lev Kopelev, an inmate. He was considered the top expert on recognizing speech, with an unerring ear for accents and a deep grasp of the physics of sound waves.

In the late autumn of 1949, at the yard of Marfino, Kopelev approached his closest friend, Alexander Solzhenitsyn, a fellow inmate, to share with him a state secret. Kopelev had successfully listened to and identified a caller who gave sensitive information to the US Embassy about the atomic bomb.[3] Kopelev was incensed.

Although he had been convicted and sentenced for expressing his disapproval of the Soviet troops' harsh treatment of the German population in 1945, Kopelev remained a devoted Communist and Soviet patriot, and he was outraged to listen to someone who had just betrayed such a big secret to the Americans. He was given four audio tapes—it turned out the speaker tried three times to reach the US Embassy and then gave up and called the Canadian Embassy once. The security services intercepted and recorded all the conversations. Kopelev was also given samples of phone conversations of three suspects. With his considerable skills and talents, Kopelev pointed the finger at one of the recorded voices, leading the authorities to a certain foreign ministry official, who was arrested. It was a major—and unexpected—victory for the sharashka. Excited, Kopelev couldn't help but tell his friend Solzhenitsyn what he had done. Kopelev coined the term *phonoscopy* for the new scientific discipline of recognizing the identity of a speaker on the phone, one that would be very valuable to the security services for many years to come.[4]

In July 1950 the secure telephone technology for Stalin was finished, as was the main assignment for Marfino. For the next two years Marfino created a manufacturing line for the equipment they had invented. When that was completed, the sharashka was essentially divided in half. The specialists on secure telephony were left there, and it was renamed to become the top-secret National Research Institute No. 2, working on the protection of Kremlin telecommunications, as it does to this day. The other half of specialists, who had worked in the acoustic laboratory, including Kopelev, were moved to Kuchino, another sharashka located outside of Moscow.

This was a fateful move that established the KGB's central role in research and development of listening devices and eavesdropping for the next half century. The transfer to Kuchino meant that the secret services would do the research on speech recognition technology in the same facility—and guided by the same people—as those working on wiretapping. They wanted to make sure they could not only intercept a conversation but also have the means to identify those who spoke on the phone. The KGB wanted full control of telecommunications, and from this time on, identifying a speaker was considered a legitimate part of Soviet surveillance.

Kuchino, surrounded by high walls seventeen miles east of Moscow, was the main research facility for Stalin's secret services in the area of special, or "operative," equipment—ranging from weapons to radio sets to, most importantly, listening devices. In one of their most ambitious and successful exploits, the experts at Kuchino planted a listening device inside a large replica of the Great Seal of the United States and presented it as a gift to the US ambassador in August 1945, and it was hung in the ambassador's study. The device transmitted sound waves out of the ambassador's study to the Soviet secret services until it was exposed in 1952.

The talented Kopelev left Kuchino in 1954, a year after Stalin died, never to return to his research in phonoscopy. He went on to become a dissident. But he left his archives behind in Kuchino, and they were carefully preserved. For a time the security services didn't know what to do with them; it seemed that the technology Kopelev invented was based on his knowledge alone and wouldn't work without him. In other words, without Kopelev's unique skills, it was useless to try to identify a speaker on the phone.[5]

But other research began to show that there was a method behind Kopelev's success. The first evidence came in 1960 when a Swedish scientist, Gunnar Fant, published a monograph, *The Acoustic Theory of Speech Production*, based on his research at MIT.[6] He had found a way to slice up a voice recording into samples and then identify them using mathematics and physics. This meant that there was a more reliable and verifiable scientific method instead of relying on Kopelev's skills. Fant's discovery, translated into Russian in 1964, led to a surge of secret research into the topic inside the Soviet Union.[7]

While the scientists pursued his theory, Fant began to be concerned that law enforcement would abuse speech recognition technology. Fant's concerns were confirmed in 1970, when FBI director J. Edgar Hoover went to Stockholm and gave an interview to the local newspaper *Dagens Nyheter* about shining prospects for using voice samples for identifying terrorists. When the newspaper asked Fant for comments on Hoover's remarks, Fant cautioned that the method he had developed was imprecise and it was premature to use to identify anyone. His rebuttal was so surprising that the newspaper printed on the front page photographs of Hoover and Fant opposite each other, presenting him, as Fant put it later, as a "possible FBI enemy number one."[8]

Soviet scientists had no such reservations. Research centers working on speech recognition opened in many cities, and the section on acoustics at the Academy of Sciences coordinated the nationwide research. But everybody knew that the true boss was the KGB.

An instrumental part of the research was in Leningrad, the Scientific Research Institute of Dalny Svyazi, or of long-distance communications, known as Dalsvyaz. This is the facility where Sergei Koval began work in 1973 on acoustics. He was always interested in the science of sound, but what was also attractive was a promised monthly salary bonus of 15 percent. He was unconcerned that the institute was shrouded in secrecy. The offices of his applied acoustics unit were always guarded by men with automatic weapons. The institute, with more than ten thousand personnel, was overseen by a ministry for industrial telecommunications, but its real purpose was to work for the military. It was top secret and harbored even more secrets inside. The applied acoustics unit of three hundred people that Koval joined was not under control of the institute at all but was instead run by the KGB, who paid these additional personnel the bonus. It was a classic Russian *matryoshka*—secrets within secrets—applied to research.

Koval soon realized the reason for such secrecy. His colleagues told him that this unit was in fact the Marfino sharashka that had been transferred to Leningrad. One day he was pointed to a bespectacled engineer who worked at a neighboring laboratory. His name was Valentin Martynov, and he had once served in Marfino along with Kopelev and Solzhenitsyn. Koval recalled that Martynov was "meticulous and stubborn." A young, enthusiastic engineer of the late 1940s, Martynov had remained devoted to speech recognition for decades. He went so far as to defend a thesis for a degree on the topic. Although he was free now, he still walked every day into the territory guarded by the men with automatic weapons and dogs to do research for the same secret services that had once sent him to prison. Koval never tried to ask him why: "It was a generation that was much more mature. It was not suitable to talk about the past."

By the 1970s Koval's applied acoustic unit became the main coordinator of research funded by the KGB in speech recognition. He recalled, "There was a section of applied problem-solving at the Academy of Sciences. This section took orders and research commissions on perspective research from all the agencies, from the Ministry of Defense and from the KGB. The section demanded money, and it always got the money. The scheme was wonderful: the money then was allocated to the applied research departments belonging to the KGB, like our department. So we were able to distribute this money right across the different academic institutions as we saw fit. We could effectively sponsor any project we wanted. I myself was the curator of the scientific program, where forty universities were involved."[9]

What began in the 1940s with seven people in the acoustic laboratory in Marfino had, by the 1970s, become a sprawling, well-funded empire of secret research. There was no clear line between KGB-sponsored research and civilian research; it was all part of the same empire. The secrecy touched everyone—numbering millions of people. The secrecy showed up in the most unexpected places. For example, the Computation Center of the Academy of Sciences on Vavilova Street in Moscow, which Ed Fredkin loved to visit in the 1980s to talk personal computers, was one of the research institutes quietly working for Koval's unit.

Vladimir Chuchupal joined the section of voice recognition of the Computation Center in 1980. He was told that the main task of the section was to apply computers to speech recognition. Chuchupal was warned that it was strictly prohibited to mention to anyone outside the Center the name of their main "customer"—the Dalsvyaz and the KGB. He was put in direct contact with Kuchino almost immediately. Chuchupal knew exactly what they worked on—one day his chief described how he was given notes from the legendary Kopelev to study.[10]

Thanks to the generous funding provided by the KGB, in the early 1980s Chuchupal's section got its first personal computers, some Soviet-made machines and a few IBM PS2s. When they arrived, the issue of speech recognition opened up a vista for surveillance the KGB had never imagined possible—applying computer technologies to phone tapping meant that not only could a speaker be identified but that what he said could be used to trigger the interception system. That, at least, was the theory. The KGB came up with the idea of using key words so that mention of "the bomb" or the "Communist Party," or anything else chosen by the KGB and put in the system would automatically initiate interception of the phone line. This option could have changed the KGB's modus operandi completely—in most previous cases the KGB needed to know the identity of the suspect to start eavesdropping on his phone; now the technology would provide the suspects. But it was also very challenging; the keyword system was an ambition, but making it a reality depended on more computing power than was available.

The Soviet research empire into speech recognition along with Dalsvyaz and the unit at the Computation Center worked actively on the issue for years. Once again, there was no clear line between the civilian and KGB research.

This empire cracked with the collapse of the Soviet Union, but it didn't go away. Initially the KGB cut its research programs. "In 1990 our funding stopped," Koval recalled, who himself left Dalsvyaz. "Two-thirds of employees quit immediately." But he did not leave the field of research. With his laboratory chief, Mikhail Khitrov, and five colleagues, he founded a private company that in 1993 became the Speech Technology Center, trademarked in the United States as SpeechPro. Each of eight founders got an equal share of 12.5 percent of the company. The speech recognition scientists tried to succeed with civilian contracts; for example, they developed a talking book for the Society for the Blind.

But soon their old friends, the security services, returned. Koval's company got its first contract from the Interior Ministry to build a system of using phonoscopy for chasing criminals. Then the FSB offered a contract to make a system that would separate voice from background noise. In the 2000s the company employed up to 350 people—roughly the size of the original Soviet department in Dalsvyaz. "I cannot say what kind of work we do for them," Koval said of the security services, "but it all continues, it's the same—what we did then, we do now."

The company has developed technology they consider unique in its capability and reach. It is able, for example, to store many millions of items of biometric data, such as voice samples and photo images, and match them to individuals by searching the world's communication channels, including video files. The voice recognition technology can identify the speaker, regardless of language, accent, or dialect, based on physical characteristics of the voice.

In 2008 the company completed its first national voice recognition project in Mexico. The system was able to use state records of human voices and biometric details—voice, face, and other characteristics—to identify individuals, and to do it from fragments of speech alone. Mexico's national database of voices was made up of speech fragments recorded from criminals, law enforcers, and many law-abiding citizens, who are obliged to supply vocal samples for state regulated activities, such as obtaining a driver's license. Thus, Kopelev's 1949 dream of creating the system that "would allow recognition of the voice in all circumstances out of any amount of voices" was realized in 2010 in Mexico. Koval was personally in charge of implementing the ambitious project. "I've been traveling to Mexico for seven years!" he exclaimed.

On a cold and snowy day in January 2012, in an almost empty café near Chernyshevsky Metro Station in St. Petersburg, Koval enthusiastically recalled to Andrei the story of his company. Koval's confidence had recently been bolstered by an investment from a source even closer to Putin than the secret services could provide. In September 2011 Gazprombank acquired 35 percent of SpeechPro. Gazprombank is also part of the vast business empire of Yuri Kovalchuk, a close friend of Vladimir Putin.

The Russian system of secret research appears to be reestablished completely. In Moscow, Chuchupal, now the chief of the sector on speech recognition at the Computation Center of the Academy of Sciences, continues to work on speech recognition, and Kuchino is among his customers. Both Koval's and Chuchupal's organizations are still working on the issue of "key words."

Koval's odyssey was repeated over and over again by other Soviet scientists and engineers, and it created a mindset among many of them. Loren Graham, a preeminent historian of Soviet and Russian science at MIT, told us, "Russian scientists and engineers are, on the whole, less interested in the ethical and moral problems of their work than many of their counterparts in Western countries."[11]

"Why is this so? I see two reasons," he added. "In the Soviet period Russian scientists and engineers learned early on that if they raised ethical and moral issues that this was seen by the authorities as 'political opposition,' and they would be punished for raising such issues. Therefore, they learned to stay silent, and after a while this silence became ingrained and even a part of their professional definition. Of course, the Soviet Union is long gone, but these attitudes have largely continued."

Second, he said, "Engineering education in Russia has been focused on technical issues, with very little attention to larger human, ethical, and moral questions. Although engineering education in the US has some of these characteristics also, it is worth noticing that at top engineering schools in the United States, such as the Massachusetts Institute of Technology—my university—every student during four years of engineering study is required to take eight courses, usually one each semester, in the humanities and social sciences. These courses open up deep questions of ethics and 'meaning,' which are not considered in technical courses.

"This is an important part of engineering education in the best universities in Western countries," Graham said. "It has important effects, leading to questions about the social responsibilities of scientists and engineers. And many of the best engineering schools in the United States also have departments of Science, Technology and Society [STS], where these problems are studied."

Anatoly Levenchuk, an engineer himself who, in the early 1990s, helped launch Relcom, told us that "I tell my students not to apply system engineering when you work for the government." Why? "It could be very dangerous. You need to know humanities to deal with the state. If you apply only engineering, you will build a prison as a result. Say you are tasked to address threats, in this case the best way to address them as engineer is to build a box, a prison, you just close everything off."[12]

Levenchuk himself ceased to cooperate with the government in 2006 and focused on teaching engineering at Moscow Institute of Physics and Technology, the major university for training engineers for the Russian nuclear industry. Levenchuk sought to present new ideas in his classroom, challenging the traditional rigid approach and urging students to be more open-minded and aware. He was soon attacked. In April 2013 he was confronted with an old and nefarious Soviet practice—a public denunciation. An open letter was published on LiveJournal.com, accusing Levenchuk of teaching "fascist" philosophy and values. Levenchuk was accused of systematic destruction of "the Soviet school of design." The denunciation then went on to demand that members of the State Duma to initiate a request to the General Prosecutor's Office to check whether Levenchuk is a foreign agent, as "pro-Western ideas" are detected in his lectures. The request was duly sent, and the institute was forced to write an official reply, protecting Levenchuk.[13]

The denunciation showed that Soviet engineers' mindset—the rigid adherence to the technical—was resurging under Putin.

Sergei Koval, so dismissive of concerns about dissidents and human rights, took his approach overseas in 2009. It was one thing to loyally and unquestioningly serve the state in the former Soviet Union, but it was quite another to deliver the same approach to other countries and security services. Koval's journey abroad took him to Colombia. There, on September 21, 2009, the secret police, Departamento Administrativo de Seguridad, or DAS, a hybrid of intelligence and law enforcement, held a press conference in Bogotá.[14]

For a year DAS had been under constant criticism, accused of illegal wiretapping of journalists, opposition politicians, human rights groups, and even Supreme Court justices. The scale of the scandal caused journalists to coin the term "Colombian Watergate."[15]

In the announcement of the press conference DAS promised to present some new crucial evidence to address the question of illegal wiretapping. The DAS director, Felipe Muñoz, a thirty-nine-year-old energetic technocrat, trained at the London School of Economics and Colombia University, appeared at the press conference with Koval sitting alongside.

Muñoz announced that DAS had conducted the internal investigation and invited an independent expert from Russia, with more than thirty years experience in the field, to examine leaked recordings of intercepted calls and compare them with the recordings made by DAS legally. He tried to prove that the agency was not involved in illegal wiretapping. Then he presented Sergei Koval.

Koval stated that he had applied more than twenty various audio characteristics in the course of examination, and the analysis showed that the recordings had been made using completely
different types of equipment. "The conclusion was unequivocal:
these wiretaps were not registered with this type of equipment,"
Koval added.[16]

If true, this would absolve the security service from having
made illegal wiretaps. Koval claimed the Colombian secret service
didn't have the necessary equipment to produce the type of recordings leaked to the media. Muñoz, in turn, was happy to point
a finger to some private unidentified spies, "We have sufficiently
strong preliminary evidence to say that there is a market for mobile equipment interception which lacks control."

Koval had come halfway around the world to speak up for the
Colombian secret police. And it turned out these public declara-
tions were wrong. A few months later a prosecutor in Colombia
declared that he had proof that a DAS team had spied on public
figures with the knowledge of officials in President Álvaro Uribe's
office.[17] Eventually some DAS officials confirmed that it was indeed
the DAS that had conducted illegal wiretapping. One employee
admitted he had received orders directly from the DAS director,
Maria del Pilar Hurtado, and the intended recipient of wiretap
transcripts was President Álvaro Uribe.[18] In late 2011 the agency was
finally disbanded, and the expert on speech recognition was long
gone from Bogotá, back to Russia, and then on to Mexico.

On the outskirts of St. Petersburg, in a glossy new business
center, there is a small company named Protei. The company's office was a bit chaotic in 2011—they had just moved in—
with tables and wires all over the place. The computers had yet
to be installed, but Protei was already making something highly
desired outside of Russia: the equipment for making sure that the
black boxes—the SORM technologies—would work in countries

like Uzbekistan and Kazakhstan, where authoritarian rulers with miserable human rights practices and intolerant of democracy and dissent were eager to use the technology to control the Internet. The company produced all kinds of technology from SORM-1 to SORM-3, from phone eavesdropping to Internet intercepts. In December 2011 WikiLeaks and Privacy International launched the Spy Files project, a database on companies that sell such surveillance gear around the world.[19] Although most of the vendors are British, Israeli, German, and American companies, it also included Koval's SpeechPro and Protei.

Andrei went to see another engineer who had made it in the world of secret services and secret surveillance. Vadim Sekeresh was head of the SORM department at Protei. A phlegmatic, forty-year-old graduate of the applied mathematics department of St. Petersburg University, he seemed unruffled by the WikiLeaks disclosure. Like so many other engineers, he did not ask deep moral or ethical questions about how his products were being used. "I didn't pay any attention to it," Sekeresh said of the report. "I didn't really look into it because the whole thing doesn't bother me. After all, we are not producing the listening devices, or bugs. And . . . we aren't the only ones producing such tech anyway."[20] A few months later he told Andrei in an e-mail, "Lots of crimes are solved thanks to technology. It's obvious that everything could be used to harm, but it's not related to the producers."

In other words, it is not the engineers' fault.

In 2012, the year Internet filtering was introduced in Russia, Protei developed a product based on DPI technology to implement the censorship of Roskomnadzor. In March 2015 Protei announced that the company had successfully deployed an Internet-filtering system based on DPI on the network of Kyrgyzstan's telecom operator MegaCom, one of the largest in the country. Russian engineers, once again, developed the hardware that brought one of the world's most intrusive Internet-filtering technologies to Central Asia.

Part II

CHAPTER 10

The Snowden Affair

I n the 1990s the global nature of the Internet meant wires. When a user got connected, he could send his e-mail or visit a website anywhere in the world. In the 2000s the Internet meant the rise of global platforms that allowed users to share the same social networks, e-mail services, search engines, and clouds. The Internet became more of a common ground for people from Argentina to Russia—they used the same Facebook, the same Twitter. That also meant that the information users exchanged was stored inside systems located far from the users—systems that could not be readily controlled by nations, their leaders, or their secret services. Most of the servers were located in the United States.

For President Vladimir Putin this was intolerable. In his mind the solution was simple: force the platforms—Facebook, Google, Twitter, and Apple among them—to locate their servers on Russian soil so Russian authorities could control them.

The challenge was how to do it.

S ince November 2012 Russia had censored and controlled the Internet extensively by using a nationwide system of filtering, but it was primitive. Rather than being based on key words, as in China, it was based on a blacklist of Internet sites in various forms. The blacklist could block Internet protocol or IP addresses, a set of numbers, such as 70.226.194; URLs, an address of a particular page, like www.agentura.ru/english; or domain names, such as google.com. The Federal Agency for Supervision of Communications, or Roskomnadzor, maintained the blacklist, was instrumental in dealing with the digital companies in Russia, and was in charge of implementing the filtering.

The head of the agency was Alexander Zharov, forty-eight, a soft-mannered but ambitious man. A physician by training who had worked as an anesthesiologist and doctor in Chelyabinsk, he wrote articles for *Family Doctor* magazine in the 1990s and moved to Moscow to become the magazine's deputy editor. He then went into public relations, working for different government agencies, rising to become spokesman for a colorless Russian premier, Mikhail Fradkov, from 2004 to 2006. Along the way Zharov built important alliances with people in power, including Igor Shchegolev, a one-time TASS correspondent in Paris who, in 2008, was put in charge of a combined ministry of communications and the media under Putin. Shchegolev invited Zharov to be his deputy and put him in charge of the news media. Shchegolev and Zharov were roughly the same age and had both come into government from public relations; Shchegolev had also been spokesman for a prime minister, Yevgeny Primakov in 1998, and held prominent positions in the presidential administration in the years since. Most importantly, Shchegolev enjoyed direct access to Putin. Both he and Zharov settled into their ministry offices on Tverskaya Street in central Moscow.

When Putin returned to the Kremlin for a third term in May 2012, he took Shchegolev out of the ministry and appointed him presidential assistant in charge of the Internet. On May 3, 2012, Zharov was appointed chief of Roskomnadzor. He was considered Shchegolev's man, and he made the agency a powerful and semi-independent body, with three thousand employees and branches across the country. In the long back-and-forth between Putin and Medvedev, Zharov always carefully sided with Putin's people—a wise decision. Zharov's agency effectively took over governing the Internet in Russia, which by 2012 meant controlling it. The reins of power were held by him and Shchegolev, who mostly worked behind the scenes.

Zharov dreamed of becoming the minister, but he also was well aware that it would be risky for his career—and not so good for his chances to become minister—if he was seen as the chief Internet censor. Three weeks after Internet filtering was started in Russia, Zharov appeared on TV Dozhd and was interviewed for an hour. In response to tough questions from journalists about the blacklist, he insisted it was for combating pornography and narcotics and said he was only implementing the law. Near the end of the interview he said the blacklist was updated every hour and at that moment included 591 banned sites. He managed to navigate the interview smoothly and, with a good sense of public relations, realized that the issue of Internet censorship could be a dark spot on his image.[1]

He turned to a new deputy, Maxim Ksenzov, and handed over to him the task of dealing with filtering and censorship. Ksenzov, thirty-nine years old, was stiff and tense. A military engineer by training, he started his career at a research center of the Defense Ministry, then worked in information technology and communications, and by 2004 was in the ministry's licensing department for mass media. In July 2012 he was appointed deputy to Zharov at Roskomnadzor. In his public comments on Twitter, Ksenzov loyally expressed the agency's line that it only implemented the law. Ksenzov also made some efforts to explain to worried ISPs the techniques of filtration; he gave a number of informative question-and-answer sessions on web platforms.

It was not long before Zharov and Ksenzov realized the incredible power of the instrument they possessed.

In September 2012, weeks before the blacklist was put in place, the agency tried to block Internet access to the video "Innocence of Muslims"—the General Prosecutor's Office deemed it extremist. A court was to rule on it in October, but before the ruling, on September 17, Roskomnadzor "recommended" that Internet operators and media not disseminate the video. In a few days three major Russian telecom operators—VimpelCom, MegaFon, and MTS—all blocked access to the video on YouTube in the southern, mostly Muslim-populated region of the North Caucasus. Only MTS was able to block access to the specific page where the video was available; the first two operators blocked the entire YouTube service.[2]

This prompted not only Russian ISPs but also global platforms like Google to rush to Roskomnadzor for consultations. They were frightened that the primitive Russian system of filtering could end up blocking their entire service. Three days after Zharov's interview on TV Dozhd, on November 24, Roskomnadzor added the Internet protocol address of the entire Google Blogspot, a blogging platform, to the blacklist. Although it was soon removed, in that time Google users complained about the loss of some Gmail, Google Drive, and Google Play functionality. However crude an instrument, the power of the blacklist was becoming more visible.

Eugene Kaspersky, who had been so dismissive of attacks on news media websites just two years before and had denied that cyber assaults even occurred, quietly changed his tune in March 2013. He came to the rescue of the troubled opposition newspaper, *Novaya Gazeta*, definitely not his most profitable client, when a tsunami of hacker traffic endangered it.

The newspaper was getting ready to celebrate its twentieth anniversary and had earned a reputation for critical coverage of the Kremlin and for thorough investigations—it expected some kind of electronic attack. The newspaper turned to Alexey Afanasyev, chief of the team working on preventing DDOS attacks at Kaspersky Lab. They had invented a traffic filtering system to counter the DDOS attacks used by pro-Kremlin hackers.[3] *Novaya Gazeta* had never been an easy client of Kaspersky's, but Afanasyev grew up during Gorbachev's perestroika years and loved the newspaper, which had Gorbachev on its board. Afanasyev admired the paper's brave journalists and was ready to defend them.

In the late evening of March 31 Afanasyev was on his way home when a colleague called with the news that the website of *Novaya Gazeta* was under DDOS attack. The attack expanded after a few hours, but the newspaper's website remained online thanks to Afanasyev and his team's efforts, using the technology Kaspersky had developed to fight off bad traffic.

The next day, however, it got worse. The traffic from hackers exploded, and the attackers changed tactics. They launched a new type of assault called DNS amplification, a popular form of DDOS in which attackers use publicly accessible open DNS servers to flood a target system. Over two days it swamped *Novaya Gazeta* at a rate of more than one thousand times normal traffic.[4] "That broke down two big data centers with our equipment, which filters incoming traffic," Afanasyev recalled. He was in a shop buying some computer stuff when a colleague called, expressing fear that the attack could cause the entire Internet in Moscow to collapse under the weight of the assault. The situation was critical, and Afanasyev decided to cut off all foreign traffic so that only users in Moscow could access *Novaya Gazeta*. By April 3 the attack reached a peak of sixty gigabits per second, an unheard of volume.

Kaspersky Lab asked two big telecom firms to help organize a special pathway for *Novaya Gazeta* in the Moscow Internet. They did, and it worked to isolate the newspaper from the digital chaos aimed at its website. At the attack's peak the website of *Novaya Gazeta* was out of service only for three hours—thanks largely to Kaspersky, who played an unlikely role. He believed that malware was evil and was ready to fight it, even if it meant defending a scrappy, critical newspaper like *Novaya Gazeta*.[5]

I n March 2013 Roskomnadzor made its first direct assault on global social networks. The agency sent a warning to Twitter when it asked the social media site to block access to five tweets and close an account, saying the offending messages were advertising narcotics and promoting suicide. On March 15 Twitter reported that the company agreed to block the tweets and deleted the account.[6] Roskomnadzor issued a special statement, expressing satisfaction with Twitter's "constructive position."[7] Then, on March 28, Roskomnadzor notified Facebook that it would be blocked unless it removed a page called "Suicide School," which contained mostly humorous information about suicide. The site was added to Russia's blacklist. Facebook took down the offending page.[8]

Gradually the Russian authorities were exerting control over the Internet; Putin's people were moving in a coordinated way. Zharov and Ksenzov at Roskomnadzor issued warnings. Meanwhile the presidential administration, a separate government body directly under Putin, held private discussions with the leaders of the digital companies, like the one that Irina Levova had been invited to earlier. Also in attendance at those discussions were Russian lawmakers who were in charge of writing repressive laws for controlling the Internet.

On May 15, 2013, Ksenzov presented to Roskomnadzor a report outlining the activities of the previous year, making it clear that he felt the government was gaining ground in its efforts to impose its will. There had been little resistance from ISPs or users. At the same time, Ksenzov expressed a worry—what if people figured out how to bypass the censorship? What if they could fool the filtering? There were methods to do this, he said, "that are relatively easy to use. . . . But the fact that it's technically possible to bypass the blocking does not mean that in practice it will be done by everybody and everywhere."[9] Trying to be helpful, Ksenzov recommended the agency be further targeted by blacklisting both the Internet protocol number and the URL of those websites to be blocked.

Zharov was even more cheerful. "Despite the loud and sometimes shocking attacks against these laws, in general, the laws and working with them can be evaluated positively," he said. He noted that "among the thousands of owners of the blocked sites," only a "very few" spoke out in public against the blacklisting. There was only one court appeal, he boasted, adding that public opinion polls showed that 82 percent of those questioned in Russia supported the law that permitted the blacklisting.[10]

Zharov and Ksenzov had found a way to put pressure on the Internet companies, and the companies did not fight back. The Internet providers' silence, first seen in Levenchuk's experience with SORM years earlier, repeated itself. Back then the issue had been the black boxes. This time the companies did not protest government censorship.

An army of volunteers boosted the agency. Since 2012 a group calling itself Cyberguards of the Safe Internet League were patrolling the Internet, hunting down the sites with "prohibited information." The League was launched by a group of Orthodox businessmen to promote Internet censorship under the pretext of protecting children from harmful content, with the blessing of Shchegolev, the minister of communications and media.[11] In 2014 the leader of the League proudly reported that they processed 37,400 complaints.[12] But that was not enough, and the Russian authorities appealed to pro-Kremlin youth organizations for help with Internet censoring, echoing the tactics used with patriotic-hackers and trolls. In February 2013 Molodaya Gvardiya, or Youth Guard, the youth wing of Putin's United Russia party, launched a special unit called Media Gvardiya, or Media Guard.[13] In March 2015 this volunteer army consisted of 3,699 members who worked to identify sites with prohibited content. Due to their efforts, 2,475 pages were taken down. The site organized a competition among the members to see who could find the most sites to report to Roskomnadzor. The main goal of this effort was not to protect children but to hunt down the sites with "extremist content," including any content unpleasant to the Kremlin.

As Putin turned the screws into Internet freedom, an event occurred in Russia he could not have predicted.

On June 23, 2013, Edward Snowden flew into Moscow's Sheremetyevo Airport. Snowden, a former contractor for the US National Security Agency, or NSA, who had once worked in information technology for the CIA, had at this point exposed the bulk of telephone and Internet metadata of millions of Americans and people around the world, obtained by the NSA. Snowden said he leaked documents about the surveillance because the US government had obtained capabilities "without any warrant to search for, seize, and read your communications. Anyone's communications at any time. That is the power to change people's fates."[14]

Snowden's revelations had a huge impact. Today the Internet is ubiquitous, connecting everything from dating to purchases to the exchange of the most sensitive and personal information. Many people have questioned whether there is such a thing as privacy anymore. Human rights organizations around the world supported Snowden as a way to push back against the surveillance state, to reclaim some privacy, and to allow information to flow freely without the threat of being monitored by the state. Snowden's revelations touched off a campaign around the globe to reexamine the issues of digital freedoms and surveillance.

But just as he made the disclosures, Snowden landed in a country with a long tradition of secrecy and suppressing freedom of speech, a landscape roiled by the secret control and surveillance he claimed to despise.

At first Snowden was stuck in the airport terminal because his passport had already been revoked by the United States and he did not have valid documents. He was supposed to be in a special transit zone, but no one could find him. What at first looked like a bad joke turned into long, dreadful weeks as Russian and international journalists scoured the airport looking for him. The journalists bought plane tickets in order to be admitted to secure areas, and some even flew to Cuba on a plane Snowden was rumored to be taking—he was not on the flight. It became obvious to the journalists that Snowden was well protected. Unlike other Moscow airports, Sheremetyevo had a special FSB detachment, established there in Soviet times when it was the only international airport in the country, as well as a normal section made up of the border guards. Snowden spent thirty-nine days, invisible, supposedly somewhere in the Sheremetyevo Airport.

On June 25, at a meeting with the president of Finland, Putin insisted that "our special services never worked with Mr. Snowden and are not working with him now." He called Snowden a "transit passenger" who "remains in the transit hall." Putin ruled out extraditing Snowden to the United States, where he was charged with leaking classified information, and declared that Snowden "has committed no crimes in the Russian Federation."[15] A week later Putin insisted, "Snowden is not our agent, never was, and isn't today."[16] Putin seemed in these early weeks to be attempting to keep his distance from Snowden, saying he was a free man, comparing him to dissidents and human rights activists. Putin said Snowden could leave Russia if he wanted to. But was that the truth?

On July 11 Tanya Lokshina, the head of the Moscow office of Human Rights Watch, was at her office in Moscow, busy preparing for a business trip to New York. Although she appears to be a fragile woman with delicate features under a mop of fiery red hair, Lokshina was a fearless human rights activist who had carried out investigations of brutal abuses in Chechnya and Dagestan and during the Russian war with Georgia.

The Kremlin was never very pleased with her organization or Lokshina personally. She received menacing phone calls, and in October 2012 anonymous threats were sent to her cell phone that included details that could have been obtained only by eavesdropping on her. At the time, she was six months pregnant. Kenneth Roth, the executive director of Human Rights Watch, declared that the people threatening her "knew where she lived, what she was doing. They made explicit reference to the fact of her pregnancy. They threatened harm to herself and to her unborn baby."[17]

Lokshina had left Russia for a while, but now she was back in Moscow and focused on her work. Her son, Nikita, was six months old.

At 5 p.m. that day her assistant, Masha, opened the door and said, "Tanya, you have a phone call from Snowden."[18] Lokshina for a moment thought it had to be some sort of joke, but Masha insisted that a man on the phone said he is calling from Sheremetyevo, represents Snowden, and that Snowden wanted to meet her; the man on the phone was providing details of the meeting. Lokshina told Masha to give the caller her e-mail but still didn't think it was really Snowden.

In five minutes she got an e-mail from ed.snowden@lavabit.com:

To: edsnowden@lavabit.com

From: edsnowden@lavabit.com

Date: 07/11/2013 04:12PM

Subject: Invitation to Edward Snowden statement
TOMORROW 12 July 2013 @ 5:00PM Moscow Time

I have been extremely fortunate to enjoy and accept many offers of support and asylum from brave countries around the world. These nations have my gratitude, and I hope to travel to each of them to extend my personal thanks to their people and leaders. By refusing to compromise their principles in the face of intimidation, they have earned the respect of the world. Unfortunately, in recent weeks we have witnessed an unlawful campaign by officials in the U.S. Government to deny my right to seek and enjoy this asylum under Article 14 of the Universal Declaration of Human Rights.[19]

The letter went on, inviting the human rights organizations and "other respected individuals" to join Snowden the next day at the airport, promising a discussion about "the next steps forward in my situation." Lokshina was instructed to meet at Terminal F, in the "centre of the arrival hall," and "someone from airport staff will be waiting there to receive you with a sign labeled 'G9.'" Lokshina thought that "9" could mean the number of people invited. An identical e-mail arrived for Sergei Nikitin, director of Amnesty International's office in Moscow.[20] Nikitin had directed Amnesty in Russia since 2003 and was also a target of the Russian authorities, who, a few months earlier, raided the organization's office, a few small rooms hidden in an obscure courtyard in a derelict old building.[21]

Lokshina thought the e-mail looked strange. It was also very formal, addressed to no one. "I thought it was false. The letter was written in strange and awkward language." She had spent years in the United States in her youth, and it looked to be written in British English: "in the *centre* of the arrival hall . . . " The telephone number was also unusual—a mobile number. Most Russian mobile numbers are registered to people, not organizations, so it was impossible, from the number, to discern anything about who was behind it. Lokshina forwarded the e-mail to her colleagues at the headquarters of Human Rights Watch as well as to a pair of friends, the Moscow correspondents of the *New York Times* and the *Daily Telegraph*. Nikitin had also sent it to his headquarters. Both were skeptical and uncertain.

Impulsively Lokshina then put the e-mail on her Facebook page. It made a huge and immediate splash in the media. The rest of the day and the next morning she felt under siege—the phone rang constantly, her son demanded her attention, and she still didn't know whether to go to the airport. When she got another call from the same person who had first phoned and was now asked for passport details to get to the secure area, she realized the invitation was for real.

The next day Lokshina took with her a tape recorder she had been given by Ellen Barry, a correspondent at the *New York Times*. When she and Nikitin arrived at Terminal F, they saw hundreds of journalists. She had plenty of experience with herds of reporters, but this one was larger than she had ever seen, like a "herd of mammoths that were going to trample me," she recalled. The human rights activists who gathered around the sign "G9" were clearly divided into several parts: the Russian representatives of independent international human rights organizations, including Lokshina and Nikitin; heads of pro-Kremlin "human rights" groups, including Vladimir Lukin, Human Rights Commissioner of Russia, appointed by Putin, and Olga Kostina, a head of the government-funded NGO Resistance; a deputy of the State Duma, Vyacheslav Nikonov; and lastly, the well-known lawyers Anatoly Kucherena and Henri Reznik. Nikitin, with all his experience, immediately concluded that Kucherena, a tall, bulky, and imposing man, was the leader, if not an organizer of the meeting.

Kucherena is a prominent lawyer as well as a member of the Public Council within the FSB, an organization established in 2007 to promote the image of the Russian security service.[22] Kucherena also serves as chairman of the Institute for Democracy and Cooperation, a front organization for Russia's propaganda machine, with branches in New York and Paris. Putin had suggested personally that such an institute be created to criticize human rights violations in the United States; the institute has an annual report called "The State of Human Rights in the United States."[23]

Lokshina, Nikitin, and the other human rights activists were shown into a room in the secure area of the terminal and eventually led onto the airfield. At this moment Lokshina suddenly remembered that Snowden wanted to fly to Venezuela, and she thought maybe the plan was to fly Snowden there and to take the human rights activists along to guarantee his safety. She panicked and called her husband with instructions for how to feed the baby if she were flown to Venezuela. Then everyone was put on a bus.

The bus made a circle and stopped near an unmarked door of the same terminal, but on the far side of the building. They were shown into a room. When they walked in, Snowden was sitting there, along with a translator and Sarah Harrison, a member of the WikiLeaks group, who had been with Snowden since he fled Hong Kong. Nikitin quickly approached Snowden and asked about his condition. He got to Snowden first because Kucherena doesn't speak English, and Nikitin seized the initiative. But then a man stood in front of them and made an announcement: "Dear gentlemen, Mr. Snowden wants to make a statement, and I ask you in the interests of his security do not record it on video." Nikitin, Kucherena, Lokshina, and Reznik sat in the first row. In the back were some young bulky men in suits. Lokshina took two photographs and sent them to Barry of the *Times* immediately. Barry at once published them on Twitter. Lokshina also put Barry's tape recorder on the table in front of her and turned it on. During the meeting Lokshina texted reports to Barry while Nikitin used an open line on his phone to transmit the audio to some journalists who were listening.

Lokshina told us later that she was certain it was not Edward Snowden who invited them. Snowden did not speak Russian and did not know the people there. Lokshina concluded it was all a show, orchestrated by the security services. "It was obvious that the comrades from the intelligence agencies gathered a group of people and made up all of this event. And they arranged the meeting, probably to legitimize the decision already made that he would be granted temporary asylum."

Kucherena, his legs crossed, sitting in the front row, attempted to ask the first question. He spoke in Russian and said, "Well, how do they treat you here?" He was cut off by Harrison, who shot back, "Please wait. First Ed Snowden had a statement to read."

Snowden used the moment to appeal for "guarantees of safe passage from the relevant nations in securing my travel to Latin America" and announced that he would also seek asylum in Russia. "I will be submitting my request to Russia today, and hope it will be accepted favorably." The rest of the meeting seemed to unfold quickly, and Lukin asked Snowden whether he had any complaints. He said no, and then lawyers started debating Snowden's status.

Nikitin gave Snowden his business card but never heard from him again. Snowden was extremely cautious, but Nikitin didn't think it was worthwhile to arrange some kind of covert communications channel; he mostly wanted to establish Snowden's condition, read Snowden's body language, and detect signs of torture—to ask the questions any human rights activist would naturally ask. Nikitin observed that Snowden was relaxed and comfortable. "I was impressed by his sangfroid. After all, he lost everything." Lokshina had the same feeling, "He did not look depressed or anxious."

The meeting participants were shown out of the room, back to the terminal, and Snowden disappeared with Harrison. Lokshina instantly remembered that she forgot her tape recorder and asked the security men to retrieve it. In thirty minutes they brought Lokshina the tape recorder, but the recording had been erased; the meeting had lasted forty-five minutes. Lokshina and Nikitin told journalists in the terminal that they supported Snowden's appeal for asylum. Kucherena, the lawyer with close connections to the FSB, said he would provide legal support for Snowden.

Did the Russian authorities stage a meeting so the human rights groups would endorse Snowden's appeal for asylum, just as Putin wanted? Although they sat in the front row at the meeting, the human rights activists had no say over the meeting's time, place, or circumstances. If there was a script, they had not written it. They heard Snowden talk, and then he disappeared. It was a clever manipulation. Snowden's revelations about mass surveillance had outraged people around the world, and their anger was directed against the US government. Now Putin was presenting himself as a defender of freedoms and the only world leader strong enough to stand up to the United States. The human rights organizations, which Putin had been suppressing for years, were made props in Putin's show, at least briefly. The meeting was a sign that Putin was not going to keep his distance from Snowden but rather would attempt to co-opt him for his own purposes.

A year later Lokshina, sitting in a coffee shop in Moscow, remarked that Snowden seems to have been trapped too. "In fact he's in prison," she said. "No doubt in a comfortable one—he is well fed there, and he did not need anything. But he does not walk the streets of this city."

Snowden may not have known or realized it, but his disclosures emboldened those in Russia who wanted more control over the Internet. The State Duma debated Snowden's revelations of mass surveillance in special hearings. Sergei Zheleznyak, a vice speaker of the Russian parliament, suggested that the Snowden disclosures meant Russian citizens should be forbidden from keeping their personal data on foreign servers. "We should provide a digital sovereignty for our country," he said. Ruslan Gattarov, chairman of one of the pro-Kremlin youth organizations and a member of the upper house of parliament, the Federation Council, invited Snowden to come to the Council to "investigate" what he described as the surrender of Russian citizens' data to the American intelligence agencies.[24]

This "digital sovereignty" claim was cover for something the Kremlin wanted all along—to force Facebook, Twitter, and Google's services, Gmail and YouTube, to be subject to Russian legislation, which meant providing backdoor access to the Russian security services. It was a way to have SORM black boxes installed on the Gmail, Facebook, and Twitter servers. Since spring of 2011 the FSB had been lamenting it had no means to intercept chats and e-mail exchanges on Facebook and Gmail, and now the chances appeared to be improved. The pretext of protecting Russian personal data—the notion of "digital sovereignty"—was raised in order to impose new controls on the Internet, bring the global platforms to heel, and put their servers on the Russian soil. Snowden's name was being invoked by those who wanted to carry out new repressive measures in Russia.

On August 1, 2013, Snowden was granted one year of asylum in Russia, and the next day he left Sheremetyevo, still evading journalists. Kucherena reported the news, saying he personally put Snowden in the car. For months to come, Snowden refused to talk to Russian and Moscow-based foreign journalists. To us, the silence seemed odd and unpleasant. After all, Snowden wasn't afraid of journalists—he had used them to leak the thousands of pages of secret documents. He also spoke to American journalists coming from the United States. Snowden was, in theory, in favor of openness. So why did he refuse to talk to those of us in Russia who, in our journalism, fought every day for openness and freedom of information? Was he being manipulated again? And if so, by whom?

On September 4, 2013, Putin said in an interview that when Snowden first approached the Russian consulate in Hong Kong, the case was immediately reported to him, but he instructed aides to send Snowden away. That part of the story hadn't been reported before, but was it true? Was Putin really that ambivalent about this former NSA contractor who had upset the United States, or was he playing a clever game?[25]

While Snowden remained out of sight, Russia's security services achieved another dramatic leap in their capability to eavesdrop on the Internet. In the autumn of 2013 new SORM technical guidelines were announced that would require phone operators and Internet providers to store information for twelve hours at a time until it could be retrieved by the authorities. The guidelines also made it possible for the security services to intercept correspondence that users send through services such as Gmail and Yahoo and the popular ICQ instant messages. The goal of the updated requirements was very clear: to expand surveillance capabilities to intercept messages and information passed through foreign Internet providers.

The reaction was surprising. On October 21 VimpelCom, one of Russia's largest telecom companies, publicly—and courageously—denounced the government's plans to expand the SORM capabilities. VimpelCom sent a letter to the Ministry of Communications, criticizing the plan as unconstitutional. Next another major provider, Mail.ru, said the requirement to keep data for twelve hours "violates the Constitution of the Russian Federation, in particular the right to privacy, confidentiality of correspondence, telephone conversations, postal, telegraph and other communications" and is "inconsistent with a number of federal laws and codes."[26] The service also protested that a facility to keep that much data might not cost $100 million, as VimpelCom suggested, but more like $400 million. "This will require approximately 30–40 petabytes of data for the entire Runet every 12 hours," said Vice President and Technical Director Vladimir Gabrielyan. Anton Nossik wrote that the "FSB wants to know about every one of our moves on the Internet: Who and what we sent, and from whom they received, what sites come in, what we have there, name and password."

Nossik also wrote that "fixing of all incoming and outgoing Internet traffic of 75 million Russian users requires, without any exaggeration, petabytes and exabytes of disk space." He warned that the new SORM requirements would force users to pay more for Internet services. But the protests did not stop the Kremlin from doing what it wanted to do. The decree implementing the new SORM requirements was signed by the minister of communications on April 16, 2014, and required all operators to install the equipment by March 31, 2015. The requirement to keep twelve hours of data remained in the decree.[27] The Ministry of Communications officials also admitted that the new SORM black boxes are strengthened by DPI, as the devices can monitor the Internet traffic on the application level.[28] The two most intrusive surveillance technologies were finally combined, to be used by the Russian security services all over the country.

When all this was happening, Snowden was silent. Although he gave some interviews to American journalists, he refused to comment on Russian affairs and dropped off the radar until April 17, 2014. We tried repeatedly to contact Snowden, and we also asked American journalist, lawyer, and author Glenn Greenwald for an interview, but Greenwald never responded to our e-mails.

On that day Putin held another of his annual question-and-answer sessions in which citizens call in on a direct line. Much had changed since 2013; the success of the Sochi Olympics and the annexation of Crimea had generated a mood of intense patriotism and anti-Western sentiment. Putin's approval ratings had soared.

As always, the call-in show was broadcast live by three major TV channels along with three radio stations, and it lasted nearly four hours. A well-staged event, it started with calls from Crimea, with "Thank you, Mr. President, on behalf of all the people of Crimea," and other displays of boosterism. Hours passed, and all of a sudden a host in the studio in charge of fielding phone

calls turned not to Putin but to the television watchers and proclaimed, "We have a surprise video call, which I would describe as
sensational. It was sent by a person who has made an information
revolution by exposing a mass surveillance program that affected
millions of people around the world."

Then, a theatrical pause.

"Mr. President, you have a question from former intelligence
agent Edward Snowden!"

Putin grinned:

"Do I really?"

Then Snowden's Skype call appeared on the screen. His first
word was in Russian: "Zdravstvuyte"—Hello.

Then he proceeded in English:

> I'd like to ask you a question about the mass surveillance of online
> communications and the bulk collection of private records by
> intelligence and law enforcement services. Recently, the United
> States, two independent White House investigations, as well as
> a federal court all concluded that these programs are ineffective
> in stopping terrorism. They also found that they unreasonably
> intrude into the private lives of ordinary citizens—individuals
> who have never been suspected of any wrongdoing or criminal
> activity; and that these kinds of programs are not the least in-
> trusive means available to such agencies for these investigative
> purposes. Now, I've seen little public discussion of Russia's own
> involvement in the policies of mass surveillance. So I'd like to
> ask you: Does Russia intercept, store, or analyze in any way the
> communications of millions of individuals, and do you believe
> that simply increasing the effectiveness of intelligence or law
> enforcement investigations can justify placing societies—rather
> than subjects—under surveillance? Thank you.[29]

The host in the studio, journalist Kirill Kleymenov, asked Putin, "Mr. President, did you get the gist of the question?"

Putin, obviously pleased with the question, replied, "Yes, by and large."

Nevertheless Kleymenov—after praising Putin's ability to speak English (Putin laughed, saying American English is slightly different)—tried to translate the question. He almost missed the introductory part about the White House investigations and mistranslated the part about the debate in Russia over surveillance, saying there is a large debate in Russia, and then posed a question about mass surveillance.

Putin began his reply with a joke. "Mr. Snowden, you are a former intelligence officer, and I,"—a pause, and the audience started to giggle—"worked for an intelligence agency too. So let's talk like two professionals." Putin then insisted that Russian laws strictly regulate the use of special equipment by the security services, including for the tapping of private conversations and for the surveillance of online communications. Putin emphasized that a court warrant is needed to use the equipment in each particular case. "So there is no, and cannot be any, indiscriminate mass surveillance under Russian law," Putin declared.

"Yes, we do surveillance on the Internet," Putin allowed, "but not on such a large scale and not arbitrarily. Besides,"—and here he smiled slyly—"we do not have such technical capabilities and funds as the United States."[30]

Putin's answer was a classic obfuscation, just like the one he gave NTV journalists more than a decade earlier in the library of the Kremlin.

At first we were encouraged that Snowden at last started talking about Russia's tightening surveillance of the Internet, hoping it could provoke a public debate about SORM—Andrei made this point in his public comments. But Snowden was heavily criticized for taking part in a Putin show, and the next day he published an op-ed in the *Guardian* answering his critics. "I was surprised that people who witnessed me risk my life to expose the surveillance practices of my own country could not believe that I might also criticize the surveillance policies of Russia, a country to which I have sworn no allegiance, without ulterior motive," he wrote. "I regret that my question could be misinterpreted, and that it enabled many to ignore the substance of the question—and Putin's evasive response—in order to speculate, wildly and incorrectly, about my motives for asking it."

Snowden added, "The investigative journalist Andrei Soldatov, perhaps the single most prominent critic of Russia's surveillance apparatus (and someone who has repeatedly criticized me in the past year), described my question as 'extremely important for Russia.' According to the *Daily Beast*, Soldatov said it could lift a de facto ban on public conversations about state eavesdropping. Others have pointed out that Putin's response appears to be the strongest denial of involvement in mass surveillance ever given by a Russian leader—a denial that is, generously speaking, likely to be revisited by journalists."[31]

In the end Snowden's question didn't provoke a debate in Russia over surveillance. Nor did it stop the Kremlin.

On May 5 Putin signed a new law aimed at tightening the controls over the many popular online bloggers in Russia who carried out lively and relatively free debates on the Internet. Widely known as the "Bloggers Law," it was a part of a broader rewrite of Russia's antiterrorism statute, started in January 2014, which expanded the already-vast clout of the country's Federal Security Service and altered penalties for terrorism and extremism crimes. The new law required bloggers with more than three thousand followers—which was many of them—to register with the government. Registration was more than a mere formality; it would give the security services a way to track them, intimidate them, or close them down. Once registered like the news media, a blogger would be subject to state regulation. In addition to the registration, the law required that bloggers could not remain anonymous and that social media would maintain computer records on Russian soil of everything posted over the previous six months. The law marked a first legislative step to force the global social media to relocate their servers to Russia. At their headquarters in California, both Twitter and Facebook said they were studying the law but would not comment further.

Russia's annexation of Crimea in 2014 presaged still more efforts to control the Internet. Ksenzov, the chief censor at Roskomnadzor, became more and more aggressive on Twitter against the demonstrators in Ukraine, whose Maidan uprising, named after the square in Kiev, had touched off the crisis. The Maidan demonstrations frightened Putin too.

Ksenzov lashed out at the US, Russian, and international media in a string of angry tweets. In one of them he accused CNN of being "insane" for quoting Zbigniew Brzezinski, the former White House national security advisor. Then, on May 16, he attacked Twitter itself, and this time it was much more serious. In an interview with *Izvestia*, the largest pro-Kremlin daily newspaper, Ksenzov claimed that Twitter promotes the interests of the United States and then added, "We can tomorrow block Twitter or Facebook in Russia. It will take few minutes. We do not see this as a big risk. If at any point we decide that the impact of disabling of social networks will be less significant compared to the harm caused by the unconstructive position of management of international companies for Russian society, we will do what is required to do by law." The threat was the most categorical yet made in public. Medvedev, serving as prime minister, criticized Ksenzov, and Roskomnadzor did not officially enforce Ksenzov's statement. But he was unrepentant. The same day on Twitter he said, "Not going to make excuses. Responsible for my words."

Twitter got the message. A few days later it blocked accounts of the radical Ukrainian party Pravy Sector for Russian users, saying the action was in response to a Russian court order. The action marked another success for the Kremlin's effort to tame the global Internet giants, but the Electronic Frontier Foundation in the United States took note and made a good point about

Twitter's decision: "There are two ways that Twitter's actions are disappointing. First, Twitter has no employees or assets in Russia, so it should not have to comply with a Russian court order at all. And the order isn't even about a Russian account—it's a Ukrainian one. Worse yet, Pravy Sector's account is plainly political. If Twitter won't stand up for political speech in a country where independent media is increasingly under attack, what *will* it stand for?"

On July 4 the State Duma passed another law prohibiting the storage of Russians' personal data anywhere but in Russia. Once again members of parliament pointed to Snowden's revelations of mass surveillance to justify the action. A member of Putin's United Russia party suggested nominating Snowden for a Nobel Prize. In effect, Russian security agencies received expanded powers over the Internet under the pretext of protecting the personal data of Russian citizens from the menace that Snowden had described.

The law stipulated that global platforms would relocate their servers to Russia by September 1, 2015. After this, all three global platforms—Google, Twitter, and Facebook—sent high-ranking representatives to Moscow. Details of their talks were kept secret. On July 28 Ksenzov, who had turned Twitter into his main channel of communication, tweeted, "They start a war against us. A full-scale Third World Information one." On August 5 he triumphantly retweeted news from the state-controlled RIA Novosti agency: "For the first time, Apple has begun to store personal user data on the Chinese soil."

The pressure on the global platforms became enormous. Of the trio, only Google had an office in Moscow. Very secretive and shielded from journalists by a hired public relations company, Google's government relations officer was Marina Zhunich. She had started her career at the Moscow office of the BBC's Russian service and then briefly joined the Organization for Security and Cooperation in Europe. Hers was a classic career for a graduate of the Moscow State Institute of International Relations, which groomed young people for service in diplomacy. In the 2000s she worked in public relations at international companies in Moscow. She joined Google in 2009, when Medvedev was president and the Internet was his most enjoyable toy. In the summer of 2012 Zhunich found herself in the eye of the storm. In July she made a statement on YouTube criticizing the proposals to block sites by their Internet protocol or IP addresses.[32] Then she attended most of the meetings at the Ministry of Communications, and some progovernment Internet businessmen openly expressed unhappiness with her active involvement in Russian policy.

Two years later, in June 2014, it was revealed that Zhunich had herself been put under surveillance by private security services hired by businessmen close to the Kremlin—she had been spied on along with journalists of TV Dozhd and *Novaya Gazeta*. When the surveillance was made public by the hacker group Anonymous, Google was silent. We tried to talk to Zhunich at a conference, but she slipped away. We then turned to Facebook to connect with her, and for two days attempted to coax her into an interview. She was very guarded, and when we asked about surveillance of her, she replied, "No, I will not take part in that."[33]

On November 14, 2014, just after 7:00 p.m. and already dark, dozens of people, mostly in their twenties and thirties, were searching for a small red-brick building in Moscow. It was not easy, as the tiny structure was in the yard of a derelict factory, with no signs to help the visitors find it. The visitors, most of them journalists working for Russian online news media, seemed to be lost, searching for the modest venue for a ceremony of the national Internet media awards named after Edward Snowden.

The Russian Association for Electronic Communications had announced in April the establishment of the new award and claimed

they had secured agreement from Snowden. But many of the journalists knew it was Alexey Venediktov who was behind the idea.
Venediktov positioned himself as a quiet intermediary between
the digital news and social media and his own high-placed contacts in the Kremlin. His personal assistant had secured the agreement of Snowden for the award. The assistant was also inserted by
Venediktov into a team of experts to work on the controversial Bloggers Law. Venediktov was an editor-in-chief of Echo Moskvy, the radio station that had been a champion of liberal democracy since the
last days of the Soviet Union, but he also maintained good contacts
in the Kremlin, including, periodically, Putin himself.

On the cold day in November chosen to award the prizes,
the mood was cheerless. Once they found the building, the journalists encountered a band that tried to raise their spirits, to no
avail. Two of the show's hosts, Tatyana Felgenhauer and Alexander Plushev, both of them journalists from Echo Moskvy, wore
long faces—the fate of the station was increasingly in doubt, in
part because of some indiscreet tweets by Plushev that drew the
ire of Putin's team. The chairman of the board of directors of the
station, Mikhail Lesin, who had tried to lay his hands on the Internet in December 1999 at the meeting with Putin, warned that
that it's "entirely possible" to fire Venediktov. Everyone at Echo
was on edge.

Plushev and Felgenhauer tried their best while giving the
awards, making some jokes, but when Plushev read a gag about
his possible firing, he laughed bitterly. The show itself was sad
and confused. Ilya Klishin, now the editor of TV Dozhd's website, was clearly shocked when he got his award, shared with an
editor of the website of Lifenews.ru, a shameless pro-Kremlin tab-
loid-style TV channel that was preparing to take up occupancy of
TV Dozhd's premises after TV Dozhd had been expelled from the
Red October complex.

One of those in the crowd was Stas Kozlovsky, leader of
the Wikipedia community in Russia and a professor in the

psychology department at Moscow State University. Kozlovsky, thirty-eight, discovered Wikipedia in 2003, when its Russian version had only a few hundred articles. He gave up his blog and started to write for Wikipedia. Though he looked a bit like a Cheshire cat, Kozlovsky was famous for being a fierce fighter for Internet freedom. He was the one who, at Irina Levova's urging, put Russian Wikipedia into a blackout in the summer of 2012 to protest Internet filtering and has been battling on behalf of Wikipedia since the authorities first tried to block the online encyclopedia.

Artem Kozlyuk, a head of Rublacklist.net, the watchdog that keeps tabs on which sites have been blacklisted, greeted him with a knowing smile: "Hi, Stas, are you ready for a blackout in May?" In May 2015 a new law was to come into force that would make it possible to block all kinds of sites if they carried information without signed agreements from authors or rights holders, a measure described as an antipiracy law. It would almost certainly lead to blocking Wikipedia. "Now any hyperlink to any text or page on the Internet can cause blocking of a website. The Russian Wikipedia contains nearly 1.2 million articles, and each has dozens of hyperlinks to the sources," Kozlovsky told us.

At the Snowden ceremony there was no sign of the man who had loaned it his name. When Andrei pointed that out to Kozlovsky, he replied with a sad smile, "Well, Snowden could have done good things globally, but for Russia he was a disaster."

Four months later, in March 2015, the Ministry of Communications convened a gathering of the biggest Russian data centers to discuss the relocation of servers. A representative of Rostelecom, a state-controlled Russian operator, stepped in to announce that Google had already relocated the servers to the operator's data center, adding, "The Company [Google] is our client now, and we are the restricted access, semi-government facility."[34] At the time Google declined to provide comments.

Snowden, a whistleblower who loved to quote the UN Declaration of Human Rights, landed in a country with a miserable record on human rights. He appealed to NGOs and investigative journalists for help, but in Russia human rights activists are branded "foreign agents" or spies, and investigative journalism is under threat of complete extinction. Snowden argued that he took risks to expose state secrets in the interests of freedom of information, but he remained a guest of a regime that for years has been suppressing freedom of information. Although he justified his actions by the need to defend the Internet from government intrusion, when he landed in Moscow, the Kremlin was in the middle of a large-scale offensive against Internet freedoms.

Snowden failed to respond to these challenges. For months he tried to pretend he was not in Russia, but just somewhere, in some limbo, that he found asylum in an unmarked country that would never extradite him to the United States. The Kremlin helped him preserve this fiction, and he was never dragged into being a tool of the Russian propaganda media outlets. He was allowed to keep out of sight.

After ten months in Moscow, Snowden asked Putin at a staged news conference about surveillance, but Putin merely deflected the question.

Since the day Snowden landed in Moscow the symbols of the global Internet—Google, Facebook, and Twitter—came under increasing pressure from the Kremlin to make the global Internet local, to destroy the very nature of the global network. Snowden didn't say a word about it except for his single call to the Putin news conference.

Snowden's revelations suggest he aspired to fight for Internet freedom not only in the United States but around the world; however, Russia was omitted from his fight. He left his home country to campaign for more transparency surrounding the intelligence agencies' activities, and found himself living in Moscow, heavily protected by Russian secret services—behind the walls, shielded from the world outside.

At the same time Snowden was in Moscow, Russia was already attempting to change the global rules of the Internet. That too seemed to escape Snowden's attention.

CHAPTER 11

Putin's Overseas Offensive

Vladimir Putin was certain that all things in the world—including the Internet—existed with a hierarchical, vertical structure. He was also certain that the Internet must have someone controlling it at the top. He viewed the United States with suspicion, thinking the Americans ruled the web and that it was a CIA project. Putin wanted to end that supremacy. Just as he attempted to change the rules inside Russia, so too did he attempt to change them for the world. The goal was to make other countries, especially the United States, accept Russia's right to control the Internet within its borders, to censor or suppress it completely if the information circulated online in any way threatened Putin's hold on power.

Andrey Krutskikh devoted his entire career in the Russian Foreign Ministry to arms control. He joined the diplomatic service in 1973, right after university, and served in the ministry for the final eighteen years of the Soviet Union's existence. He admired the diplomatic style of the stolid and uncompromising foreign minister, Andrei Gromyko, known informally in the West as Mr. Nyet. Krutskikh often called Gromyko "great."

From the very beginning of his service Krutskikh's work centered on disarmament, nuclear weapons, and the so-called main adversaries, the United States and Canada. When he was twenty-four years old, in 1975, he was sent to Salt Lake City as a member of the Soviet delegation to negotiate strategic nuclear arms control. Krutskikh's experience at the negotiations in Salt Lake City left a strong impression on him. It was a time when Soviet diplomats had stature; they decided the fate of the world and spoke on equal terms with the Americans. After the Soviet collapse and into the late 1990s Krutskikh continued to focus on arms-control issues and rose through the ranks of the ministry. He was not a smooth or slick diplomat; he had a rather agitated manner—expressive, his hands always in motion. Krutskikh soon wondered whether arms control could be useful in the emerging realm of cyber conflict.

Among a particular group of Russian generals who represented FAPSI, the powerful electronic intelligence agency that had grown out of the KGB, a similar mindset was developing. The agency's headquarters was located in a stark, modern terraced building with giant antenna globes on the roof not far from the KGB headquarters. Like the US NSA, FAPSI was responsible for information security, signals, and electronic intelligence. For many years their generals watched the growth of the Internet with suspicion, thinking it was a threat to Russia's national security, because in the early days the Russian Internet was built with Western technology, and they were obsessed with the fear that it would be thoroughly penetrated by the Americans.

The leader of this group of suspicious generals was Vladislav Sherstyuk, a colonel-general in the intelligence wing of the agency and a KGB officer since 1966. By the 1990s he became head of the very mysterious and powerful Third Department of FAPSI, in charge of spying on foreign telecommunications. All Russian centers of electronic espionage abroad were subordinated to this department, including the radio interception center at Lourdes in Cuba, which was in charge of monitoring and intercepting radio communications from the United States. Sherstyuk was a spymaster, determined to exploit communications to steal US secrets and protect Russia against espionage of the same kind. This naturally made him wary of the Internet, where so much was beyond his control.

When the war in Chechnya began, Sherstyuk was put in charge of FAPSI's group there, and he organized the interception of Chechens' communications. In December 1998 he was appointed director of FAPSI, a mighty intelligence service in its own right that competed head-to-head with the FSB. Among other things, they had a very special role in controlling the government's most sensitive communications networks.

Krutskikh and the FAPSI generals spoke the same language of suspicion—a language of threats posed by the Internet. In early 1999 Krutskikh was helping to draft a resolution for the UN General Assembly that reflected these views and warned that information—the Internet—could be misused for "criminal or terrorist purposes" and could undermine "the security of States." In other words, information technologies had to be controlled because they could be dangerous. The resolution was adopted without a vote.[1]

Krutskikh and the generals viewed the Internet as a battleground for information warfare. (This term should not be mixed with cyberwarfare, which is mostly about protecting a nation's critical digital networks from hackers.) For Krutskikh and the generals, information warfare encompasses something political and menacing, including "disinformation and tendentious information" that is spread to incite psychological warfare, used for altering how people make decisions and how societies see the world.[2] In contrast to those who celebrate free media and the Internet as a glorious information superhighway that opens limitless possibilities for discovery, Krutskikh and the generals worried that it could become the front lines of conflict between nations and hostile groups.

In December 1999 Sherstyuk moved out of FAPSI to the Russian Security Council, an advisory group to the president on security. Once there, he supervised a department for information security, which included the Internet, and brought his ideas with him. The Security Council normally is made up of top officials, including the president, and meets periodically, but it also has an influential staff, which Sherstyuk joined. In 2000 his team composed the "Doctrine of the Information Security of the Russian Federation," which included an unusually broad list of threats, ranging from "compromising of keys and cryptographic protection of information" to "devaluation of spiritual values," "reduction of spiritual, moral and creative potential of the Russian population," as well as "manipulation of information (disinformation, concealment or misrepresentation)." Quite ominously, it identified one source of the threats as "the desire of some countries to dominate and infringe the interests of Russia in the global information space."[3] Putin approved the doctrine on December 9, 2000.

In 2003 FAPSI was disbanded, but not the ideas of the suspicious generals. Sherstyuk remained at the Security Council, and some of his views were reinforced when a like-minded top official from the FSB, Nikolai Klimashin, was moved to the Security Council. Sherstyuk founded and headed the Information Security Institute at Moscow State University, which he built into a major think tank to define Russian foreign policy on information security. Meanwhile, Krutskikh rose to become deputy chief of the Department for Security and Disarmament Issues at the ministry.

For years at international meetings Krutskikh had been driving home that Russia wanted to govern its own space on the Internet. Whereas others, including the United States, saw the Internet as a wide-open expanse of freedom for the whole world, Krutskikh insisted that Russia should be able to control what was said online within its borders. He expressed fear that, without such control, hostile forces might use the Internet to harm Russia and its people. "If through the Internet we would be forced to forget our mighty great Russian language, and speak only using curse words, we should not agree with that," he told us, echoing Putin's deep suspicions about the Internet and who was behind it. Krutskikh repeatedly proposed some kind of international agreement or treaty that would give Russia the control it sought over the Internet. Influenced by his own career in arms-control negotiations, he was convinced that such an agreement must be between Russia and the United States. He wasn't anti-American, but he grew emotionally attached to the idea that the two former Cold War superpowers could somehow make a pact that would give Russia control over its digital space. The United States, however, never warmed to the idea—the US government never attempted to control content on the Internet, and many of the first Internet pioneers in America were very open about the Internet as a symbol of how information should roam free—but what Krutskikh wanted most was to be taken seriously and to have his views treated with respect, as they were during the Cold War.

But he didn't get much respect. At a bilateral meeting in March 2009 in Vienna, Krutskikh delivered a long monologue arguing that Russia and the United States—and perhaps other nations—should collaborate to regulate the Internet as nations and governments. He expressed fear that the Internet was building beyond their control, that there could be an arms race in cyber space, and it was time for governments to take charge.

Russian generals felt they were losing the global cyber arms race and wanted to put some limits on the United States' offensive capabilities. But Krutskikh's speech fell on deaf ears. An American diplomat cabled back an account of the meeting, saying, "There was little change, if any, between U.S. and Russian long-held views" on the subject. Krutskikh desperately wanted some sort of joint statement with the United States, but the US administration was reluctant to sign anything.[4]

But he didn't give up. In 2010 Kaspersky Lab investigated Stuxnet, the US-Israeli worm that wrecked nearly a thousand Iranian centrifuges.[5] Krutskikh seized on the incident—with its destructive malware, designed in part by the United States—as a justification for a ban on cyber weapons.[6] In 2011 Kaspersky, who was highly regarded in Russia as an Internet entrepreneur, added his voice to the idea of a ban on cyber weapons, and in November he wrote on his blog, "Considering the fact that peace and world stability strongly relies on the internet, an international organization needs to be created in order to control cyber-weapons. A kind of International Atomic Energy Agency but dedicated to the cyberspace."[7]

In the Bavarian Alps a small mountain resort town, Garmisch-Partenkirchen, is famous for its spectacular views and NATO's Marshall Center for Security Studies, which is based there. Nearby is a pretty hotel, Atlas, with a traditional Bavarian three-story lodge that is a twenty-minute walk from the Marshall Center. Founded in the early sixteenth century as a tavern, the hotel proudly lists among its previous guests Duke Ludwig from Bavaria, the Prince of Wales, and the King of Jordan. Every April, for almost a week, the hotel hangs a Russian flag from its balcony, hung personally by Sherstyuk, who, since 2007, has been bringing to the lodge a group of Russian and American generals and high-placed officials to talk quietly about information security and cyber conflict. The first two days are always reserved for general discussions, mostly on cyber security and what kind of research is required. Russians gathered in one part of the hotel, and non-Russians gathered in another, partly because many Russians didn't speak English, and most Americans didn't speak Russian. The third day was devoted to individual meetings. The real business was conducted in closed rooms with only a few participants. Klimashin was among the guests, as well as Krutskikh, who never tired of making speeches and arguing for agreement on "terms and definitions" in cyberspace and for greater UN involvement in Internet governance. He favored the United Nations because it was filled with governments, not companies, and many of them were sympathetic to Russia's desire to control the Internet within their borders.[8]

The US government took the gatherings in Garmisch very seriously every year. High-level officials were sent; in 2010 the US delegation included Christopher Painter, the second-ranking White House official on cyber security, and Judith Strotz, the director of the State Department's Office of Cyber Affairs.[9]

Russian officials in charge of information security often spoke bitterly of US domination of the Internet, believing all the tools and mechanisms for technical control were in US hands. Their main target was the Internet Corporation for Assigned Names and Numbers, known as ICANN, a nonprofit organization headquartered in California. In 1997 President Clinton directed the secretary of commerce to privatize the management of the domain name system, a critical part of the Internet that serves as a giant warehouse of web addresses looked up every time a user wants to go somewhere online. The Defense Advanced Research Projects Agency, the National Science Foundation, and other US research agencies had previously performed this task. On September 18, 1998, ICANN was created and given a contract with the US Department of Commerce to oversee a number of Internet-related tasks, but the most important among them was to manage the distribution of domain names worldwide. In the 2000s other nations campaigned to have a greater role in ICANN, but the Kremlin's idea was more radical: to strip ICANN of its powers.

The president of ICANN, Paul Twomey, hastened to the second gathering in Garmisch in 2008. He and other high-ranking

ICANN representatives tried to keep open channels of communications with the Russians. One of the top US ICANN representatives who made sure always to attend was George Sadowsky. Looking always professorial, he taught mathematics at Harvard and was a technical adviser to the United Nations in the 1970s. In 2001 Sadowsky became executive director of the Global Internet Policy Initiative, which promoted Internet freedoms in the former Soviet Union and Central Asia. In 2009 he was selected to the board of directors of ICANN. Sadowsky had a great deal of experience in dealing with Russian officials. He found the endless discussions to be frustrating, as both sides saw the world differently and had trouble even agreeing to a common language about the Internet; there were very basic divisions over definitions regarding the Internet. "Is it a communications service or is it an information service?" he recalled. "And this went on, and on, and on."[10] In Garmisch both Russians and Americans tried to be pleasant and friendly, but they were at a stalemate. And with each passing year the discussions became increasingly difficult—after the conference in 2010 Sadowsky admitted, "The Russians have a dramatically different definition of information security than we do; it's a broader notion, and they really mean state security."[11]

When the Russian officials failed to get an agreement with the United States about ICANN, they shifted strategy, looking for a new way to assert more sovereignty over the Internet. This new approach led them to the International Telecommunications Union, or ITU. With headquarters in Geneva, the organization was originally established in 1895 to regulate the telephone and telegraph. It is a specialized UN agency, and as such, it is dependent on the member states.

The ITU was not involved in Internet governance until late 2006, when Hamadoun I. Touré was elected its secretary general.

Touré made the Internet a central issue for the ITU from the start of his tenure. A citizen of Mali, he speaks fluent Russian and studied at the Communications Institute in Leningrad, the same institute where Boris Goldstein, one of the main Russian experts on SORM, studied and has been working for decades. Touré was well known in and maintained close ties with Russia—he was first elected and then, in 2010, reelected with the full support of Russia. As secretary general of ITU, he became very critical of ICANN, and in August 2010 he even refused Rod Beckstrom, then chief executive and president of ICANN, permission to attend an ITU conference.

Krutskikh spotted all this jockeying and, frustrated by the failures to change ICANN, moved to promote a larger role for the ITU. This was a surprising development for Sadowsky. When he met Krutskikh at a Moscow conference in 2008, the Russian official was pleasant and restrained. But it was another story two years later when they met again at the same conference. Sadowsky said something unfavorable about the ITU, and Krutskikh responded emotionally and forcefully, interrupting the American midremarks.

For Sadowsky, it seemed like Krutskikh—and Russia—had wagered a big bet on the ITU.

The tumultuous uprisings of the Arab Spring that threw out long-serving authoritarian leaders—uprisings that Internet communications accelerated—suddenly made the issue of Internet governance more urgent for Putin. In June 2011 Putin went to Geneva to talk to Touré. They met at the large hall at the UN Office, and Putin reminded Touré that Russia cofounded the ITU and went on to say that Russia intended to actively participate in "establishing international control over the internet" by using the capabilities of the ITU.[12] It was an audacious idea: to control the Internet using a century-old UN agency.

Krutskikh, in preparation for the new effort, moved in August 2011 to another department inside the Foreign Ministry. The department was closely tied to the security services and had once been supervised by a former first deputy director of the FSB. Then in March of the following year he was made a special coordinator for issues regarding political use of information and telecommunication technologies—the Internet—and given a rank of ambassador. He was to be Putin's point man on a campaign to wrest more control of the Internet from the United States.

The next major ITU conference was scheduled for December 2012 in Dubai. The top ITU officials intended to use the gathering to change the rules for the Internet globally through a review of an existing global treaty, which was last updated in 1988, before the digital era. The ITU intended to amend the treaty to include the Internet and, thus, make it subject to ITU regulation. And the Kremlin decided to make the conference in Dubai the launch pad for a general offensive against US domination of the Internet.

Krutskikh went to work recruiting other countries to support Russia. He won nods of agreement from China, where the Internet is rigidly and widely censored, and from Central Asian nations that were former Soviet republics and also largely authoritarian. In May 2012 Krutskikh won backing directly from the Kremlin. The former minister of communications Igor Shchegolev moved to the administration as Putin's adviser on the Internet, and he fully shared Krutskikh's ideas about the ITU and ICANN. Shchegolev had accompanied Putin in June 2011 to Geneva and took part in the meeting with Touré.[13] The new communications minister, Nikolai Nikiforov, twenty-nine, was technically savvy but inexperienced. He was appointed to his position from Kazan, Tatarstan, where he had served as Tatarstan's minister of communications. He was far from being an independent political figure.

Krutskikh plotted his strategy for the Dubai meeting in an office near the foreign ministry's twenty-seven-story tower in central Moscow. His office building next door looked like a giant, seven-story cube with an oblique angle. From there, on the fourth floor, with an Andreevsky Flag (two blue stripes crossed diagonally on white, the insignia of the Russian fleet) on the wall and a spaceship model on his desk, with his papers always carefully sorted, Krutskikh laid out the battle plan, drafting dozens of proposals for the ITU summit.

Google launched a campaign against the Russian offensive. In May 2012 Vint Cerf, "chief Internet evangelist" at Google and widely recognized as one of the fathers of the Internet, published an op-ed in the *New York Times* headlined "Keep the Internet Open."[14] He referred to Putin's remark at the meeting with Touré in 2011 and criticized a proposal submitted by China, Russia, Tajikistan, and Uzbekistan to the UN General Assembly that sought to establish government-led "international norms and rules" in cyberspace. Cerf proclaimed, "The decisions taken in Dubai in December have the potential to put government handcuffs on the Net." He appealed for action against it.

But Russia was undeterred, and preparations became more intense. In June the first draft of the Russian proposals to the ITU conference were leaked to the press. They were couched in jargon, but the point was crystal clear: Russia proposed to give countries the right to control the Internet in cases in which it was used "for the purpose of interfering in the internal affairs or undermining the sovereignty, national security, territorial integrity and public safety of other states, or to divulge information of a sensitive nature." This would give nations the right to censor on the slimmest of pretexts.[15] Then, just two weeks before the conference started in Dubai, there was another leak of Russian proposals, and then another one. The direction of the drafts was the same, giving nations "the sovereign right . . . to regulate the national Internet segment."[16]

The two-week ITU conference started on Monday, December 3, at the Dubai World Trade Center, a thirty-nine-story rectangular tower built in 1978 at the city's Trade Centre Roundabout. More than nineteen hundred participants from 193 countries attended.[17] Krutskikh hoped this would be his triumphal moment.

The Russian delegation was led by the minister of communications, Nikiforov, with Krutskikh as a member of his team. Touré at once appointed Nikiforov one of the vice chairs of the conference. Russia's hopes looked promising: the Russian team had already secured private pledges of support from China and eighty-seven other countries for the draft proposals, and Krutskikh was determined to win over other countries.

Throughout the first week of the conference the participants debated the leaked Russian drafts in the corridors and meeting rooms as they waited anxiously for the official Russian proposal to come.[18] Tensions were high, as the United States opposed talking about Internet regulation at the ITU conference at all. On Thursday, December 6, the head of the US delegation, Ambassador Terry Kramer, convened a special briefing. Kramer was not a career diplomat but rather a top company manager with a twenty-five-year career in the private sector and telecommunications, mostly at Vodafone, and was specifically appointed by President Obama to head the delegation. Kramer didn't hesitate to use strong words. "Fundamentally, the conference, to us, should not be dealing with the internet sector," he declared. "That carries significant implications that could open the doors to things such as content censorship." He dismissed the Russian proposals out of hand. "What can happen is what are seemingly harmless proposals can open the door to censorship, because people can then say, listen, as part of internet security, we see traffic and content that we don't like."[19]

On Friday, December 7, a twenty-two-page document was passed to the conference's organizer, the ITU. It was headed, "Russia, UAE, China, Saudi Arabia, Algeria, Sudan, and Egypt. PROPOSALS FOR THE WORK OF THE CONFERENCE." The document had the insignia of the ITU globe at the top and was dated December 5, 2012. Although the document was written in English, it had been edited by someone with a computer in Cyrillic. Some of the editing changes were made by Maria Ivankovich, an expert at the Radio Research and Development Institute within the Russian Ministry of Communications, one of three major research centers involved in developing SORM, the Russian system of communications interception.

A day later, on December 8, the website wcitleaks.org made a splash in the media by publishing a link to the latest Russian proposal, which declared that member states have "the sovereign right to establish and implement public policy, including international policy, on matters of Internet governance."[20] The proposal drew condemnation from around the world, and Krutskikh's dream began to fall apart; the Egyptian delegation announced that despite the fact that its name was on it, it "never supported the document." On December 10, without explanation, the Russian delegation withdrew it. It was reported that Touré talked personally to Nikiforov to persuade Russia to withdraw the proposal following American threats to walk out of the conference if the document was formally submitted.[21] Touré feared that the proposal could break up the conference completely, and he wanted the new treaty to be signed.

The Russian initiative failed spectacularly—strongly opposed by the United States and other Western governments.

At the last day of the conference, on Friday, December 14, a new treaty was offered for signing, and eighty-nine countries endorsed the document, including Russia. Much of the language of the earlier drafts had been taken out, but the final document still contained Article 5B, which stated, "Member states should endeavour to take necessary measures to prevent the propagation of unsolicited bulk electronic communications and minimize its impact on international telecommunication services."

It sounded rather unobjectionable. But the Western delegations were certain that this clause was intended, among other things, to support actions by governments that want to control content on the Internet, as Russia was striving to do. Kramer said the treaty was "seeking to insert governmental control over Internet governance" and, in a dramatic moment, walked out of the hall, destroying any prospects for a treaty.[22] On the whole, fifty-five countries refused to sign the new treaty, including Western European and Anglo-Saxon nations, and their refusal to sign the new treaty meant that the document simply could not be implemented.

Krutskikh was the only Russian official in Dubai willing to comment. "The Americans are the fathers and mothers of the Internet, and we have to appreciate that," he said with bitterness. "But words like 'Internet' and 'security' should not be treated like curse words. They have been treated like curse words by some delegations at this conference."[23]

The Kremlin had sought to recruit nations from around the world to change the rules of the Internet to give authoritarian countries the ability to censor it. But it didn't work. The nations involved in building the Internet, chiefly the United States, were dead set against it.

Krutskikh's dream slipped away.

A few months after the ITU disaster Krutskikh took part in a conference on information security in Russia. He spoke at length about the threats to Russia on the Internet, and when he finished, Irina approached him and asked for a comment about what had happened in Dubai. He was both angry and passionate, stating that the Russian initiative didn't fail because it was never officially on the table. Then he exclaimed, "We have not lost! Eighty-nine countries support us!" He vowed that Russia would continue to promote its model of global Internet regulation in every possible forum.

Snowden's revelations of mass surveillance of Internet and telephone metadata in 2013 prompted other countries to start thinking in terms of "national sovereignty" on the Internet, and the United States faced widespread condemnation and criticism. Brazil's communications minister said that local ISPs could be required to store data on servers within the country, saying local control over data was a "matter of national sovereignty." Later, Germany's Deutsche Telekom declared that it wanted to create a national Internet to protect Germany from privacy infringements. In February 2014 German chancellor Angela Merkel, furious at the disclosure that the NSA had monitored her cell phone, raised the prospect with French president François Hollande to build a European network so as to avoid data passing through US servers.

In June 2013 Presidents Obama and Putin agreed to establish a new working group within the US-Russia Bilateral Presidential Commission as part of a cyber security confidence-building measure between the two countries. To chair the group from the Russian side Putin appointed deputy secretary of the Security Council Klimashin, and Krutskikh was made the group's cocoordinator.[24] Putin clearly still trusted Krutskikh and his generals. The new working group gathered for the first time in November in Washington; the participants, our sources told us, consciously left Snowden's name out of the talks.

Krutskikh got a second chance. In February 2014 Putin appointed him his special representative for international negotiations on Internet regulation. On April 23–24, in São Paulo, Brazil, a conference was held, NETmundial. Provoked by Edward Snowden's revelations, it was a two-day global meeting on the topic of Internet governance. Nikiforov, the Russian minister of communications, noted that the conference delivered a standing ovation after a speaker expressed words of gratitude to Snowden. Nikiforov delivered welcoming remarks prepared by Krutskikh, and they had all his usual hallmarks—attacks on ICANN and calls to hand over all powers to the ITU. But against Nikiforov's expectations, the speech didn't go over well—the participants simply ignored Russia's proposals.

The very next day in Moscow Putin declared that the Internet was a "CIA project" and that Russia needed to be protected from it.[25] His remarks were reported far and wide, overshadowing the Russian presentation at the conference, and Nikiforov's speech was omitted from the documents of NETmundial. The Russian ministry was outraged and published a protest on its site.[26]

Many countries were unhappy with the way the Internet was governed, but it didn't mean they would march in lockstep with Russia. They could be very critical of US dominance on the Internet or the way their citizens' personal data was circulated, but they were not ready to turn the global network into a collection of local Internets under the control of national governments.

The Kremlin's attempt to change the global rules of the Internet fell flat. But there were other ways Putin could experiment with digital sovereignty—for example, in a small, beautiful town on the Black Sea.

CHAPTER 12

Watch Your Back

I n the center of Toronto, on Bloor Street, on a cold day in March 2013 we walked up the steps of a two-story English-style mansion with a tall round tower attached to it. During World War II the building was used to train pilots to identify weather patterns, but now it is part of the University of Toronto. Inside we found a bunch of geeks and researchers who worked to identify surveillance and filtering equipment on communications around the world.

We were met by Professor Ron Deibert, forty-nine years old, who, as a scholar, was deeply interested in the impact of the Internet on world politics. In the mid-1990s he moved to the University of Toronto because it had been the home of Canadian communications theorists Harold Innis and Marshall McLuhan. In 2001 the Ford Foundation offered him a $250,000 grant to conduct research on the Internet and international security, giving rise to a research center known as the Citizen Lab.[1] Deibert recruited ex-hackers, programmers, and researchers in an effort to discover hidden surveillance and content filtering on global networks.

In a few years Citizen Lab emerged as a primary source of data on repressive regimes' Internet intrusions and attacks on their critics and opponents. In 2009 they identified a massive intrusion into the computers of the Tibetan leader, the Dalai Lama, and on computers in 103 countries. The intrusion was called "GhostNet" and was believed to have emanated from China. Citizen Lab also revealed malware campaigns against Syrian activists and exposed how a remote intrusion and surveillance software called FinFisher was used against protesters in Bahrain and political dissidents in Malaysia and Ethiopia.

We met that day in the tower on Bloor Street. The group also included Masashi Nishihata and Sarah McKune from Citizen Lab as well as Eric King of Privacy International, the British organization concerned with privacy issues. Deibert showed us into the turret room under the ceiling of the tower, known to the staff as the Jedi Council. We joined the group to plan an investigation into Russian surveillance in the upcoming Olympic Games, scheduled for February 2014 at Sochi on the Black Sea.

The games were a showcase for Vladimir Putin. In 2007 he had personally presented, in English, Russia's bid to the International Olympic Committee, and Russia won. In the years before the games Putin put the FSB in charge of providing security for the Olympics. In 2010 an FSB general, Oleg Syromolotov, was appointed as the chairman of the Russian group that would oversee security at the games. We described to the others at the meeting how Syromolotov, inside the FSB, was not in charge of counterterrorism operations, as might be expected; rather, he was a top counterintelligence officer at Lubyanka since 2000. He spent his entire career in the KGB and then the FSB, and for thirteen years he had directed FSB efforts to hunt down foreign spies. Now he was put in charge of providing security for a major international gathering that would host athletes, journalists, and political leaders from around the world. We told the group that Syromolotov's appointment was significant. It could mean that Russia viewed the games as an opportunity to collect intelligence.

We obtained a PowerPoint presentation about security at the games that was primarily concerned with the communications challenges, and we found something revealing on its final pages, which we shared with our colleagues. The slides revealed how SORM—the black boxes of the FSB that were placed on all kind of communications connections—were being deployed to Sochi to cover all communications at the games. The next to last slide gave a list of the black boxes' basic requirements, including that they should be able to "intercept all segments of the network," that the fact of SORM's presence there should be completely se-cret, that there should be an iron-clad system to avoid anyone dis-covering that they were being intercepted, and that they should be hidden from the personnel of phone companies and ISPs. We suggested to our colleagues that Russia was preparing to use sur-veillance of the same intensity that China had in the 2008 Sum-mer Games in Beijing.

King, of Privacy International and a world-renowned expert in spotting the presence of surveillance equipment suppliers, had made it his passion to attend every expo on surveillance through-out the globe. He knew what SORM was about—he had come across this technology in Central Asia. He asked us, "What does it mean that it is being upgraded for the Olympics? Does that mean that SORM will be combined with deep packet inspection [the system of infiltrating the content of communications]? If they were used together, would that transform the targeted surveillance into mass surveillance? In other words, would it help to identify and track, say, activists by words they use?"

We just didn't know. We thought there might be clues if we could find out what hardware and equipment was being used, but that would take some digging.

One thing we did know was that the FSB and Interior Minis-try officials spoke openly and increasingly about their experiences in the 1980 Moscow Olympics more than three decades earlier. Officials had learned certain lessons about both surveillance and physical security of the Games. The lesson for surveillance was to monitor as much as possible; the lesson for physical security was to isolate the Games as much as possible.

In 1980 the Olympic Games were secured in a way that was only possible in the totalitarian Soviet state—Moscow was ruthlessly cleansed of any possible troublemakers, who were sent out of the capital, and the city stood empty for the two weeks of the competitions, surrounded by troops and with KGB officers at every corner. When some of the sporting events were underattended, the authorities just sent troops to fill the stands. The Moscow Olympics was surrounded by paranoia; the KGB prepared dozens of reports of foreign intelligence services' "hostile intentions" to undermine the games.

We underscored to the group in Toronto that the appointment of Syromolotov, a top counterintelligence officer in the FSB, seemed to echo this Soviet-style approach. It was clear that in Sochi the authorities wanted to combine the KGB's traditional methods with cutting-edge surveillance technologies.

Those who gathered in Citizen Lab's tower that day knew how quickly the pace of electronic surveillance was growing in Russia. The FSB's supervision of the Olympics security meant that all measures were to be carried out under a veil of secrecy. For years it had been impossible to obtain comments from the FSB; the press office was effectively shut off from journalists' requests. Not only officials but also companies contracted by the authorities to provide security solutions were reluctant to talk.

Under the turret that day we acknowledged with the others that there were many unknowns. We felt that Russia was preparing something large and menacing in surveillance, but we didn't know how it would be actually used, how it would work, and what was the goal for the FSB: to gather intelligence using interception and surveillance, to stop protesters from reaching the site of the games, or maybe to use the surveillance measures as a big stick to intimidate and frighten possible troublemakers?

We also wondered about the future of SORM and what the Russian authorities wanted to do after the games ended. Was Sochi intended to be a laboratory to be replicated all over the country? After all, many security measures, first tested in Moscow in 1980, were then introduced on the national level. Even the anti-riot police units known as OMON, which had beaten protesters during the demonstrations in 2011–2012, were formed because of the Moscow Olympics. What kind of legacy would Sochi leave in terms of surveillance and control of information?

The information games were afoot.

Once we got back to Moscow we decided to make a point of examining all kinds of open sources, including technical documents published on the government's procurement agency website, zakupki.gov.ru; Russian law requires all government agencies, including the secret services, to buy their equipment through this site. We also scrutinized presentations and public statements made by government officials and top managers of firms involved with the Olympics and security for the city of Sochi. We reviewed public records of government oversight agencies such as the telecoms watchdog Roskomnadzor. Soon we found out that our suspicions about upgrading SORM were correct.

The Russian Supreme Court keeps statistics about court orders issued for interception, but they are held deeply inside the court's filing system and are not in the open. For years finding such information was impossible; members of parliament told us they could not get it. Then a lawyer gave us a hint on how to mine the data out of the computers. We followed the lawyer's advice and discovered what we were looking for—the court's statistics. We found that in six years Russia's use of SORM had skyrocketed: the number of intercepted phone conversations and e-mail messages doubled in six years, from 265,937 in 2007 to 539,864 in 2012. These figures do not include counterintelligence eavesdropping on Russian citizens and foreigners, the area of Syromolotov's department.

It was hard to find specific details about SORM deployment in Sochi, so we turned to the data of Roskomnadzor, the communications watchdog that was very busy making sure SORM equipment was properly installed in the Sochi region. We discovered that several local ISPs were fined for having failed to install Omega, the SORM black box recommended by the FSB. One document from Roskomnadzor showed that in November 2012 the ISP Sochi-Online was officially warned for "failing to introduce the required technical equipment to ensure the functioning of SORM."

Our suspicions about SORM deepened on April 8 when Gus Hosein, director of Privacy International, forwarded us a US State Department warning for Americans wanting to attend the Olympics in Sochi. The document, issued by the department's Bureau of Diplomatic Security, carried the title, "Russian SORM Factsheet, Winter Olympics; Surveillance; Cyber," and it warned that when traveling to Russia, people "should be aware that their telephone and electronic communications may be subject to surveillance, potentially compromising sensitive information." The warning then went into details describing SORM, stating that the system "permits the monitoring, retention and analysis of all data that traverses Russian communications networks." The document warned people heading to Sochi to be extremely careful:

> Consider traveling with "clean" electronic devices—if you do not need the device, do not take it. Otherwise, essential devices should have all personal identifying information and sensitive files removed or "sanitized." Devices with wireless connection capabilities should have the Wi-Fi turned off at all times. Do not check business or personal electronic devices with your luggage

at the airport. . . . Do not connect to local ISPs at cafes, coffee shops, hotels, airports, or other local venues. . . . Change all your passwords before and after your trip. . . . Be sure to remove the battery from your Smartphone when not in use. Technology is commercially available that can geo-track your location and activate the microphone on your phone. Assume any electronic device you take can be exploited. . . . If you must utilize a phone during travel consider using a "burn phone" that uses a SIM card purchased locally with cash. Sanitize sensitive conversations as necessary.[2]

When we read this, we wondered what the Americans knew about SORM that we didn't.

A year before, in August 2012, the Americans were the most numerous spectators at the London Olympics, with over sixty-six thousand Americans attending the games.[3] It was clear that Americans would come by the thousands to Russia in February 2014.

Although we worried about the use of surveillance and interception in Sochi, it had a legitimate purpose in fighting terrorism. The threat and the reality of terrorism cast a long shadow over Sochi, and then it happened.

On April 15, 2013, Boston hosted its annual marathon, and 23,000 runners took part. About two hours after the winner crossed the finish line but with more than 5,700 runners yet to finish, two bombs detonated on Boylston Street. Three people were killed and more than 250 injured. The same day, using surveillance cameras, police identified two brothers as suspects, Tamerlan and Dzhokhar Tsarnaev. After a manhunt, the older brother, Tamerlan, was killed, and Dzhokhar captured. It was soon discovered that over a decade before the attack, their parents, ethnic Chechens, had moved the family to the United States from Dagestan, a Russian internal republic in the North Caucasus.

The terrorist attack had a lasting impact on the way the terrorist threat to the Sochi Olympics was viewed in the United States and around the world. It was long assumed that the militants in the North Caucasus were not interested in attacking Western targets. Since the 1990s the Chechen movement shifted from a nationalist agenda to make Chechnya independent, to one embracing radical Islam. The Chechen's top commander, Dokku Umarov, proclaimed an Islamic state in the North Caucasus, the Caucasus Emirate, in October 2007, and since then militants spread across the republics of the North Caucasus, but primarily in Dagestan. They continued to attack Russians—developing a clear terrorist strategy, attacking civilians on the Russian mainland, including in Moscow, and killing law enforcement personnel in the North Caucasus. But foreigners were not in their crosshairs.

The Boston bombing raised questions about whether that had changed. To make things worse, in a few months thousands of Americans would fly close to the Islamists' stronghold; Sochi, one of the most beautiful places in South Russia, on the coast of the Black Sea, is geographically located at the foot of the Caucasus Mountains.

Soon it became known that the Russian FSB had sent messages in 2011 to the FBI and CIA about Tamerlan Tsarnaev.[4] Though these letters were not real warnings—rather, the FSB asked for information on Tsarnaev, fearing he could join the militants in Dagestan—this information inflamed public opinion in the United States, and there were calls for more cooperation between Russian and American security services. Putin and Obama spoke twice by phone in the wake of the marathon bombing.[5] A White House statement said Obama praised the "close cooperation" Washington received on counterterrorism from Moscow, stating, "Both sides underlined their interest in deepening the close cooperation of the Russian and US special services in the fight against international terrorism."[6] On May 11 British prime minister David Cameron said that the Russian and British security services would cooperate in the build-up to the Winter Olympics in Sochi after his talks with Putin, adding that Britain would be providing "limited" security support at the Olympic Games. "We both want the Sochi Games to be a safe and secure Games," he said.[7]

This was a bad time to be asking questions about surveillance at the Olympics. The bombings in Boston made many people more tolerant of surveillance because of tangible fears of terrorism.

Six months before the Olympics were to open, on August 19, 2013, Putin signed an executive order, No. 686, that effectively turned the Olympics venue into a fortress.[8] It banned the entry of all vehicles and cars apart from those specially registered to Sochi from January 7 to March 21, 2014. Putin's order also prohibited any protests in the area of the Games during this period. But some of the fortress wasn't visible.

All those who wanted to visit the Olympics were required to pass through advance screening by the security services. The Russian authorities introduced a new security measure, a spectator pass that all visitors of the Games would need to have. To get it, a visitor was required to post his or her passport data and photo on a special website and wait for the FSB to check their information. If there were no suspicions, an applicant could receive a spectator pass, which bore his or her photo and name. Only with the spectator pass in hand could a visitor buy tickets to the Olympic competitions. The procedure was clearly aimed at gathering data on tens of thousands of people from across the globe.

In August 2013 Irina decided to get a spectator pass, so she went on the official Olympic website. Because the procedure required taking a photo, Irina clicked the function to do this. Her computer then warned her that the site "is requesting access to your camera and microphone. If you click 'Allow,' you may be recorded." This seemed suspicious, so we asked Citizen Lab's researcher Byron Sonne to look at the site more closely. "This image, where the Flash entity on the site is asking for access to your camera and microphone, does indeed appear pretty intrusive and downright creepy," he responded. We wondered whether this procedure was intended to collect legitimate information or to send a message that everybody was being watched.

We analyzed dozens of open-source technical documents published on the government procurement agency website as well as public records of government oversight agencies and presentations of companies contracted by the government. We confirmed that SORM had been greatly strengthened in Sochi for the Olympics.

In November 2012 it was announced that there would be free WiFi access at all the competition venues "for the first time in Olympic history" as well as in the media centers and media hotels. But all users were required to login and provide their spectator pass details—the FSB wanted to make sure nobody went unrecognized.

Conventional security measures would be high at Sochi, with more than forty thousand police on duty and more than five thousand surveillance cameras installed across the city. To gather data from cameras, in 2009–2011 Sochi had a federal program called "Safe Sochi," and a centralized command and control center was built in the city. The cost of the program was more than 1.5 billion rubles (over $48 million), and 1.2 billion of that was provided by MegaFon, one of three national mobile operators. We also discovered that Sochi was to be the first Olympics that would use surveillance drones, with both the FSB and the Interior Ministry acquiring drones. The FSB also purchased sonar systems to detect submarines so as to prevent a sea-launched terror attack.

We wanted our investigation to come out before the Olympics, as we hoped that the international and national media attention to Sochi could help prompt the conversation about

out-of-control surveillance throughout Russia. But where could we publish the story? When dealing with sensitive stories, Russian media preferred not to be the initial source. In our investigation project "Russia's Surveillance State," most of our stories were first published in *Wired* and only then translated and picked up by Russian media.

The *Guardian* seemed to us the obvious choice. The British newspaper put a great deal of effort into covering surveillance issues. In these months the *Guardian* had been running Snowden's revelations almost on a weekly basis, and the *Guardian*'s Luke Harding had been our friend since his days as a Moscow correspondent.

We wrote to Luke in early September, describing what we had. "Sochi is a terrific story," he answered. He forwarded our e-mail to the *Guardian*'s foreign editor and put us in touch with their new Moscow correspondent, Shaun Walker, whom we met at a Moscow café to discuss the story and possible repercussions. It was a very sensitive story, and we didn't know how the Kremlin might react to such an account in a Western newspaper; the Games were Putin's personal project, guarded by the FSB. The decision was not easy for Shaun either; though he had been living for years in Moscow, it was his very first week as the *Guardian* Moscow's correspondent, and the FSB had expelled his predecessor, Luke Harding, from Russia two years before.

We spent three weeks editing and repackaging our investigation. Meanwhile Shaun worked on getting comments. But it was slow and painful. Finally Shaun said that the *Guardian* had decided to run the story on October 1. Then it was delayed. And then, a surprising development: on the morning of October 2 the authorities announced that there was to be a press conference about security measures at the Olympics, that day at 2:00 p.m. Shaun rushed to the RIA Novosti building, where the press conference was to take place. FSB official Alexey Lavrishchev was listed among the participants and stated, "No, the city of Sochi will not be like a concentration camp." He then recalled the London Olympics: "Video surveillance cameras were mounted everywhere, even, excuse me, in the toilets. None of this will happen in Sochi!" He stressed that security in Sochi will be "invisible and unnoticeable."[9] Shaun sent us a quick message, "Amazing press conference! He read off a sheet of paper for 15 minutes, then they had questions, but only Russian outlets." He added, "He scuttled off like a crab at the end."

The *Guardian* ran our investigation on Sunday, October 6, placing it on the front page and headlined, "Russia to Monitor 'All Communications' at Winter Olympics in Sochi." It added, "Exclusive: Investigation Uncovers FSB Surveillance System—Branded 'PRISM on Steroids'—to Listen to all Athletes and Visitors." The term "PRISM on Steroids" was coined by Ron Deibert, with PRISM referring to the especially intrusive NSA program designed to intercept communications without the knowledge of communications services providers, exposed by Snowden.

Three days after the *Guardian* piece was published, the major English-language Russian government propaganda outlet, the *Voice of Russia*, ran an interview with a pro-Kremlin expert about the story, full of personal attacks against us and Shaun Walker.[10] We had expected as much. But the next day the position was changed: the same *Voice of Russia* published a story that seemed to come clean about what we were reporting. We were stunned at the admissions, particularly the headline that admitted that the authorities were tapping the phones. "Don't Be Scared of Phone Tapping During Sochi-2014, It's for Your Own Safety—Experts."[11] We were further surprised when these experts talked openly about the equipment installed. They admitted that "technological equipment of special services provides for eavesdropping on telephone conversations, as well as for analyzing social network and e-mail correspondence" and said that "this kind of control is the best way to spot terrorist activity and nip the problem in the bud."[12]

We began to wonder: Why was this being acknowledged so openly? Were all these sophisticated technologies going to be actually used at Sochi, or was it something else? Was it just the threat of surveillance being used to intimidate and deter? What really puzzled us was that the story was not met with the usual denials and silence; instead, the authorities were talking about it.

Even as the acknowledgment of the surveillance plans surprised us, we did a double-take on November 8, 2013, when Prime Minister Dmitry Medvedev signed an instruction listing all the parties who would be subject to FSB surveillance, including the organizers of the Games, all the athletes from around the world, judges for the competitions, and the thousands of journalists who would converge on Sochi.[13] The decree provided for the creation of a database for the users of all types of communication, including Internet services at public WiFi locations "in a volume equal to the volume of information contained in the Olympic and Paralympic identity and accreditation cards"; that is, the database contained not only each subscriber's full name but also detailed information guaranteed to establish his or her identity. The database contained "data on payments for communications services rendered, including connections, traffic, and subscriber payment," meaning it contained all information on who called whom or sent messages during the Games as well as the location of each call. In the language of intelligence agencies this is called "gathering metadata," the same kind of data-harvesting that the US NSA carried out and Snowden exposed.

It was the openness of Medvedev's instruction that shocked us—it was posted on the government's website. What's more, it seemed to us that the authorities were trying, somehow, to signal that at the Olympics, watch your back, because we are watching you.

Medvedev's instruction required the government to store the data collected during the Games for three years and said the FSB must be provided "round-the-clock remote access to the subscriber database." That means the FSB, operating from a remote location, will have three years to explore by whom, when, and how often athletes, judges, and journalists attending the Games were contacted.

On November 13 three members of the European parliament tabled written questions that raised concerns about surveillance at the Sochi Olympics, referring in particular to our investigation. "Given that everybody seems to be spying on everyone else these days, it seems legitimate to ask questions not only about the EU and the United States but about Russia as well," said Sophie in 't Veld, a Dutch member of the European parliament and the author of the questions. "Russia is a particular problem because of the Olympics, which it is using as a pretext for stepping up surveillance, with no court oversight." She added, "I hope this will act as a wake-up call."[14]

On December 29, at 12:45 a.m., a suicide bomber walked in the hall of the railway station in Volgograd, about six hundred miles from the venue of the Olympics, and blew himself up. Eighteen people were killed. The next day around 8:30 a.m., a trolleybus that connects a suburb to Volgograd's downtown area was hit by a suicide bomber, killing sixteen people. Volgograd is a large city located in the South Federal District of Russia, the same district as Sochi. Militants from Dagestan organized the bombings, which raised fears that the Russian authorities would be unable to secure the Games and that the "ring of steel" Putin had declared was built around Sochi would not stop terrorists. The stakes were high, and Western leaders hastened to offer Putin more help in providing security. Privacy concerns were set aside.

On Sunday, January 19, the Islamic militants in Dagestan claimed responsibility for the bombings. They also delivered a direct threat to the Olympics. In a video posted online two men addressed Putin, "If you hold these Olympics, we will give you a present for the innocent Muslim blood being spilled all around the world: in Afghanistan, in Somalia, in Syria." One of them added, "For the tourists who come, there will be a present, too."[15]

A few days before the video was posted, Dokku Umarov, a leader of Islamist extremists on the North Caucasus, was reported to have been killed by Russian forces, but it didn't eliminate the threat. The Olympics presented a tempting target for militants. In the 2000s strong censorship in the Russian media had deprived the militants of attention, and the movement was in decline. But for the Olympics the eyes of all major global news organizations were to be focused on Sochi.

At the time journalists spotted wanted posters with the images of three women who were suspected suicide bombers, so-called black widows, at the airport and in the Sochi hotels. Police launched an urgent search for possible suicide bombers and distributed the posters further. For months the Russian media had been under pressure to report everything around the Olympics in positive way, and now they were hesitant to report the news that black widows were being sought inside the "ring of steel." Then a local blog, blogsochi.ru, posted information about these suicide bombers. When NBC reported the news, the Russian media picked up the story. The authorities felt clearly uncomfortable; they had failed to prevent the news from spreading.

Meanwhile, after the publication of our investigation in the *Guardian*, dozens of Western journalists came to us, asking anxious questions about their communications before traveling to Sochi. Some of them were on their way back from Sochi to Moscow and told us stories of odd happenings with their phones and laptops in Sochi. Wacek Radziwiniwicz from the Polish newspaper

Gazeta Wyborcza could not connect with the server in Warsaw, and his phone received wrong SMSs. "Our technicians told us not to use public Wi-Fi," said Nataliya Vasilyeva, Moscow correspondent for the Associated Press. "But sometimes we used it, and every time the system required to provide all details for identification. It was like enter and say, 'Hello, it's me.'"[16] Andrei opted not to bring his laptop to Sochi when he traveled to the city with an NBC crew in early January.

Boris Nemtsov, an opposition leader in Moscow and a former deputy prime minister, had written a report, published in 2013 and prepared with help from Nikolai Levshits, a civil activist, that documented some of the corruption surrounding contracts for the Olympics. He suggested that more than half of the $50 billion spent on the Games had disappeared. Just before the Games, in January 2014, Levshits applied for a spectator pass to the Olympics. He tried twice, but every time the website sent him the same message: "Your application is rejected." He also noticed that the website tried to take control of his laptop.[17]

On February 5, two days before the opening ceremonies, Dmitry Kozak, the deputy prime minister responsible for the Olympic preparations, made a tour with foreign journalists around Sochi. Kozak had a surprising response to some criticism expressed by journalists about the conditions in the hotel rooms: "We have surveillance video from the hotels that shows people turn on the shower, direct the nozzle at the wall, and then leave the room for the whole day," he said.[18] His statement was bizarre but also struck us as containing a fascinating warning: we are watching you, even in the shower.

The Games opened on February 7, and the grand opening ceremony at the Fisht Olympic Stadium lasted for three hours. Forty thousand spectators came to watch the event, and Putin personally greeted the athletes. The official theme of the ceremony was "Dreams of Russia," and the mood was festive.

That same day the website nosochi2014.com, which had been launched in 2007 to protest the Sochi Olympics and to serve as a reminder of ethnic cleansing carried out against Sochi's native people—the Circassians—by Czarist Russia, was hacked and infected by malware.[19] Citizen Lab experts looked at the site and discovered that the site included a malicious JavaScript hosted on the domain e094bcfdc2d.com, which at the time of investigation, was hosted at an address registered to the Russian State Institute of Information Technologies and Telecommunications in St. Petersburg.

On February 19, four days before the Games ended, the protest band Pussy Riot made a trip to Sochi to perform and planned to record a new video clip. They knew it could be difficult: after the group performed a punk prayer, "Mother of God, Chase Putin Away," in Moscow's Cathedral of Christ the Savior, they were considered an enemy of the state, and three of them were imprisoned. Anastasia Kirilenko, a journalist for *Radio Liberty*, was to accompany Pussy Riot in Sochi. They were well aware of surveillance and had talked details of the coming trip via ChatSecure, an encrypted smartphone messenger. One of the group's supporters gave them new cell phones that, in Sochi, they used exclusively. But it did not help Pussy Riot avoid surveillance. Video cameras spotted their car, and the police detained them a few times under false pretexts.[20]

Nevertheless, Pussy Riot managed to perform in Sochi twice. Five girls in colorful balaclavas started to shout out "Putin will teach you to love the Motherland" in front of the Sochi-2014 banner and were immediately attacked by a group of Cossacks, who beat them with whips, ripped their masks off, and threw the group's guitar away. Journalists recorded the group's performance and the Cossacks' intrusion. A bit later the group held another performance in central Sochi next to the Olympic rings in front of the city hall. Although police watched the event, they did not intervene. The video of the clip went viral.

The Russian secret services have had a long tradition of using spying techniques not merely to spy on people but to intimidate them. The KGB had a method of "overt surveillance" in which they followed a target without concealing themselves. It was used against dissidents. After all of the evidence we found of investments in cutting-edge surveillance technologies, the FSB primarily used them for intimidation; they wanted to showcase their surveillance and did not hide it, like the "overt surveillance" of the KGB. The authorities didn't deny our investigation—in fact, it was confirmed by the *Voice of Russia*, and Medvedev's decree, openly posted, also sent a strong signal. Even Kozak's comment, though extremely bizarre, seems to make the same point—in Sochi we are watching you everywhere.

But the intimidation didn't work. Committed bloggers, foreign journalists, Pussy Riot, and activists all managed to do their thing without much restraint. If the surveillance was built to prevent protests or bottle up information, then the surveillance state built in Sochi was a paper tiger. Still, publicly Sochi became a great personal success for Putin; he got support domestically and around the world. After all, nobody wanted to question the enormous $50 billion cost of the Games.[21] It was all justified by success: Russia was back. The games went off largely without a hitch—there was no terrorism and a great deal of national pride on display.

We don't know with any degree of detail how much interception or surveillance was carried out at Sochi using such things as SORM and other technology. But we think there is another possibility, equally disturbing: the Russian secret services gathered large amounts of personal data on all visitors to the Games, including diplomats, journalists, and all kinds of officials. And these efforts were planned and conducted under guidance of the top counterintelligence official in the country, and counterintelligence officers tend to play a long game. It cannot be ruled out that someday, long after the closing ceremony of the Olympic Games, any one of these people could be approached with the information collected in February 2014 in Sochi.

CHAPTER 13

The Big Red Button

On February 23, 2014, the day the Sochi Olympics ended, Putin was not entirely happy. One of his guests, a close ally, who was with him at the opening ceremony of the games had gone missing from Sochi. Viktor Yanukovych, the Ukrainian president, had disappeared from his capital, Kiev, a day before. After months of protests against Yanukovych on the Maidan, the central square of Kiev, no one knew where the president had gone. Television broadcasts showed that some government buildings in the capital had been abandoned; the headquarters of the Ukranian secret police was also empty, and police were nowhere to be seen. Protesters had pulled down a monument to Lenin. The demonstrations and the sudden dissolution of Yanukovych's presidency appeared to Putin to be far more serious than the public uprisings known as "color revolutions" over the previous decade in Ukraine and Georgia, and, beginning in 2010, the Arab Spring; this time it looked more like August of 1991, when the Soviet Union teetered on the abyss. For Putin, the events in Ukraine suggested that the elites of the country had split, and some of them had betrayed Yanukovych, a frightening prospect for the Russian president. Putin had invested his personal prestige in Yanukovych and sent his intelligence officers to Kiev under the guidance of a colonel general of the FSB to show his support. When Yanukovych fled, Putin saw it as proof of a conspiracy by the West to undermine Russia's sphere of influence, which, in his mind, included Ukraine.[1]

In a week the Russian military transported Yanukovych to Rostov-on-Don and unmarked Russian troops occupied Crimea, which had been part of Ukraine. On March 1 Putin obtained permission from the cheering Russian parliament to use troops in Ukraine as well.[2] They unleashed an unprecedented campaign of propaganda, calling the Ukrainian protesters "fascists" and warning that Russians living in eastern Ukraine were threatened.[3] This was the start of a major armed conflict that engulfed eastern Ukraine in the months ahead as Russian-backed separatists battled Ukrainian troops for control of several provinces. Thousands of people were killed and injured in the war, inciting sharp protests and Western sanctions imposed on Russia.

As soon as the crisis began, the Russian authorities tightened control of information online. Since 2012 the Kremlin had been actively building mechanisms and tools of control of the Internet, and now the moment came to test their effectiveness. On March 3 Roskomnadzor rushed to block thirteen pages of groups linked to the Ukrainian protest movement on the Russian-based social network VKontakte.[4]

On March 8 pro-Kremlin activists launched a new website that pointed a finger at "national traitors." It was established on the domain predatel.net, where *predatel* stands for a traitor, and domain extension .net for *nyet*, or no: *no traitors*. It sought to gather the public statements of liberals deemed unpatriotic and then threaten them. The first name on the list was Navalny, and it also included the opposition leader Boris Nemtsov, journalist Sergei Parkhomenko, artists and writers, and some civil activists and journalists who took part in Moscow protests in 2011–2012.

A week later a popular Russian news site, Lenta.ru, suddenly faced the traditional methods of intimidation by the authorities. On the morning of March 12 Roskomnadzor issued the website a warning for publishing material of an "extremist nature," citing an interview with one of the leaders of the far right Ukrainian party, Pravy Sector. The interview was conducted by Ilya Azar, the reporter who had exposed the carousel voting fraud during the Russian parliamentary elections in December 2012. On the same day as the warning the owner of Lenta.ru, Alexander Mamut, called the editor, Galina Timchenko, and demanded Azar be fired. Timchenko refused, so Mamut immediately fired Timchenko. All thirty-nine journalists of Lenta.ru left the publication in protest, along with Timchenko.[5]

On March 16 a hurried referendum in Crimea resulted in a call to join Russia. Two days later Putin summoned both houses of the Russian parliament to the Kremlin for what was to be one of his most memorable and emotional speeches celebrating the taking of Crimea, with its big Russian-speaking population, from Ukraine. To effusive applause Putin spoke emotionally about the destiny of Russia. And then, finally, he turned to the West, noting that Russia's actions had already drawn threats of sanctions that might cause disruption inside Russia. He paused and then asked ominously, "I would like to know what it is they have in mind exactly: action by the fifth column, this disparate bunch of 'national traitors,' or are they hoping to put us in a worsening social and economic situation so as to provoke public discontent?" He promised to "respond accordingly."[6]

Earlier, on March 13, Roskomnadzor had blocked three independent opposition news media—Kasparov.ru, Ej.ru, and Grani.ru—along with Navalny's blog on LiveJournal.com.[7] Maxim Ksenzov from Roskomnadzor was quick to explain that the sites were blocked because of "extremist calls." He added that Navalny was no longer allowed to use communications and post anything on the Internet: "Wherever the materials appear under his name—there will be blocking."[8]

The political commentary site Ej.ru represents *Ezhednevny Journal*, or Daily Journal, and was launched in 2005 in a desperate attempt to save a team of journalists thrown out of *Itogi* magazine during the annihilation of Gusinsky's media empire. With a simple design, it published three stories per day along with some short news items. Along with Grani.ru, it was a platform for prominent liberal commentators in the country, from satirist Viktor Shenderovich, to military experts and political analysts expelled from traditional media in the 2000s. The site enjoyed popularity among the liberal-minded intelligentsia.

Since February Ej.ru had come under fierce attack from Putin's supporters after it had published a column by Shenderovich in which he questioned the whole wave of intense patriotism ignited by the Sochi Olympics.[9] Despite the attacks, Ej.ru continued functioning, and on this day it had a story that dissected Russian propaganda and the televised euphoria surrounding the annexation of Crimea by Russia. That same day Navalny posted the results of phone polls conducted by his activists about Crimea and Ukraine, revealing that Russians' attitudes were dramatically contrary to the propaganda. Navalny said his surveys showed that 84.5 percent of those asked viewed Ukraine as a friendly country.

From this day onward all three sites and a blog were blocked on Russian soil.

The night of Putin's speech, worried journalists of the liberal and independent media arranged an urgent meeting. They chose to meet at the Sakharov Center, the venue of human rights organizations, named after the Soviet dissident Andrei Sakharov, on Thursday, March 21. The center occupies two buildings—a two-story mansion and a tiny exposition hall on the embankment of the Moscow River. It was given the premises in the early 1990s by the first Russian government, which felt in some debt to Soviet dissidents, and for years the center was used to host talks and debates on human rights issues.

That evening Sergei Lukashevsky, the thirty-nine-year-old director of the center who had brought his children to the demonstration on Bolotnaya Square in 2012, was waiting for the journalists and bloggers to gather on the second floor of the Sakharov Center, in a room filled with chairs set in a circle. All editors of the blocked websites came to the meeting, including Alexander Ryklin of Ej.ru; Vladimir Korsunsky, editor of Grani.ru, and Kirill Samodurov, editor of Kasparov.ru. Galina Timchenko, a former editor of Lenta .ru, was among the first to arrive. Anton Nossik walked in, followed by Grigory Okhotin from OVD-Info. Olga Romanova, from Russia Behind Bars, who had collected money via Yandex Money for the protests in 2011, also appeared. There was also Nikolai Lyaskin, one of Chief Navalny's lieutenants, and Lena Bereznitskaya-Bruni, the editor of Newsru.com who had helped us withstand FSB pressure in 2002. All in all, dozens of journalists and bloggers came along with some liberal lawyers.

The day they had all feared had finally arrived. Since November 2012 the filtering in Russia expanded to areas way beyond protecting children from harmful content. By March 2014 Russia had four official blacklists of banned websites and pages: the first one to deal with sites deemed extremist; the second to block sites containing child pornography, suicide, and drugs; the third to block sites with copyright problems; and the fourth, the most recent one, created in February 2014, lists the sites blocked—without a court order—because they call for demonstrations that had not been approved by the authorities. There is also an unofficial fifth blacklist aimed not at sites but at hosting companies based abroad that Roskomnadzor considers to be uncooperative and, thus, need to be blocked.

The fourth blacklist, which included Ej.ru, Kasparov.ru, Grani.ru, and the Navalny blog, exists thanks to the efforts of

Andrei Lugovoi, a former KGB officer best known for his involvement in the poisoning of another former Russian security agent, Alexander Litvinenko, who fled to London in 2000 and was assassinated in 2006. The British authorities accused Lugovoi of conducting the poisoning by radioactive polonium, allegations he vehemently denied. Instead, he accused the British intelligence of carrying out the poisoning and got a seat in the Russian parliament. He was made a member of the Security Committee, in charge of writing legislation for the Russian secret services, of the State Duma. Putin approved Lugovoi's blacklist in December 30, 2013, and it came into force on February 1, 2014.

The discussion at the Sakharov Center was emotional. Roskomnadzor's failure to provide any reason for the blocking outraged editors of the blocked sites. In the letters they all received they were simply told, with no explanation, that they would be blocked. Korsunsky remarked darkly, "Websites are blocked just because they are suppressed as enemy information sources. Putin said it openly: 'The enemies.' He's going to fight with this. But legally, there is still a possibility—as long as we breathe, we need to do something. As well as to keep working." But he urged, "We should be ready to work in a state of war."

The editors debated possible legal avenues of resistance and technical solutions that could bypass the blocking. The odds of winning in court seemed slim. Ryklin angrily said that everybody should finally understand that their sites are blocked forever, and even if the lawyers would be able to win in court, the next day the General Prosecutor's Office would find another article to use as pretext for blocking.[10]

Olga Pashkova from Ej.ru suggested launching a united platform for all blocked sites. Other journalists thought about posting extracts of the stories on Facebook. Nossik exclaimed, "Forget about Facebook—it would be blocked in a month. We are walking in the direction of North Korea!" Timchenko insisted that the blocked sites should turn to social media, "Launch your campaign in social networks and contact the administrators of large groups, for example in VKontakte. That's all. This is a very big resource."

The journalists thought of some joint action they might take, a campaign for the blocked websites, but it was clear this was not a good option. An editor of the Echo Moskvy website, which might have been counted upon to take up the campaign, was at the meeting but was conspicuously silent. Nossik was not discouraged, arguing that they all have an advantage: "We all work with bytes, right? And we can all interact with the same bytes." He said that they don't need to meet somewhere regularly to coordinate efforts; it's enough to meet on Facebook. And when Facebook would be shut down, somewhere else.

But they all urgently needed to find a way to bypass the blocking. There was a lot of talk about Tor, a circumvention tool in widespread use around the world and essentially a network of virtual tunnels: instead of taking a direct route from source to destination, data packets on the Tor network take a random pathway through several relays that cover a user's tracks so nobody at any single point can tell where the data came from or where it's going. In the case of the blocked sites, it meant that people who came to the blocked sites couldn't be seen as coming from Russia, thus evading Roskomnadzor's blocking. It's easy to use, and the only problem with Tor is that a user must install Tor software on the computer to use its network.

That posed a fundamental problem: How could they teach readers to use circumvention tools? The blocked sites already lost thousands of readers, and although a committed audience would find a way to get to the sites, the question remained: How would they reach the rest?

Nossik came up with the idea to promote Tor and other circumvention tools on his page on LiveJournal.com and called others to follow his example. Some suggested to remember the Soviet dissident practice of disseminating information on carbon-copied typescript known as *samizdat*. Some offered to print leaflets.

One of those at the meeting was Artem Kozlyuk, a thirty-five-year-old born in Cherepovets in central Russia to a military family. He studied at the Cherepovets military school, spent a few years in the army, and soon moved to Moscow, where he joined the Pirate Party in 2011. The idea of Internet censorship shocked him, and the day the blacklist came into force, on November 1, 2012, he launched a project against filtering. It was called *Roskomsvoboda*, or Freedom from Roskomnadzor, and was also known as Rublacklist.net. On the home page of the website there is a link to the major treasure of the project—the total of how many sites are blocked and a list of sites blocked by mistake.

Ksenzov and Zharov, the brains behind Roskomnadzor, had made the official blacklist secret, ostensibly to avoid promoting the blocked sites and pages. The list is available only to authorized ISPs so they can check the lists daily. Kozlyuk was certain that the primitive system of filtering inevitably led to the blocking of innocent sites that happen to be hosted on the same IP address, so he made his cause to find a way to check the blacklist against the real numbers of blocked sites. Some liberal ISPs shared the data from the blacklists, and Kozlyuk was able to check how many sites are blocked along with the sites targeted by Roskomnadzor. The difference in numbers was astonishing—whereas Roskomnadzor insisted that only a few thousand sites were blocked, Kozlyuk's figures showed tens of thousands of sites. Kozlyuk knew better than anyone in the room how the filtering was organized, and he was hopeful. He described how one day he wanted to go to a prohibited site, Grani.ru. When he did this, the page was blank—it was blocked. But his home ISP had defiantly put a message on the blank page, saying, "To bypass the censorship, click here." The link then took the user to a site with a list of circumvention tools. Kozlyuk's point was that many friendly ISPs might be enlisted to help bypass the censorship. Kozlyuk's idea drew support, but few in the room believed it would be able to solve the problem of blocking.

But soon a technical solution was found, one that was much more effective at evading the blacklists.

Ruslan Leviev, then twenty-seven years old, is a computer geek and a lawyer by training. Short and thin, with earrings in both of his earlobes and often with a radical haircut, he was born in the Russian Far East, where he worked for an NGO providing poor citizens with legal support in court. In 2009 Leviev moved to Moscow, and two years later he joined the protests in Moscow against fraud in the parliamentary elections and was detained along with hundreds of outraged Muscovites. He spent two days in prison, and when he left the detention center, he decided to volunteer to help Navalny build his online projects. The first was the online elections watchdog Navalny launched.

When the law on filtering was debated in 2012, Leviev attended the meetings at Roskomnadzor as Navalny's representative, and he got to know Ksenzov. Leviev tried to explain why the filtering was such a bad idea, and he invited Ksenzov to talk to the audience of Habrahabr, the biggest Russian web community of programmers, where Leviev published extracts of Navalny's blog on fighting corruption. On January 4, 2013, Ksenzov started answering the participants' questions and posted his answers for a few days. Leviev thought this was a very good sign—he even asked the audience to be polite with Ksenzov because he could not imagine an official from any other ministry department willing to talk to them.

When Navalny's blog on LiveJournal was blocked on March 18, 2014—the blog on which Leviev had worked so hard—Leviev came to realize that the cooperation with the authorities was pointless. Everything seemed to change so quickly; Ksenzov at once started to attack Leviev, calling him a foreign agent and the fifth column because Leviev had volunteered for Navalny.

Leviev felt desperate, but one day a friend gave him an idea of how to bypass the blocking. When someone visits an Internet

site, such as Lenta.ru, the domain name is linked to one or more
Internet protocol addresses, which are a set of numbers. Sometimes there can be a whole list of these addresses linked to one
domain. By changing the list of the Internet protocol addresses
assigned to the domain on the site of domain names registration
center, Leviev found that he could trick the blocking—even send
it off in another direction entirely. In an experiment he manipulated the numbers so that when Roskomnadzor tried to block Navalny, they instead blocked a pro-Kremlin site called Lifenews.ru.
Next he tried redirecting the censorship to block Roskomnadzor's
own internal list of sites that were currently blocked, paralyzing
Roskomnadzor.[11] "It was like the blacklist blocked itself," Leviev
recalled.

It was a bright victory for Leviev's team: the system of technical
filtering had gaps, and Leviev thought about how to exploit them,
not to harass Roskomnadzor but to keep Navalny's blog online.

They set up a domain, navalny.us, with lots of subdomains—
the technical mechanism of blocking does not block all subdomains. Leviev called for help: on the site of navalny.us he posted
instructions on how to make a subdomain, and urged people to
make them and send word to Navalny. Over sixty volunteers responded, many with several subdomains, and Leviev got a network of 150 to 200 possible subdomains, ready to go.

The system became known as the "Big Red Button of Navalny"—the user gets to navalny.us, sees a big red button, pushes
it, and it leads him or her to one of the subdomains. Navalny's
blog survives.

Next Leviev went to war against Roskomnadzor's censors. He
figured out how to identify who inside the agency was responsible
for the search-and-destroy missions against Navalny and others.[12]
In April Leviev published a large post with a scheme, logs, and detailed explanations of who was in charge inside of Roskomnadzor
for checking the blocked sites.[13] By exposing them, he made their
lives difficult, often trapping them into long, pointless dead ends.

When the censors came to work and started to check whether the Navalny blog was working, their screens were filled with images of cats and ponies—a wicked retaliation.

Leviev was pleasantly surprised one day when Roskomnadzor officials acknowledged to the newspaper *Vedomosti* that they saw a cat instead of Navalny's blog.[14] It was a triumph—a rare one—for the digital revolutionaries. Despite all of Roskomnadzor's efforts, Navalny's blog was alive and accessible, and no one needed special software like Tor to access the site.

Leviev was sitting in the offices of TV Dozhd in the Red October compound when he told Irina about his success in evading the censors. Leviev's small company, Newscaster, was broadcasting online from an antiwar street demonstration in Moscow for TV Dozhd. Newscaster provided the broadcast to TV Dozhd for free because Leviev thought its content was important. The TV Dozhd premises were almost deserted because the channel was on the move after having come under constant pressure. In the patriotic hysterics that were already evident in January 2014, TV Dozhd was accused of being unpatriotic for conducting a controversial online poll that asked viewers whether Leningrad, now St. Petersburg, should have been surrendered to the Nazis in 1941 in order to spare its citizens the mass agony of a brutal nine-hundred-day siege. The poll took place on Sunday, January 26, a day before the seventieth anniversary of the lifting of the siege. Pro-Kremlin bloggers immediately attacked the channel, and in thirty minutes Ilya Klishin, now editor of the channel's site, removed the poll and apologized for the wording. On Monday Putin was in St. Petersburg to take part in official celebrations.[15] He was on his way to the Piskarev cemetery where his brother, who had died during the blockade, is buried, when he was shown the TV Dozhd poll.[16]

On January 27 Sindeeva, the founder of TV Dozhd, was sitting in her glass office at Red October. She started getting calls and e-mails from viewers that the channel was going off the air in different regions. A cable operator, who said it was his patriotic duty to throw TV Dozhd off his package, began the attack, and soon others followed.[17] By then TV Dozhd was present in 18 million homes and enjoyed a monthly audience of 12 million viewers. Every day an estimated 1.1 million people watched it. The audience in regions was on the rise, and Sindeeva's contacts told her that the presidential administration was worried about the growth in viewers; TV Dozhd had ceased being just a Moscow hipster's thing. Some operators called Sindeeva and explained that they got phone calls from the Kremlin and could not resist the pressure.[18] "It was a snowball," Sindeeva said. When, on January 29, Putin's spokesperson Dmitry Peskov said, "TV Dozhd crossed the line of the permissible," all other cable operators followed suit and switched off TV Dozhd.[19] The channel lost millions of viewers—its lifeline.

Sindeeva desperately tried to find a way to get the channel back on cable. The channel held a press conference, and Sindeeva talked about the pressure. She asked for a personal meeting with Putin and was initially told that Putin agreed. However, Volodin intervened, and the meeting never happened. Journalists of the channel went to Putin's press conferences and asked questions about the fate of TV Dozhd, and on April 17 Putin said something encouraging but it led nowhere.[20] In June a TV Dozhd reporter tried again, but the result was the same. Putin simply shrugged, "I don't know who gave the command to switch you off from the cable, I didn't give such a command."[21] It looked like a déjà vu—his words echoed his meeting with NTV journalists in January 2001.

From this time forward TV Dozhd was available only on the Internet. It lost many advertisers, and Sindeeva was forced to introduce a paid model for TV Dozhd content.

In March TV Dozhd got a letter from its headquarters' landlord: in a few months they were to be expelled from its premises on Red October, the symbol of the modernized hipsters of Medvedev's time. For some months journalists of TV Dozhd had to broadcast from their apartments. But they broadcast nevertheless.[22]

On August 2, 2014, Ksenzov's agency, Roskomnadzor, reached a new level, attempting to censor the Internet beyond the Russian borders. The agency sent a request to fourteen websites to block information about an unapproved march in Novosibirsk to support greater autonomy for Siberia from the Moscow central authorities. The march was organized by Artem Loskutov, a twenty-eight-year-old performance artist in Novosibirsk who played out political themes in his art. He wanted to protest Russia's interference in Ukraine by mimicking the Kremlin's rhetoric about "federalization" of Ukraine to justify the separatists' war there.[23] The news of Loskutov's planned demonstration went viral, and the Russian BBC interviewed Loskutov. At once the service received a request from Roskomnadzor to remove the interview from its site. Ksenzov confirmed that the request was valid but declined to explain. In response, the BBC made the request public and refused to remove the interview.[24] Roskomnadzor threatened to block the site bbcrussian.com on Russian soil, but never followed through.

Most of the fourteen sites complied with Roskomnadzor's request. Among them were Ukrainian websites. One of them was the site TSN.ua, whose editors said they were acting "to maintain accessibility of the entire site for the Russian audience."[25] Other sites, like obozrevatel.com, glavcom.ua, and delo.ua, refused to comply, so Roskomnadzor blocked them on Russian soil.

On August 6 the German Internet hosting provider Hetzner Online AG received an e-mail from Roskomnadzor requesting they suspend hosting of the popular Ukrainian news media site glavkom.ua. Hetzner agreed and sent a warning letter to the editors of glavkom.ua. Immediately the letter was posted on-line, triggering protests—people were outraged that a request from Russia to a firm in Germany could take down a website in Ukraine. Hetzner was forced to apologize.

In December 2014, however, Roskomnadzor sent a warning to the American news site BuzzFeed for posting a video the Russian authorities deemed extremist. The video was removed not by BuzzFeed but by Google, which owns YouTube.[26]

This was an important victory for Roskomnadzor, marking the first time the agency openly and shamelessly blocked foreign websites for expressing political views regarding Russia.

But in late December 2014 Roskomnadzor made another move, this time against Facebook. On December 19 activists opened an event group on Facebook in support of Alexey Navalny. Navalny, along with his younger brother, was facing trumped-up accusations of fraud. The case was used to keep Navalny under pressure as well as a pretext to keep him under house arrest for months. Prosecutors had asked the court to sentence Navalny to ten years in jail, and the verdict was expected in few days. The event on Facebook was actually an invitation to gather in the center of Moscow to protest against the verdict, as there was no doubt he would be found guilty. The prosecutor's office immediately issued a request to Roskomnadzor to block the event, and Roskomnadzor forwarded the document to Facebook's office in London.[27] Facebook complied, blocking the group on December 20.[28]

The outraged activists launched several new groups, and Leviev, in few hours, added a new "big red button" on the site navalny.us that linked to the current, unblocked event group on Facebook. Facebook's decision to comply with the Russian censor triggered a great deal of outrage in Moscow and abroad.[29] Following the outcry, Facebook and Twitter decided not to block the event groups launched by Navalny's supporters.[30]

The online protest forced the authorities to change their plans: instead of January 15, the Navalny brothers' verdict was announced on December 30. Alexey Navalny was given three and a half years of suspended sentence, and his younger brother, Oleg Navalny, was sent to prison for three and a half years.[31] If the authorities had hoped to discourage protesters by shifting the verdict to December 30, the day before New Year's Eve, they miscalculated. That cold night thousands of Muscovites assembled on Tverskaya Street, two hundred meters from the Kremlin, to protest Navalny's verdict. Navalny, who was still under house arrest, made it to Tverskaya but was detained shortly after he appeared along with some of his close supporters.

Almost twenty-five years prior, Relcom and Demos programmers didn't wait for someone to tell them what to do during the putsch. Likewise, in December 2014 activists didn't wait for a leader's decision—in this case, Navalny—to start launching groups to support him on Facebook. It was a horizontal structure, a network, that made all of that possible. It repeated itself time and again.

Although Navalny stood as a symbol of Moscow's protests in December 2011, he was under lock and key most of December. It was activists and journalists who took over organizing protest rallies. Three years later, in December 2014, Navalny was again under lock and key, placed under house arrest, and he couldn't take part in organizing efforts. But again it didn't matter. The group on Facebook was launched first by a Navalny friend, Leonid Volkov, and when this first group was blocked, a dozen new groups were launched, this time by people with no ties to Navalny who were simply outraged by censorship.

The authorities who sought to block, filter, and censor simply did not know what to do with the forces behind the "big red button."

CHAPTER 14

Moscow's Long Shadow

On November 21, 2013, Mustafa Nayyem, a thirty-two-year-old liberal television journalist, had been deeply disappointed by Ukrainian president Viktor Yanukovych's decision to postpone the integration of Ukraine into the European Union. Yanukovych hesitated to sign an agreement with the EU because of pressure from Vladimir Putin, who wanted to hold Ukraine close to Russia and opposed any pact with Europe.

Nayyem posted an angry message on Facebook. "Well, let's get serious," he wrote. "Who today is ready to come to Maidan before midnight? 'Likes' don't count. Only comments under this post with the words, 'I am ready.' As soon as we get more than a thousand, we will organize ourselves."

This Facebook post started the Ukrainian revolution. Thousands went to Independence Square, popularly known as Maidan, and stayed there. In the months that followed, the Maidan was turned into an improvised fortress, surrounded by barricades, fires, and smoking tires and guarded day and night by protesters. The protesters wanted closer ties with Europe—a sentiment that was shared by part of Ukraine's population, largely in the western portion of the country, whereas the east felt aligned to Russia, not in the least because most spoke Russian as their first language. The protests in Kiev were a seminal crisis for Putin, who felt a move by Ukraine toward Europe would be intolerable—it would bring the West to Russia's borders.

On November 30 the Ukrainian riot police, the Berkut, launched an offensive against the protesters on the Maidan, and dozens were severely beaten. The protesters were forcibly dispersed. Some of them took refuge in St. Michael's Cathedral, an elegant gold-domed monastery not far from the square. The police then besieged the monastery.

Sasha Romantsova worked at a bank in Kiev, but she harbored the soul of a popular organizer. At twenty-seven, she had already successfully created a large student movement at her university and was deeply interested in events at the Maidan. She had joined one of the first marches in favor of Ukraine's integration with Europe.

When the protests were dispersed into the monastery, Romantsova received a desperate text message from a friend hiding inside, who said the Berkut were battering down the monastery's doors. Romantsova was frightened for her friend and angry at the use of force against the protesters. She called the Center of Civil Liberties of Kiev and volunteered to do something—anything— to help to defend the protesters. The center, based in a residential apartment in the center of Kiev, was at that moment thinking the same thing; a workshop was under way on human rights. They decided to form a volunteer service to help locate the detained and wounded from the Berkut crackdown and to open a telephone hotline to gather information from those in trouble.

But one of the most important decisions made that day was to open a group on Facebook, called Euromaidan SOS, which immediately gathered over ten thousand followers. When Romantsova called the center to volunteer, she was told, "We opened a phone hotline, and we need a volunteer to sit here from 4:00 a.m. to 8:00 a.m." Romantsova enthusiastically accepted. She had to be at work at 9:00 a.m. but was more than willing to work the hotline for four hours first. She stayed there for months during the Maidan uprising, shuttling between the office and the hospital where the wounded were treated. When a few radio stations and a major television channel advertised the phone numbers for the hotline—actually three cell phones—the project expanded rapidly. It began with the intention of locating casualties, but it soon became an information service, fielding calls from all over the city. People called in to report eyewitness spottings of the Berkut, which were then posted on the Euromaidan SOS page, asking those who lived nearby to verify them and report back.[1]

To an extent this must have made Putin pale—the digital pathways were enabling the protest against authority. The Euromaidan SOS experiment on Facebook took advantage of the horizontal structure of a network, allowing people to share information readily and disseminating it where it was needed without the need for an established organization behind it. What happened in Kiev was reminiscent of Relcom's request in August 1991 for users to look out their windows and report back troop movements, but this time it was not e-mails but Facebook that provided the platform. The authorities knew where the Euromaidan SOS was based, but the speed of the network took them by surprise. The Euromaidan SOS group on Facebook thrived and grew with the protests. Soon Euromaidan SOS had created comprehensive lists of the wounded or those missing or detained by the Berkut, and the lists were frequently checked and updated. Along with Romantsova, 250 volunteers worked on Euromaidan SOS, searching for the missing and keeping a direct telephone line open to the Maidan protest organizers on the square. Regular announcements were made by megaphone at the square regarding those who were missing or detained.

Yet there was a dark side to this political conflict: the digital pathways that enabled protest could also be used against the protesters. The night of January 21, 2014, was frosty and only about 10 degrees at the Maidan. Most of the protesters were sleeping in tents. Suddenly, *all* their cell phones vibrated with a new text message. The number was disguised as a service message, and it read, "Dear subscriber, you are registered as a participant in a mass disturbance."

The identical message went to users of each of the three mobile operators in the city—Kyivstar, MTS, and Life. But it went only to people who were on Independence Square. The phrasing of the message echoed language in a new Ukraine law that made it illegal to take part in a protest deemed violent. The law had taken effect that very morning.

The sense of the message was clear: the protesters had been identified. The text message was a means of intimidation.

Romantsova also received the text. She wasn't taken aback by it, but she and the protesters saw it as a new trick by the authorities against the protesters. Many of the Maidan protesters quickly took a screen shot of the message and posted it online—the network answered back, defiantly.

In fact, the texts appeared to have little effect. The text messages outraged many Ukrainians and were widely reported.[2] All three Ukrainian mobile operators immediately denied they had sent the text messages. So the question emerged: If the message was not sent by the mobile operators, how it was done?

Kyivstar suggested that it was the work of a "pirate" cell phone tower set up in the area. This could have referred to something called an IMSI-catcher, a device that can emit a signal over an area of nearly four square miles, forcing hundreds of cell phones per minute to release their unique IMSI and IMEI identification codes, which can then be used to track a person's movements in real time. Every phone has such identification codes, although most people are not aware of it. This technology also can be used to intercept text messages and phone calls by duping cell phones within range into operating with a false cellular tower. A transceiver around the size of a suitcase can be placed in a vehicle or at another static location and then operated remotely by security agents wirelessly.

However, the telephone carriers could offer no evidence that a pirate tower was used, but there is another possibility: SORM—the black boxes, which can monitor both Internet and cellular communications—could identify the protesters and send the message. If security services had SORM, they could use it as a back door into the Ukrainian mobile networks, giving them the ability to carry out such an operation without being detected.

A fascinating clue then emerged. A Kiev city court had ordered Kyivstar to disclose to the police which cell phones in their network were turned on outside the courthouse during a protest that occurred on January 10.[3] The warrant, No. 759, which we obtained, was issued by a Kiev district court on January 13. Its goal was to identify people in the particular area of the protest. Further, the police specifically requested that a representative of Kyivstar be excluded from the proceedings to keep the operation secret. The judge agreed with the police request.

This warrant made clear that the Security Service of Ukraine (SBU) and other law enforcement agencies had the capability to eavesdrop on communications networks without the telecom operator's knowledge. Thus, the security services could have used their surveillance systems against protesters. On February 3 the communications regulatory agency of Ukraine reported that it could not determine who had sent the text messages to protesters in January. Secrecy prevailed.

After March 1, the day Russia annexed Crimea, many Western experts told us at different cyber security gatherings that they expected a massive denial-of-service attack to be launched against Ukrainian websites. The fears were well founded: every Russian conflict with a neighboring country in the 2000s—including Georgia and Estonia—had been accompanied by such relatively crude onslaughts against the countries' online resources.[4] For a while the Ukraine conflict developed along the same lines. On March 3 the Ukrainian information agency UNIAN reported a powerful denial-of-service attack, causing the agency's website to be temporarily taken offline.[5] The Internet infrastructure of the country seemed weak, almost begging cyber hackers to try their hand. Ukrainians clearly understood this vulnerability. That same day Konstantin Korsun, an SBU cyber-security officer in 1996–2006 and now in the cyber security business, working as the head of the NGO Ukrainian Information Security Group and supporting Maidan, appealed for help. "Because of the military intervention of Russia against Ukraine I ask everybody who has the technical ability to counter the enemy in the information war, to contact me and be prepared for a fight," he wrote on LinkedIn. "Will talk to the security forces to work together against the external enemy."

Almost immediately he received a reply from Maxim Litvinov, head of the cyber crime department in the Interior Ministry of Ukraine: "You can count on me." Litvinov said he had analysts, a laboratory, and loyal personnel, and he didn't want to wait until the country was already under attack.[6]

But the large and much-feared cyber attack on Ukraine did not come as it had been anticipated; instead it came from another direction, a tidal wave of propaganda spread on social networks.[7] The Kremlin launched a massive campaign to infiltrate social networks—first of all, VKontakte—and exploit the digital pathways for its own purposes. Russia possessed certain natural advantages on this information battleground. First, both Russia and Ukraine shared a common cultural and historical legacy in the Soviet Union, such as the experience of World War II and the shared Russian language, used widely in Ukraine. Second, the Russian-based social network VKontakte is the most popular social network in Ukraine, with more than 20 million users. Russian officials knew how to frame the messages they wanted to send and had all but taken control of VKontakte. They then decided to take their information combat to the enemy, fighting on Twitter, YouTube, and anywhere the digital revolutionaries had previously raised a victory flag.

From the Kremlin an army was unleashed, a fighting force whose weapons were words. Legions of trolls, people who disrupt online discussions by deliberately posting inflammatory, extraneous, or off-topic messages, were deployed to provoke and intimidate people. The trolls are not usually volunteers but paid propagandists. In the 2000s they were used inside Russia against liberal and independent media and bloggers. Now this army, hundreds of people, was directed outside.

The trolls often appear in the comments section of traditional news media and social media. Katarina Aistova, a former hotel receptionist, then twenty-one years old, was one of them. In April 2014 she spotted something negative written about Putin on WorldNetDaily. "You are against Putin!" she exclaimed in response to another user. "Do you actually know what he does for his country and for people?? The fact is that Obama is losing ground as a leader." A lot of the commentary was much more strident.

The *Guardian* was among the first in the Western media to find itself in the Russian trolls' crosshairs. On May 4 the newspaper reported that a particularly nasty strain emerged in the midst of the conflict in Ukraine, "which infests comment threads on the *Guardian* and elsewhere, despite the best efforts of moderators." Readers and reporters became concerned that these comments came from "those paid to troll, and to denigrate in abusive terms anyone criticising Russia or President Vladimir Putin." The first complaint to the moderators of the *Guardian* was reported on March 6, when a reader complained, "In the past weeks [I] have become incredibly frustrated and disillusioned by your inability to effectively police the waves of Nashibot trolls who've been relentlessly posting pro-Putin propaganda in the comments on Ukraine v Russia coverage." The *Guardian* replied that there was no conclusive evidence about who was behind the trolling, although *Guardian* moderators, who deal with forty thousand comments a day, believed there was an orchestrated campaign.[8]

In 2014 French and then Italian journalists told the authors that they were attacked by trolls when they published critical stories on Russia. In both countries the onslaughts were carried out in fluent and faultless French and Italian, and the trolls attacking the critical reporting from Russia were the same ones who separately were known to write xenophobic and anti-immigrant posts, which led French journalists to suspect that the comments could be coming from a community of far-right-wing activists.

In May, Ilya Klishin, the editor of the TV Dozhd website, shed some light on the trolls focused on the Western media. On May 21 Klishin exposed in *Vedomosti* the organization of trolls that had been directed to target the American audience.[9] He reported that the team serving under Vyacheslav Volodin, the deputy chief of the presidential administration in Moscow, who had replaced Surkov at the peak of the 2012 protests, had proposed a "systematic manipulation of public opinion through social media."

Sources close to the presidential administration told Klishin that preliminary work began in the fall of 2013 and that Volodin personally approved the strategy. Volodin also moved Konstantin Kostin—the Kremlin official who once had been on the other end of a phone line, pressuring the Yandex News team to shape their news report to fit Kremlin wishes—into a key position at the Civil Society Development Foundation, a pro-Kremlin organization, although Kostin remained directly subordinate to Volodin.[10] In the summer of 2013 he announced the launch of a new, large system for social network monitoring called "Mediaimpuls."

It was an ambitious attempt to monitor and manipulate social networks. Kostin boasted that they joined efforts with the Boston-based firm Crimson Hexagon, using a system designed to figure out consumer trends on social networks. According to Kostin, Mediaimpuls could monitor LiveJournal and Twitter along with Russian social networks. But it was cursed with the same trouble the Russian secret services had been lamenting since 2011: it could not deal with Facebook because Facebook does not give up the data.[11]

In the fall of 2013 the newspaper *Novaya Gazeta* exposed a "farm" of trolls writing away in a suburb of St. Petersburg known as Olgino. There the employees were paid over 25,000 rubles a month, then equivalent to about $900, to post comments on blogs and news articles. The troll farm occupied two rooms in a posh home with large glass walls. According to the report, employees in one room wrote blog posts for social networks, while those in the other room worked on comments. The troll farm had close ties with pro-Kremlin youth movements. Among those working in the glass-walled house was Katarina Aistova, the young woman mentioned above.

Anonymous International publicized the internal reports of this group in May 2014, with documents consisting of dozens of analytical briefs detailing the way the comments were dealt with on US media sites. There were also recommendations, such as this one for the site Politico: "In the future, there should be more provocative comments to start the discussion with the audience."

The documents show that the masterminds of the troll movement were curious about legitimate online movements—the documents included, for example, a detailed analysis of Barack Obama support communities on Facebook and Twitter. They were also aware of the perils of being deleted by moderators; one brief cautions about "Censorship on the American Internet." But the most interesting document was one that all but acknowledged that users in the United States could easily spot the troll campaigns supporting Russia, rendering the postings useless. "In the study of major US media, some pro-Russian comments were seen. After a detailed study, it became clear that such comments are extremely negatively perceived by the audience. In addition, users suggest that these comments were written either for ideological reasons or were paid."

Although the campaign may not have worked well in the United States and Britain, Ukraine was different. False reports from the east of Ukraine and fake photographs of purported atrocities and victims flooded VKontakte and Facebook. Photographs of casualties from the war in Syria were doctored and presented as coming from the Ukraine provinces of Luhansk or Donetsk. The trolls claimed the violence was caused by Ukrainian "fascists" and sometimes borrowed images from war movies to make their point. There was a heart-wrenching photograph of a grieving young girl, sitting by the body of a dead woman sprawled on the ground and carrying the caption, "This is democracy, baby, Ukrainian army is killing Donbass people." It went viral on social networks under the hashtag #SaveDonbassPeople. In fact, however, the photo was borrowed from a famous Russian film, *Brest Fortress*, released in 2010, about the Nazi invasion of the Soviet Union in 1941.

Although this and many other postings in the troll campaigns were filled with deceptions, they also struck a nerve, appealing to the historical memory of the Soviet Union—a country that lost over 30 million people in World War II—and carrying a highly emotional message to the Internet audience: fascists were coming again, this time with backing from the West, and there could be no questions asked, no place for skepticism, doubt, or opposition in this fight to the death.

By the end of 2014 the army of trolls enjoyed a major boost. The trolls at Olgino left the glass-walled house and moved to a four-story building in the same suburb of St. Petersburg in order to accommodate their growing numbers, now 250 people.[12] They worked in twelve-hour shifts and were required to post 135 comments a day.[13] New initiatives were launched, such as a quasi-news agency, like ANNA News, which was registered in Abkhazia, a breakaway region of Georgia. The agency set up accounts on a Russian replica of YouTube, known as Rutube; on YouTube itself; and on VKontakte, Facebook, Twitter, Google+, and Odnoklassniki. They posted videos that were presented as news but were largely propagandistic, including videos celebrating fighting by separatists in Ukraine. Another faux news agency, Novorossia television, set up accounts in social networks, posted videos on a daily basis, and collected money for separatists. The videos were then picked up by conventional pro-Kremlin TV channels and disseminated domestically and internationally. The efforts of these fake news agencies were combined with those of dozens of online communities positioned as blogs of patriotic citizens.

Some of the individual trolls enjoyed large, committed audiences. One of them writes under the name Lev Mishkin, taking his name from a character in Fyodor Dostoyevsky's famous novel *The Idiot*. The character in the novel is a symbol of Russian humility and kindness, but the troll Lev Mishkin is different. No one knows his true identity, but he is very active online as a Russian propagandist. On Facebook he lists among his friends some prominent pro-Kremlin spin doctors and often mocks Ukraine's political leaders. His message is bitterly anti-American and anti-Western, and he frequently publishes doctored photographs to make his point. As of this writing, he had almost five thousand followers on Facebook and over twenty-six hundred on Twitter, and more than a million people have watched his videos on YouTube. For all his activity, however, Mishkin's biggest coup appeared to be something that almost escaped notice.

On February 4 the audio recording of an intercepted phone conversation between Victoria Nuland, the US assistant secretary of state for Europe, and Geoffrey Pyatt, the US ambassador to Ukraine, was posted on YouTube and the next day reposted by Mishkin, opening a new front on the digital battlefield.

The recording was explosive, a conversation between two US diplomats, discussing how to resolve the ongoing standoff between the Ukrainian government and protesters. In the private conversation, recorded in January 2014, Nuland cursed the European Union, expressing frustration at the EU's handling of the Kiev crisis. According to our sources, Pyatt in Kiev used an ordinary cell phone for this conversation, not an encrypted one. Although the recording was embarrassing to the United States, as Nuland declared "Fuck the EU," another aspect of it proved incendiary. Nuland expressed a preference for who should enter the new Ukrainian government—proof positive, in the Kremlin's view, that the United States was calling the shots in Ukraine. It isn't known precisely who obtained the conversation, but it was someone who wanted to embarrass the United States and had the means to intercept and record a telephone call.

The audio was initially uploaded on the YouTube channel "Re Post," which had been mostly uploading anti-Maidan videos and smearing Ukrainian politicians. In some videos the voice of the cameraman is heard, he speaks in Russian and pretends to be a journalist, but he is very focused on documenting protesters' faces, weapons (self-made batons and the like), and actions. Most of the videos got only a few hundred views on YouTube.

Quite suddenly, on February 4, the channel's moderators uploaded the conversation, along with another conversation between European officials.[14] Two days passed, and no one noticed. Finally, on February 6, Christopher Miller, then the editor of English-language Ukrainian daily *Kyiv Post*, received an e-mail with a link to the Nuland video. The person who sent it to him, an acquaintance in the security service, asked, "Did you see this?"

Miller was thrown at first. The video had been viewed only three times before Miller watched it, and he wondered whether it was authentic. But the more he listened to it, the more he came to realize it was genuine. He called the embassy to get a comment and asked if it was real. They had no idea what he was talking about and were shocked.[15] Miller at once published the story, on February 6, quoting the intercept on the website of the *Kyiv Post*.[16]

But a strange thing happened on the way to a public uproar over the Nuland comments: Miller was not the only recipient. In fact, before he published his article, the hot intercept had fallen into the hands of the mysterious troll Lev Mishkin, who posted it on his YouTube channel a day before Miller, on February 5. And when Mishkin uploaded it, the video went viral.

The story of the recording—a murky one of phone calls recorded and mysterious uploads—highlights a larger picture depicting the security services, both in Russia and Ukraine, attempting to influence the political course of events with underhanded means. The eavesdropping on Nuland and Pyatt was probably made possible by SORM technology in Ukraine identical to Russia's. The recording was then passed from one hand to another until it became public, in the process removing any fingerprints of who originally made the interception and recording. That's the way combat in the shadows of the digital world is done.

The call created a sensation, but the Ukrainian security service, the SBU, denied any involvement. In two days the SBU held a press conference in Kiev. When asked about the Nuland recording, Maxim Lenko, a senior investigations official in the SBU, who was present at the conference, stepped forward and said, "The Ukrainian Security Service is not conducting any investigation into the matter at this time."[17]

The video was extensively used by Russian propaganda outlets to portray Maidan as an American conspiracy. The circumstances of the intercept and its circuitous route to the media suggest that it was the SBU, not the Russian secret services, that conducted the interception. It is impossible to know for sure, but we think some SBU officers likely intercepted the Nuland call and then shopped around until they found a colleague or friend who would post it on YouTube. When the scheme didn't ignite a media storm, they kept shopping for an alternative outlet and eventually found one.

Time and again intercepted conversations in Ukraine were used to compromise political opponents, and surveillance on telecommunications was used as a means of intimidation. This strategy provoked a great deal of speculation about conspiracies; for months a Ukrainian mobile operator was accused of sending Ukrainian citizens' personal data to Russia and maintaining their servers in Moscow. No proof was ever found.

The truth, however, might be much simpler, tracing back to SORM, the black boxes first deployed in Russia years earlier to monitor telecommunications and Internet traffic. Ukraine's security services possess their own SORM; except for a period after the Orange Revolution in 2005–2010, they always kept close ties with the Russian security services. The two countries' security officers carried out joint operations and exchanged information, and that special relationship ended, rather spectacularly, only in February of 2014 when the SBU exposed the names of FSB generals who were present in Kiev on the day Yanukovych fled his capital.

Ukraine's version of SORM was even more intrusive than Russia's. "The Ukrainian SORM is tougher—they have the right to interrupt the conversation and we have no such powers," said Victor Shlyapobersky, a chief of the SORM-testing laboratory at the St. Petersburg branch of the Central Research Institute of Communications, one of three main Russian research centers working on SORM development. To be stuck in the Soviet legacy means to be dependent on Russian supplies of surveillance. When Ukraine updated its national needs for SORM equipment in 2010, the Russian company IskraUraltel, a manufacturer of SORM equipment, was happy to announce that it had successfully tested its SORM devices under the new requirements, and it had been approved by the SBU.[18]

Although Ukraine hewed to Russia's eavesdropping system with equipment supplied by Russia, this does not necessarily mean that Russian secret services conducted all sensitive interceptions, but this option cannot be ruled out. But it does suggest that the Ukrainian security services modeled their surveillance capabilities after the most opaque and nontransparent example, with origins tracing back to the KGB.

Ukraine possessed not only the same equipment as Russia but also used the same terminology. In two decades of independence Ukraine didn't modify the basic terms used to label its surveillance departments. In the Soviet KGB the unit in charge of surveillance was called the OTU (*Operativno-Technicheskoye Upravlenie*, or the Operative-Technical Department), and eavesdropping and surveillance operations were identified in official documentation as ORM. That Soviet-style euphemism means *Operativno-Rozisknie meropriatiya*, or Operative-Search Measures.

In the 1990s the Russian FSB changed the name of the department to the UOTM (adding the word Measures to its title), but for years Ukraine remained attached to the Soviet acronym OTU. Now this department is called the DOTM (the Department of Operative-Technical Measures), echoing the Russian experience.

In late February in Kiev the chief of DOTM was fired along with Maxim Lenko, who had denied SBU's role in intercepting the US diplomats' conversation just three weeks before.[19] In July the chief of DOTM was changed again.[20] This musical chairs of the DOTM indicated that the new Ukrainian authorities didn't accept that the SBU had had nothing to do with the eavesdropping.

The saga of the Nuland interception and the larger battle for the digital space in Ukraine also reflects the reality throughout the former Soviet Union. Some of the nations that became independent in 1991 simply preserved the methods they inherited from the old regime. "Ukraine, Kazakhstan, Belarus, and Uzbekistan, they all use a system that is much closer to SORM than to the European or American systems," Shlyapobersky told us. In our own investigations we found documents confirming that Belarus, Ukraine, Uzbekistan, Kazakhstan, and Kyrgyzstan all have their national SORM systems. And in most cases this means their legislation and equipment has also been copied and imported from Russia.[21]

In September 2014, seven months after Maidan, Kiev was back to near normal. Independence Square was cleared; there was no sign of the barricades or burning tires that had once clogged the streets. It was time for the parliamentary elections, and Mustafa Nayyem, who had done so much to launch the Maidan movement with his post on Facebook, was one of the candidates. Andrei had difficulty catching up with his busy schedule, so Nayyem suggested they meet at the city court.

Nayyem had found out that a Ukrainian oligarch was trying to run for parliament despite the fact he had spent most of the 2000s out of the country, and this was against Ukrainian law. So Mustafa went to the court, and on the day we met, the hearings were under way.

The shabby Soviet-style building on Moskovskya Street, where the city court occupies a few floors, posed a striking contrast to the Moscow city court, which is all marble, statues, and expensive furniture. In a tiny room packed with journalists, a bald-headed Mustafa, wearing all black, with his two lawyers, faced three judges.

Mustafa's lawyer was in the middle of a long peroration, full of details. The main judge turned left and whispered something to his colleague.

Mustafa's lawyer exclaimed, "You should listen carefully to what I'm saying!"

"Well, the entire country listens to you now," the judge said apologetically.

And he obviously didn't mean only the lawyer. The digital revolutionaries had found their voice.

CHAPTER 15

Information Runs Free

Along with the pressure on global platforms such as Facebook, Google+, and Twitter, the Kremlin also wanted to ratchet up the pressure on two very popular Russian platforms—the social network VKontakte, with massive user groups of thousands of people involved in political events, and the search engine Yandex, which carried news headlines on its home page that had become essential daily reading for millions of Russians. Both enjoyed widespread use beyond Russia's borders in the former Soviet Union. When Russian authorities set out in 2014 to win the hearts and minds of Russian-speaking populations at home and abroad and to persuade them to accept the Kremlin's version of the conflict in Ukraine, controlling these two homegrown platforms became crucial.

The year began in confusion for VKontakte. On January 24 Pavel Durov, the primary founder, sold 12 percent of the company—his share—to a friend, Ivan Tavrin, CEO of Mega-Fon, one of the biggest telecommunications companies in Russia, and offered odd explanations for the sale in a post on his page on VKontakte, saying that "what you own, sooner or later, owns you." Reclusive, Durov communicated almost entirely with the outside world by posting on his page. In the same post, however, he stressed that he would remain CEO of VKontakte. "It's my responsibility to [take] care of and protect this network," he wrote.

VKontakte was modeled after Facebook, and Durov even chose the same fonts and colors, blue and white, for his network, but with a more primitive design. The network itself is a strange mix of contradictions: although a user is required to provide a genuine identity to register with VKontakte, the network has been famous for years as a safe haven for pirates, and many used it as a source of watching movies and listening to music for free.[1] It was Russia's most popular social network in 2012, earning over $15 million in net profit that year.

VKontakte was caught in the middle of a conflict over control of the company between two of its biggest shareholders, both oligarchs: Igor Sechin and Alisher Usmanov. Sechin was a personal friend of Putin; Usmanov was a pro-Kremlin oligarch who had gathered a vast media empire of formerly liberal news outlets—he started with Gazeta.ru, then acquired *Kommersant*, and later turned to the Internet—and absorbed LiveJournal.com, the most popular blogging platform, as well as Mail.ru, the most popular e-mail service, and was believed to want to acquire some of Yandex too.

When caught in the squeeze between the two oligarchs, Durov was feeling the pressure personally. Some shareholders reportedly launched an internal investigation at the behest of one of the oligarchs into Durov's business expense accounts, for reasons that were unclear.[2] In spring 2014 the pressure took its toll on Durov, who was still only twenty-nine years old. His moves became frantic. On March 11 he posted, "Seven Reasons to Stay in Russia," in which he wrote, "In recent months the topic of emigration from Russia has become fashionable. But I go against the trend, and here are my seven reasons to stay in the country." He listed low taxes, talented people, beautiful girls, and so on.

On April 1, out of the blue, Durov announced he was resigning as CEO of VKontakte. Then, two days later, he disavowed his resignation statement, and four days after that he posted a new message, lamenting bitterly the situation inside the company. He said he had filed a lawsuit to try to get back on the board of directors.

Whereas Durov's previous posts had largely been about the company's internal ownership conflict, the posts that he put up on April 16 carried a more ominous tone; they potentially applied to everybody who used the network. The first was posted at 9:36 p.m.:

On December 13, 2013, the FSB requested us to hand over the personal data of organizers of the Euromaidan groups. Our response was and is a categorical "No." Russian jurisdiction cannot include our Ukrainian users of VKontakte. Delivery of personal data of Ukrainians to Russian authorities would have been not only illegal, but a treason of all those millions of Ukrainians who trust us. In the process, I sacrificed a lot. I sold my share in the company. Since December 2013, I have had no property, but I have a clear conscience and ideals I'm ready to defend.

He then posted a scan of the FSB letter, exactly in the same manner as he had in December 2011, when he refused to cooperate with them about the protests in Moscow.

The second posting, two hours later, declared, "On March 13, 2014, the Prosecutor's office requested me to close down the anticorruption group of Alexey Navalny. I didn't close this group in December 2011, and certainly, I did not close it now. In recent weeks, I was under pressure from different angles. We managed to gain over a month, but it's time to state—neither myself, nor my team are going to conduct political censorship. . . . Freedom of information is the inalienable right of the post-industrial society."

On April 21 Durov was fired as chief executive. He learned the news from journalists. He claimed he was fired because of his public refusal to cooperate with the authorities. The next day TechCrunch, a website, asked Durov in an e-mail about his future plans. "I'm out of Russia and have no plans to go back," he wrote back. Durov left the country.

With Durov gone, the company was firmly under the control of two loyal oligarchs; the Kremlin had managed to repeat the tactic it had used earlier with traditional media, like Gusinsky's Media-Most in the 2000s. This time it was even easier, as there were neither journalists to demand a personal meeting with Putin nor users who might come to demonstrations on Moscow's streets. At this time the Kremlin believed they fully controlled the VKontakte company and its network—they foresaw no surprises. What the Kremlin miscalculated was that a social network is different from either television or newspapers. Although journalists generate the content in traditional media by working in the editorial office, users, often widely dispersed, create the content on social media, and they don't care who owns the network.

These legions of dispersed users would soon prove VKontakte's strength.

O n April 24 Putin fired a shot that had wide reverberations at the second-largest Internet company in Russia. He was in St. Petersburg at a media forum organized by the All-Russia People's Front, an ultrapatriotic, populist movement Putin had urgently launched in 2011 to corral political support from the provinces and other quarters when his United Russia Party, largely made up of bureaucrats, lost the respect of many voters. The new People's Front, consciously evoking symbols and names of the Soviet era, had a modern political purpose for Putin: to counter the liberal-minded, Westernized intelligentsia of the big cities.

It was a staged event in the round, and in the middle of the discussion a pro-Kremlin blogger, Viktor Levanov, addressed Putin with an unusually long statement about the Internet. Levanov first attacked the United States—"It is an open secret that the United States controls the Internet"—then went after Google specifically. "Why can't they build servers here?" he said, echoing the Kremlin line. "I do not want my personal data and information about politicians that run my country to go to the United States."

Putin weighed in and answered as he had before, referring to Snowden and NSA, saying that the servers should be relocated to Russia. Then Putin asserted that the Internet began "as a special CIA project. And this is the way it is developing."

Next Levanov did something unexpected. He asked a question about the Russian company Yandex, one of the most recognizable brands and popular websites in the country. "It is not quite clear what Yandex is: on the one hand we know it as a search engine; but on the other hand it is a kind of media, because all the time, every day the top five news items Yandex collects from other sources are viewed by millions of people. Meanwhile, Yandex does not have a media license and cannot be held liable under the law as a media outlet because it is a search engine."[3]

This was not a casual allegation. By raising the question of whether Yandex was a media organization, the blogger was aiming a knife at its heart. Forcing Yandex to register as media would make the company subject to Russian media legislation and libel law, under which, if the media gets two warnings from the government, it could be closed down. Until this point Yandex had operated outside this control.

Putin eagerly pursued the theme. He claimed that Yandex, when it was formed, had been "forced" to accept Americans and Europeans in its company's management. "And they had to agree to this," he said. He also lamented that the company was partially registered abroad. Then Putin bore down on the real culprit he had in mind: "As I have said, this was all created by the Americans and they want to retain their monopoly."[4]

Putin's message was ominous, suggesting that one of the most successful Internet companies in Russia was under American control, which in turn controls the Internet. Putin had already warned with great fervor in his Crimea speech about traitors and "fifth columns," and now his comments seemed to suggest there was something wrong with Yandex having foreigners around.

The next day Yandex NV, the Dutch-registered parent company of Russia's search giant, fell 16 percent on the NASDAQ, and American investors rushed to Moscow to talk to Yandex's management.[5] Yandex responded to Putin by saying that international investors' participation was normal for a tech start-up and that, as a public company with a 70 percent free float, no single shareholder could exert pressure.[6] Yandex reminded Putin that Russia was one of the few countries where domestic Internet brands were stronger than global ones.

In early May a worried Yandex recruited to its board German Gref, CEO of the huge state-owned Sberbank and who is thought to be personally close to Putin.[7]

It soon was evident that Putin had not idly raised questions about Yandex. In May Andrei Lugovoi, the parliamentarian who authored legislation making it possible to block Ej.ru, Grani.ru, Kasparov.ru, and Navalny's blog in March, announced a new initiative to force Yandex to register as a media company.[8] It was an unmistakable threat.

In a week the Russian Investigative Committee, an increasingly powerful law enforcement body, sent representatives to Yandex offices with a search warrant.[9] The pretext for the warrant was a criminal investigation conducted by the committee against Alexey Navalny—the committee alleged Navalny had stolen money he had gathered via the online service Yandex, money intended for his campaign for Moscow mayor the previous autumn. But the raid was a shocking development and went way beyond the reasons cited for the search warrant. Yandex was one of the most famous Russian companies and inspired pride in Russia. Its profitability came not from oil and gas, the traditional sources of Russian wealth, but through building a business based on technology, and here, in this field, Russian engineers successfully competed with American companies—Yandex had a bigger share of the Russian search market than Google.

Many people felt uneasy about Putin's eagerness to target the pride of the Russian tech business. Russian high-tech companies often had foreigners on their boards—it was a ticket to world markets and foreign investments, and for years it signaled success. Now the Russian president had made foreign board members look suspicious, almost as if they were agents of a foreign state.

The campus of Kaspersky Lab headquarters in Moscow fills three modern semitransparent buildings, surrounded by green lawns and the shimmering surface of a nearby reservoir. The tableau suggests nothing more than an ambition to be like Google or Apple—a big multinational, respected everywhere. Kaspersky Lab is one of Russia's most recognizable brands. On the day Irina went there in May 2014, children frolicked on the grass in front of the company's green and red corporate logo. Andrey Yarnikh, head of government relations, said it was the day employees could bring children to the office.

While Irina was walking around with Andrey Yarnikh, a big black SUV braked suddenly behind them. A man of medium height and graying wavy hair, wearing a bright shirt and jeans, jumped out of the car and approached us. It was Eugene Kaspersky, founder and CEO of Kaspersky Lab.

"Hi," he greeted Yarnikh and shook his hand.

"Hi Genya!" said Yarnikh. And then Kaspersky disappeared even faster than he emerged.[10]

Yarnikh explained that Kaspersky didn't like formality either in conversation or clothes, and in the early years of the company, when the laboratory was a relatively small entity, he used to kiss all female employees and shake hands with every man he met.

But this placid surface concealed anxieties behind the glass walls of the headquarters. Putin's remarks about foreigners at

Yandex made its way through Kaspersky Lab like a bolt of lightning. Although based in Moscow, Kaspersky boasts that 400 million people worldwide are protected by its cyber-threat and antivirus products. At one point a foreign investment firm, General Atlantic, owned part of Kaspersky Lab.[11] And in February 2014 Kaspersky had established an international advisory board and recruited several Americans, including Howard Schmidt, former cyber adviser to Presidents Bush and Obama. If having Americans involved in an Internet company was going to be a problem, then Kaspersky, like Yandex, would not be immune to scrutiny.

Kaspersky Lab has offices everywhere, from Australia to Germany, South Africa to the United States. Just like Yandex, Kaspersky Lab is registered abroad, in the United Kingdom.[12] And just as Volozh built Yandex, when Kaspersky built up his company, he didn't exploit government connections and has not been promoted by the state.

Kaspersky was a complex and sometimes obscure figure in the world of the Russian Internet. When the first digital attacks were made on the media, he looked the other way. But then he came to the rescue of *Novaya Gazeta*. At other times he took positions that showed sympathy for the Kremlin approach to the Internet. For example, in February 2011 Kaspersky Lab joined the Safe Internet League, an Orthodox-dominated NGO that promotes Internet censorship under the pretext of protecting children from harmful content.[13] The League advanced weird ideas of creating "white lists" of sites approved in advance by them, and cyber *druzhinas* (from the Russian word that means the feudal prince's armed guardsmen) patrolling the Internet.[14] The League has been working closely with Roskomnadzor.[15]

On the day Irina visited, people at Kaspersky were debating Anatoly Karachinsky's decision to move his software company, Luxoft, out of Russia. It prompted a natural question about whether any large international companies could stay. Irina's sources in the company said that many people at Kaspersky Lab regarded Putin's words about the Internet and CIA—and the offensive on Yandex—as a hidden threat. They wondered what to do.

I n the center of Moscow a modern office building was erected in 2007 at a time of massive renovation around the city. The building, which houses Silver-City, a business center, has all the hallmarks of that period: all glass and concrete, with ugly rectangular forms that hark back to the 1970s, defined in outlandish orange stripes. It was at this building on June 10, 2014, that Putin was to meet with the leaders of the Russian Internet for the first time in fifteen years; the last and only previous meeting was in December 1999.

Back then people spoke openly in front of Putin and were not afraid to oppose what they saw as the government's power-grab to control the Internet. They did not fear Putin in those days, and by the end of the meeting Putin had supported those who objected to the government intrusion. At that time the Internet was new, and so was the hodge-podge of entrepreneurs who met with Putin. A decade and a half later the Russian Internet had grown into a $143 billion annual business, employing over 1.3 million professionals, generating 8.5 percent of Russia's gross domestic product and accounting for 2.5 percent of all its trade.[16] In those same years Putin's government had imposed surveillance on the Internet—the SORM black boxes and, ultimately, filtering and censorship.

The security at the meeting was strict, and journalists were admitted only with special identity cards issued just for this event. Before Putin arrived, there was a session about the future of the Internet. It was more like a wake. No one jumped from a chair and shouted about the lack of Internet freedom. In fact, the subject of state control over the Internet was never mentioned; rather, it was evident that Putin, not yet in the room, held the upper hand. This reality weighed heavily on those who were present, including Volozh, the founder of Yandex, who had also been present fifteen years earlier and walked out of that meeting with the pencil. At this very moment Volozh was feeling the Kremlin pressure on the business he had built, and everybody knew it.

They could see a powerful reminder in the chair marked "VKontakte." In the chair was not Durov, the founder; instead, there was Boris Dobrodeyev, then deputy chief executive of VKontakte, whose presence underscored the growing clout of the Kremlin. Dobrodeyev is a scion of the post-Soviet media establishment; his father, Oleg, is head of the television colossus known as the All-Russia State Television and Radio Broadcasting Company.[17] When Dobrodeyev sat in the chair, it was a sign that other chairs could also suffer the same fate—the founders could be replaced. The blogger Leviev, who had invented Alexey Navalny's big red button, was present at the meeting because his company was broadcasting it. When he saw how Durov's chair had been filled, he immediately thought of the peril that faced Volozh and Yandex. "Yandex's business, all its 'circulatory system,' is in Russia: data centers, offices, the staff. Yes, there are offices abroad, but it is a drop in the sea, insignificant. If Volozh was to say something wrong—it will be very easy to take his business away," he told us later.

Putin was late, as usual, and when he did arrive, he didn't immediately enter the conference room; rather, he was shown a small exhibition of Internet start-ups in the hall. He was escorted by Kirill Varlamov, who had grown up in Ekaterinburg, graduated from the local technical university, and joined Uralmash, the mammoth metallurgical factory, as an engineer. In the early 2000s he founded a small software company and soon moved to Moscow. In 2011 he caught the eye of some people at one of Putin's pet projects, the Agency of Strategic Initiatives. It was launched when Putin was prime minister and was designed to be a high-tech incubator, just like a much-publicized effort by Medvedev known as Skolkovo. Varlamov joined the agency, and it proved to be a wise decision; he was introduced to Putin. In the same year, when Putin formed the

All-Russia People's Front, Varlamov joined. He was included on a list of nearly five hundred people who were prominent Putin political supporters, most of them celebrities; he was the only one with an Internet background. After Putin was elected president, Varlamov was made the head of a state-funded venture capital fund, giving him power over the budget available to Internet start-ups. By then Medvedev's Skolkovo was in clear decline. Varlamov maintained a key position at the All-Russia People's Front.

Russia had produced an entire generation of bright entrepreneurs in the first years of the digital revolution, but Putin was not interested in them. He wanted, most of all, someone loyal. Varlamov's appearance at the June meeting signaled that Putin had triumphed. Varlamov's fund had even organized the meeting, and when Putin appeared, Varlamov sat on his right—there was no doubt that Varlamov was the star of the show. Volozh, who was a genuine Internet legend in Russia, looked uneasy. He was exceedingly cautious and repeated his line that there are very few countries in the world where the local Internet companies dominate, and these companies became prominent not because of protection but because they were left alone.

The sole question about repressive measures on the Internet was raised by Dmitry Grishin of Mail.ru, Russia's leading e-mail service. An engineer by training, Grishin, thirty-five years old, was nervous as he looked at Putin. He began by saying that most Russian software advances had happened because the state left the inventors alone. "And we have this mentality," he said. "We have this mentality that we count on ourselves." He added that any contacts with the authorities can't lead to good things, and "in principle, if you can hide, it is better to hide."

Putin sternly interrupted him. "It's wrong," he said, shaking his head. "First of all, you can't hide from us." The remark said everything about the state of the Internet in Russia: it had grown immensely, had enabled appeals for freedom, and yet there was no place to hide.

Grishin reddened and said excitedly, "We often hear that all Internet users are from another planet. But we do love our country; we want to help to make it comfortable to live and work in. And we understand that the Internet has grown and it is now an integral part of the society. Therefore, in principle, we understand that the regulation, it's necessary. And often the ideas in the regulation, they are very correct. But, unfortunately, sometimes it happens that realization, in general, is frightening. And it would be great to develop some sort of process that allows us not only to listen but also to be listened to. It would be very, very important!"[18]

It was a polite appeal but, in its timidity, reflected the reality of Putin and the Internet. The entrepreneurs and businessmen were not challenging the Kremlin; there were no new proposals that day, no confrontations. And some of those present were worried that a discussion might have been started about a project called Cheburashka, to create a purely domestic Internet—inaccessible from abroad—named after a popular children's cartoon character. The project was suggested by a Russian senator in April, but, thankfully, it did not come up.

The real beneficiary on June 10 was Putin's political machine, the All-Russia People's Front, and Kirill Varlamov. The genuine Internet market leaders were invited not to talk to Putin but to lend legitimacy to a government-funded pet project. And they did.

Although Yandex had once resisted pressure from the Kremlin, now it gave some ground. On September 12, 2014, Yandex announced that the company agreed to formally register three of its online services—Yandex's cloud service, its social network Moi Krug, and its mail system. They were put on a special list of Roskomnadzor consisting of online services required to keep users' metadata for six months and to provide remote access to this data for the Russian security services. Mail.ru and VKontakte were also included on the list.[19] The scope of SORM had just expanded.

Yandex also attempted to tread carefully in the minefield of the Ukraine war. In March the service started offering different maps of Ukraine for Russian and Ukrainian users. The Russians would see a map showing Crimea as part of Russia, while a user in Ukraine would see the peninsula as still part of Ukraine. Yandex explained it by saying Crimea would be shown according to the official position of the country in which the map was viewed.[20]

The Kremlin pressure to control the Internet was not always visible. It did not always appear in black-and-white threats. Sometimes the battle was waged in the mists. Those who believed in keeping the Internet out of the hands of the state tried to survive any way they could. Andrei Kolesnikov learned the game firsthand, and he was a very good player. CEO of an NGO that had been set up in 2001 to oversee Internet domain names, Kolesnikov has a long history with the Russian Internet; in 1992 he was one of eight people who signed the agreement that established the domain .ru. He was present at the meeting with Putin in December 1999, and he also attended the meeting with Putin in June 2014, though this time he was not invited to join the panel.

Kolesnikov was the first Russian expert who joined ICANN's governing bodies, and he was acutely aware of the Kremlin's ideas about the Internet and what the Kremlin thought of NGOs as a whole. To avoid interference, he devoted a lot of time to attending public meetings on Internet security and offered repeatedly to be a technical expert to people who were in charge of setting policy on the Internet. His position was fragile. When Andrei visited him in September 2014, Kolesnikov argued with great fervor that repressive laws were, in fact, in "a parallel reality," and they had no impact on the Internet at all. After half an hour of wrangling, he insisted that what the authorities had done to the Internet was entirely immaterial: "Look, did it affect your morning coffee?"[21]

But the next morning brought disturbing news. The business daily *Vedomosti* exposed a Kremlin plan to gather the Russian Security Council, the advisory group to the president on security, in three days to discuss the option of shutting the country off from the global Internet in case of an emergency.

The centralized structure of the Russian Internet has led the authorities to believe that it is entirely possible and that the international traffic can be cut off either by the operators that control cross-border fiber-optic cables or at the Internet exchange points, where the international traffic joins the national Internet.

Even two decades after the collapse of the Soviet Union, Russian telecommunications remain largely centralized. Russia is connected with the outside world by fiber-optic cables, most of them laid by five Russian national operators, with the state-controlled Rostelecom enjoying the largest Internet backbone network in the country. Russia has only a dozen Internet exchange points (compared with more than eighty in the United States).[22] And nearly half of the Russian Internet traffic passes through one of them, MSK-IX. The MSK-IX itself is based on the premises of the phone station M9, which is owned by Rostelecom.

The geography of Russia doesn't help. Although most of the world's Internet traffic is passed via underwater cables, Russia connects with the West through the terrestrial cross-border fiber-optic cables laid from Moscow to St. Petersburg to Helsinki and Stockholm, and only recently did Rostelecom lay cables in a new direction, from Moscow to Frankfurt, Germany. In the east there are also some lines to China, Japan, and Iran, but overall the connections to the outside world are sparse.

Although it didn't get as much attention, the Security Council also wanted to talk about a second option—to hand over the powers of administering Russian domains from Kolesnikov's center to the government. If approved, it would mean that all Russian domains were under direct government control—or, rather, direct control of most websites in the country.

This time the initiative was not approved, but the message was strong and clear.

In 2014 Putin had one big secret he wanted to keep: Russian troops were in Ukraine. The Russian security services hunted down people around the country who tried to expose Putin's secret, relying on the same technology the secret police had used almost seventy years earlier.

On April 17, 2014, Svetlana Davydova heard something on the street in the city of Vyazma, about 150 miles west of Moscow, and grabbed her phone. She was a mother of six children and pregnant with the seventh. She knew that outside the small town the Russian military intelligence service had a base, and she had just overheard talk at a bus stop that small groups of officers were being sent to Moscow and then Ukraine.

At that moment Russia was backing an undeclared war by Ukrainian separatists. Davydova had no access to secret information about the military unit; she simply overheard what people were saying on their cell phones at the bus stop. She was very interested in events in Ukraine and personally opposed to the Russian military presence there. She told her husband, Anatoly, what she had heard—and what it might mean. Then she wrote down what she knew.

That day, around 2:00 p.m., she called a hotline to the embassy of Ukraine in Moscow on her cell phone. She told the embassy she had information about the deployment of Russian military intelligence officers to Ukraine, and not much more. Nine minutes later the first secretary of the embassy called her back and asked her to provide details. Davydova relayed all she knew—just rumors she had heard on the street.

Davydova didn't know it, but the FSB was monitoring the hotline, and the Russian security service recorded Davydova's voice on the line to the embassy. The FSB immediately went to work to identify who she was. They had no difficulty—Davydova's phone number was easily traced.

Then nothing happened for a while. Davydova was not questioned about the call. The war in Ukraine grew more intense.

Six months later Davydova had given birth to a baby girl. In two months, on January 21, 2015, there was a knock at the door of her apartment, and when Anatoly opened it, a group of special operations soldiers dressed in black burst in. The group was led by a top official of the FSB sent from Moscow. Davydova was detained, taken away, and the officers searched her small apartment, taking her computer, notebooks, and other materials as the family looked on. Davydova was brought directly to Moscow's Lefortovo prison, the main prison the FSB used for high-profile investigations and detentions. Davydova was frightened—and worried, not least of all about the two-month-old baby she had been torn away from.

Six days later she was charged with treason, which can carry a sentence of twelve to twenty years in prison. She was told that her call to the embassy of Ukraine had been intercepted. She was given a state-appointed lawyer who advised her to plead guilty. Overwrought with emotion and scared, at first she complied.

For the FSB it was not enough to have just a guilty plea, however; they needed to prove she had made the call. For this the security service needed a sample of her voice to compare with the recording of the call. But Davydova refused to give the voice sample.

At this point, in early 2015, her case gained widespread attention in Russia, and human rights activists visited her in Lefortovo, a common practice. When they came to the prison to see her, the FSB illicitly made a video, without telling her or the activists.

Then the FSB reached back to technology that had been created and perfected since 1949 in the work at Marfino and Kuchino. From this video recording they compared her voice on the intercepted phone call.[23]

Davydova was not a spy—she was a housewife. But she was caught up in something larger—the secret services were repeating practices of wiretapping and examining voices, all in an effort to keep the lid on a closed society, to lock up information, even if it was just a rumor a housewife had overheard at a bus stop.

After two weeks in prison and a public outcry, Davydova was released, and the charges were later dropped.

In the summer of 2014 Russian and Ukrainian journalists started to find dozens of profiles of Russian soldiers on VKontakte— and many who had been posted to Ukraine had added to their pages photographs from their posting. The Russian military commanders were not aware the soldiers were posting boastful comments and photographs, identifying their units and their geographic positions.

The pictures and comments revealed a lie that Putin had been spouting about the war. Journalists in Russia's northwestern city Pskov, bordering Latvia and Estonia, found online, on VKontakte, profiles of soldiers from a paratrooper base in the region. The soldiers, who had visited their pages for the last time on August 15–16, posted photographs from Ukraine.

Then the soldiers disappeared. There were awful rumors that dozens of Pskov's paratroopers had been killed in an ambush in Ukraine. On August 22 journalists found a new post on the VKontakte page of one of the soldiers, Leonid Kichatkin:

"Life has stopped!!"

Then, a bit later: "Dear friends!!!!!!!!!! Leonid was killed [. . .] funeral[']s Monday at 10am in Vibutah. Who wants to say goodbye to him, please come over. My phone number 8953254066. A wife[,] Oksana[.]"

Soon the post reporting the tragedy was removed and replaced by a cheerful post depicting a family celebration. When journalists called the number, a male voice on the phone answered that he was Leonid, alive and well.

But journalists attended the funerals and found the two new graves, and one of them bears the inscription: "Leonid Kichatkin, 30.09.1984–19.08.2014."

When two TV Dozhd journalists and a *Novaya Gazeta* reporter went to the Pskov cemetery, they were attacked by unknown men in balaclavas, and a local parliamentary deputy was beaten up because he had exposed the postings in the local newspaper. But it didn't prevent other leaks about Russian soldiers in Ukraine, and VKontakte turned out to be indispensable—for the soldiers posting and for all the others who would be reading. The soldiers chose VKontakte because it was easy to use and was there, always online. On July 23 a Russian soldier conscript from Samara in southern Russia posted photographs of his artillery pieces on VKontakte, with the words, "All night we were shooting at Ukraine." It went viral.

The Russian seizure of Crimea in early 2014 was carried out bloodlessly by unmarked soldiers. It was relatively clean and swift and heralded as a new kind of warfare. But the two graves in Pskov shattered this image of a bloodless new kind of warfare. The reality that soldiers were being killed on the battlefield in Ukraine exposed the cover-up and deception about Russia's role in the violence in the Donbass. The losses, inevitable lies, and cover-ups didn't work in large part because Russian soldiers as well as their relatives and friends kept posting on VKontakte.

After all the Kremlin efforts to control information, the information about Ukraine freed itself. The primary source of sensitive data on the violence in Ukraine was not journalists, nongovernmental organizations, opposition leaders, activists, or even

bloggers; it was soldiers. Inexperienced young men, who had been schooled by state-sponsored television propaganda, were electrified by it and went to war, boasting of their exploits.

The network enabled the information to move freely, unhindered, to millions.

EPILOGUE

On December 19, 2011, LifeNews, a website of yellow journalism and Kremlin propaganda, published a report with a photograph of the former deputy prime minister and opposition leader Boris Nemtsov, with the headline, "Lifenews Publishes Secret Talks of Nemtsov."[1] The site boasted that they had acquired more than six hours of audio recordings of Nemtsov's phone calls and posted nine of the recordings online, including those in which Nemtsov made candid and sometimes embarrassing comments about his opposition colleagues. How did they get these private conversations? There can be only one answer. Nemtsov told us back then that the Russian security services had eavesdropped on his cell phone conversations and then someone leaked the recordings to harm him. Nemtsov was subjected to SORM.

Three years later, on February 27, 2015, late in the evening, Nemtsov was walking with his girlfriend across the Bolshoi Moskvoretsky Bridge, a stone's throw from the Kremlin wall. They were heading over the bridge, away from the Kremlin, when they reached a stairwell that runs down the side. A man appeared behind Nemtsov and opened fire, shooting four bullets into his back. Nemtsov died instantly. The shooter escaped in a passing car.

Two days later we joined the crowds gathering in the center of Moscow to honor Nemtsov's life and memory. It was a cloudy and somber afternoon. People carried flowers—white roses, yellow chrysanthemums, and red carnations. In contrast to the boisterous protests of recent years, the crowd was quiet; almost nobody spoke of the killing or showed their anger. Some carried Russian flags with a black ribbon in a sign of mourning; others brought placards that said simply, "I do not fear."

The wiretapping of Nemtsov in 2011 and his murder just over three years later are two strands in a larger narrative about Russia today, one that was well understood by us and thousands of others as we expressed sorrow and rage for his loss. The interception of his calls and their release was an attempt to unnerve Nemtsov and send a message to Putin's opposition. The killing of a charismatic politician near the Kremlin wall was an attempt to send a message to fear to everyone. Both events spoke volumes about how the Kremlin has wielded power in recent years and, in particular, how Putin has confronted the rise of the Internet.

Fear—and self-censorship caused by fear—were for centuries essential to the system of government in Russia, from imperial times through the Soviet period and into the present. The leaders often dealt in the currency of threats and intimidation. Since 1999 we have chronicled the activities of Russian secret services, in the product of which is our 2010 book, *The New Nobility*. For years we've been trying to understand the main impact of former Soviet KGB officers' presence in today's corridors of power. We believe it has come to dominate the way Putin views the world. He and his colleagues from the security services brought to their governance the old mindset that threats existed and had to be countered. First and foremost they had to fight any threat to the stability of the political regime, which meant any threat to their hold on power.

This mindset came into full bloom in 2011 when Putin announced he would return to the Kremlin, touching off widespread protests by voters who felt insulted and angry at how the decision was made, apparently without their participation. The subsequent uprisings, lasting well into 2012, brought tens of thousands of people to the streets and were the largest public protests in Moscow during his presidency and the first really mass demonstrations against him in a dozen years. For Putin, the sense of threat resided in something invisible and ubiquitous in the prosperous Russia he had presided over since 2000: the Internet. The vibrant digital channels that existed, especially in Moscow, proved vital to mobilizing the demonstrations that echoed off the Kremlin walls.

On the surface, the system the Kremlin created was technically advanced and well-orchestrated, with special roles assigned to different actors. Parliament was tasked with producing a flow of repressive legislation. Pro-Kremlin hacktivists and trolls were hired to attack and harass liberals online. To spy on and intercept the opposition, the security services got a nod. Roskomnadzor was handed the power to censor and filter the Internet. Friendly oligarchs were asked to bankroll and take over media companies, both traditional and new media, to bring them to heel as well as called upon to take over Russia's Internet companies when necessary to strengthen the Kremlin's hand with services that were popular among tens of millions of people. Finally, to provide surveillance equipment, manufacturers were selected, both domestic and international. What Putin brought that tied it together was an outlook of unabashed paranoia that saw enemies all around.

In practice Putin's tactics were never fully exploited. The Internet filtering in Russia turned out to be unsophisticated; thousands of sites were blocked by mistake, and users could easily find ways to make an end-run around it. At the same time, very few people in Russia were actually sent to jail for posting criticism of the government online. This is a far cry from the frequent and brutal persecution of people in China and Turkey, for example, for their opinions. Even with all the mechanisms available, relatively few new media organizations were actually closed down; many more were simply brought to heel. Those media that were blocked were left alone, their offices not raided by police nor their journalists sent to prison; Russia did not need to be as repressive or technically sophisticated as, say, China. Putin did not need to carry out mass repression against journalists or activists; he could get results just as effectively by using the tools of threat and intimidation, which is what he did. He carried a big stick, but he didn't always use it.

Putin could be remarkably effective with the threat of the big stick. Russian Internet freedom has been deeply curtailed. The thriving Internet companies, many of them started in Russia from scratch in an environment of a free and open Internet, agreed to work under state censorship without creating much of a fuss. When invited to talk to Putin, they were so intimidated that they avoided raising the issue of sustaining Internet freedoms. When the security state, acting largely in secret, planned to install intrusive surveillance equipment in Russia, thus creating back doors to the messages and content of the entire country, the ISPs hardly murmured a complaint. There was also little resistance when the state imposed four blacklists of Internet sites.

The Putin approach is all about intimidation, more often than actual coercion, as an instrument of control. To intimidate, legislation was drafted as broadly as possible, the restrictions constantly expanded; companies, ISPs, and the media rushed to the Kremlin to ask what was now allowed. The authorities threatened to block entire services like YouTube—and the Internet giants came running, offering technical solutions, often at their own expense. More often than not this intimidation was aimed at pressuring individuals to do what the Kremlin wanted rather than attacking a whole network or company. When the authorities wanted to control VKontakte, they ousted its founder. They twisted arms more often than they cut wires.

Putin's system is effective as long as people are certain the Kremlin is in control, that the stability of the political regime is unperturbed. Intimidation is essential in this environment, and it sends an unmistakable message: we are watching you, we are in charge, and there is no way to hide from us. But during a crisis of confidence, an upheaval, or an emergency, the dynamic is transformed. In a crisis a tidal wave of content is generated and shared in real time. A single message can be copied by millions, and here the Putin system of control cannot cope. It is built to zero in on a few troublemakers, not millions of average users. In times of instability it is average users who spread the information, and the Putin system then breaks down.

There was a larger failure in the Putin strategy. He was accustomed to dealing with hierarchy and organizations that could be coerced by going after the bosses. But networks have no tops; they are horizontal creatures. Everyone can participate without authorization. The content is generated not by the companies that operate websites and social media but by the users. Putin and his team never fully grasped this.

The Internet today is the printing press of the past. Just as the invention of a printed page once enabled a free flow of ideas, so now simple tools like VKontakte and Facebook, widely used every day by average people in Russia, have created an environment in which information cannot be stopped. The British historian of the Civil War in England, Christopher Hill, described this in *The World Turned Upside Down*, a work devoted to the radical thinkers of the time. He explained why the Revolution caused such a "fascinating flood of radical ideas": "During the brief years of extensive liberty of the press in England it may have been easier to eccentrics to get into print than ever before or since. Before 1641 and after 1660, there was a strict censorship. In the intervening years of freedom, a printing press was a relatively cheap and portable piece of equipment. Publishing had not yet developed as a capitalist industry."[2]

Today the Internet is the everyman's platform. To control it, Putin would have to control the mind of every single user, which simply isn't possible. Information runs free like water or air on a network, not easily captured. The Russian conscript soldiers who posted their photographs taken in Ukraine did more to expose the Kremlin's lies about the conflict than journalists or activists. The network enabled them.

ACKNOWLEDGMENTS

Writing books takes a lot of time, and the work on this one was a rather long journey. It probably started in 1996 in Moscow, when the Internet was the very first topic Andrei was assigned to cover as a journalist at the newspaper *Segodnya*, or in 1997 when Irina decided to move to the newspaper department that conducted investigations. Along the way many colleagues supported us. We owe much to Lyudmila Telen and Michael Shevelev, whom we met in 2004 at *Moskovskie Novosti* and who have encouraged us ever since. Marina Latysheva, our best friend for many years, has been a source of constant and never-ending support. Nick Fielding never hesitated to offer his much-appreciated advice. Mort Rosenblum was a source of inspiration about journalism. We are grateful to Olga Pashkova, the courageous and flamboyant director of the website Ezhednevny Journal, or Ej.ru, who invited us to write for the website and was always willing to accept our ideas, including the 2009 project, "Control Over Society: Methods of the Kremlin," which laid the first research groundwork for the book. Ej.ru has been blocked in Russia since March 2014 but remains alive and online.

As it is getting more difficult to publish journalistic investigations in Russia, we are very grateful to our colleagues and friends at OpenDemocracy, Wired.com, *World Policy Journal*, and the *Guardian*. With their help, our stories on surveillance and censorship in Russia were published and eventually found their way back to a Russian audience.

We began working on the topic of the book intensively in 2012, and since then we were very lucky to find new friends in Russia and beyond. We are very grateful to Alexander Verkhovsky, an extremely brave director of the SOVA Center, who is the best expert on Russian nationalist movements, a dangerous topic for research. He helped us when we needed it most. Our thanks also go out to Sergei Lukashevsky and Lena Kaluzhskaya, at the Sakharov Center, who very generously gave us an opportunity to test our ideas in a series of discussions at the center in 2012–2014 and who made it possible to bring our friends from international organizations concerned with privacy and surveillance issues to Moscow to exchange ideas and information.

We are very grateful to Ron Deibert and his group at Citizen Lab as well as Gus Hosein and his team at Privacy International. They proved to be good friends, and we enjoyed working together. Our special thanks go to Max Kashulinsky, at Slon.ru, whom we worked with at *Segodnya* back in the 1990s; Max helped us secure a series of interviews crucial for this book. And Svetlana Reiter, at RBC, was extremely generous with her contacts and insights.

We would like to thank the officials in the Russian Ministry of Communications, former and acting, who shared their knowledge and opinions with us. Many of them are genuinely concerned not with a fictional threat to Russia's "digital sovereignty" but that the country they worked to open in the 1990s is trying to shut itself off from the world.

We are deeply indebted to Clive Priddle of PublicAffairs, who never flagged in his trust in us and our ideas. This book could not have been possible without PublicAffairs' founder, Peter Osnos, who has been a key source of support since he published our first book, *The New Nobility*, five years ago.

Special appreciation is due to David Hoffman, a contributing editor at the *Washington Post*, who spent a year assisting us as we developed the idea into the book and then spent two very hard weeks with us in Moscow helping to frame and edit the man-uscript. We are very grateful to Michael Birnbaum, the *Post*'s Moscow bureau chief, for his hospitality as we hammered out the manuscript. And, as always, we thank Robert Guinsler, our agent at Sterling Lord Literistic.

We would be remiss not to add that we are indebted to Mikhail Gorbachev, who did more than anyone else to free information in our country.

NOTES

PROLOGUE

1. Pew Research Center, "Internet Seen as Positive Influence on Education but Negative on Morality in Emerging and Developing Nations," PewGlobal, March 19, 2015, www.pewglobal.org/2015/03/19/internet-seen-as-positive-influence-on -education-but-negative-influence-on-morality-in-emerging-and-developing -nations.

CHAPTER 1: THE PRISON OF INFORMATION

1. The details of Trakhtman's biography are largely drawn from the memoirs published online by the Vinitsky family; Trakhtman was a friend of the family for decades. See: http://arkady-vinitsky-100years.weebly.com; also, see Russian Jewish Encyclopedia, http://www.rujen.ru.

2. Konstantin Kalachev, *V kruge tretiem* [In the Third Circle]. Kalachev worked as a researcher at Marfino from 1947 to 1996, and in 1999 he wrote a history of the Marfino project. When the authors of this book called the Research Institute of Automation (http://niia.ru/eng.htm), a successor to the sharashka that occupies the building in Marfino to this day, we were told that Kalachev's book is the only authoritative source of information. The book was published and is available only at http://anmal.narod.ru/kniga/kniga.html.

3. The general was Foma Zhelezov, chief of the department in the security service in charge of developing various kinds of technology, from radios and weapons to listening devices. Lev Kopelev, *Utili moi pechaly* [Soothe My Sorrows] (Moscow: Novaya Gazeta, 2011), 234.

4. Editorial, "Ob Odnoy antipatrioticheskoy gruppe teatralnikh critikov" [About one group of unpatriotic theatrical critics], *Pravda*, January 28, 1949, www.ihst.ru/projects/sohist/books/cosmopolit/100.htm.

5. Kopelev, *Utili moi pechaly* [Soothe My Sorrows], 239.

6. Vladimir Fridkin, interview with authors, September 2014.

7. Chester Carlson, an American physicist and inventor, created a dry photocopying technique in 1938 and patented his invention on October 6, 1942. US Patent, US 2297691 A, via Google Patents, www.google.com/patents /US2297691.

8. Joseph Stalin, "Pechat kak Kollektivny Organizator" [The Press as Collective Organizer], *Pravda*, May 6, 1923.

9. Yevgenia Albats, *The State Within a State: The KGB and Its Hold on Russia—Past, Present, and Future* (New York: Farrar Straus & Giroux, 1994), 234. A photocopy of the document is in the Russian edition of the book, *Mina zamedlennogo deistvia. Politichesky portret KGB* (Moscow, 1992), 314.

10. Rimantas Pleikis, "Radiocenzura" [Radio Censorship], Agentura.ru, 2003, www.agentura.ru/equipment/radiocenzura.

11. Maria Orlova (Kopelev's daughter), interview with authors, October 2014.

12. Yuri Andropov, "Ob Ispolzovanii evreiskimi natcionalistami mezjnudarod-nogo telephonnogo kanala svyazi" [About the Use of International Phone Calls by Jewish Nationalists], order No. 1428-A, June 1975, quoted in *Evreiskaya emigratsia v svete novikh documentov*, ed. B. Morozov, 41–44 (Tel Aviv: The Cummings Center for Russian and Eastern European Studies, Tel Aviv University, 1998).

13. Ibid., 41–44.

14. Ibid.

15. Alexander Paritsky, communications with authors, October 2014.

16. Gennady Kudryavtsev, interview with authors, October 2014.

17. In 1989 Kudryavtsev finally found a way to bypass the restrictions. Denis Thatcher, the husband of British prime minister Margaret Thatcher, was a counsel to Cable & Wireless, the British telecom company. Kudryavtsev suggested to him that they launch a joint project in Moscow to establish dozens of phone boxes for automatic international connection in hotels and airports. The project was given a green light, and once again automatic international calls were possible from Moscow, at least in a very limited way. But the hour was late; these were the final years before the Soviet collapse.

18. Edward Fredkin, interview with authors, October 2014.

19. Yevgeny Velikhov, interview with authors, September to November 2014.

CHAPTER 2: THE FIRST CONNECTION

1. For details of the history of Kurchatov Institute see "Kurchatov Institute: Current Life of the Institute Celebrating Jubilees," www.iter.org/doc/www /content/com/Lists/Stories/Attachments/1575/Kurchatov_Institute.pdf.

2. Velikhov, interview with authors, September 2014.

3. Alexander Solzhenitsyn, *The Oak and the Calf: Memoirs of a Literary Life* (New York: Harper & Row, 1980), 142.

4. At the same time, Alexandrov hid a fact about his past that could have called into question his loyalty: when he was sixteen years old, he joined the White Army and fought the Communists during the Russian Civil War. Anatoly P.

Alexandrov, *Akademik Anatoly Petrovich Alexandrov: Pryamaya Rech* [*Academician Anatoly Alexandrov: Direct Speech*] (Moscow: Nauka, 2002), 15.

5. Bardin, interview with authors, August 2014; and recollections of Demos employees published at http://news.demos.su/private/demos.html.

6. Alexey Soldatov and Valery Bardin, interviews with authors, August–October 2014.

7. The programmers from Kurchatov Institute worked in conjuction with colleagues at the Ministry of Car Manufacturing.

8. Soldatov and Velikhov, interviews with authors, September 2014.

9. Bardin, interview with authors, August 2014.

10. The headquarters of the Twelfth Department on Varsonofyevsky Lane was first described in Boris Gulko, Yuri Felshtinsky, Vladimir Popov, and Viktor Kortschnoi, "The KGB Plays Chess: The Soviet Secret Police and the Fight for the World Chess Crown," Russell Enterprises, 2010.

11. Andrei Bykov (deputy director of the FSB from 1992 to 1998), interview with authors, September 2014.

12. Kalgin's activities are described in a report of the KGB internal comission investigating the events of August 1991 under director Vadim Bakatin. The report, made public in 2000, is available at http://shieldandsword.mozohin.ru /documents/solution.htm. A photocopy of the report of one of the women, Tatyana Lanina, was published by Yevgenia Albats in the Russian version of her book, *Mina zamedlennogo deistvia. Politichesky portret KGB* (Moscow, 1992), later published in English as *The State Within a State: The KGB and Its Hold on Russia—Past, Present, and Future* (New York: Farrar Straus & Giroux, 1994).

13. The account is based on the book written by Urushadze Georgy, "Izbrannie mesta iz perepiski s vragami" [Selected Passages from Correspondence with Enemies] (St. Petersburg: European House, 1995), 348–349. After the putsch Urushadze was given access to the documentation of the internal investigation of the KGB and put copies of employees' reports of the Twelfth Department in the book.

14. T. A. Lapina, E. B. Kuznetsova, E. V. Timofeeva, and E. A. Volodchenko reported personally to Kalgin and the head of the controllers. Then, at Kalgin's orders, they put the information of interest in the reports to be delivered to Kryuchkov. See *Novaya Gazeta*, August 6, 2001, http://2001.novayagazeta.ru /nomer/2001/55n/n55n-s14.shtml.

15. Larry Press, professor of computer information systems at California State University, has posted these messages on a website at the California State University, Dominguez Hills. See som.csudh.edu.

16. Larry Press, interview with authors, October 2014.

17. Vladimir Bulgak, interview with authors, August, 2014.

18. The account is based on the authors' copy of the indictment of the general prosecutor of the Russian Federation No. 18/6214–01 (the case of the attempt of the coup d'état), 158.

19. Gennady Kudryavtsev, who had fought so hard to expand the international phone lines into the Soviet Union in 1980, was named communications minister of the Soviet Union in March 1991 by Gorbachev. He was flying to Belgrade on August 19 when the coup attempt began. On his plane a crew commander told Kudryavtsev about the putsch. But he ordered the pilot not to change course. Kudryavtsev apparently decided it was not his fight—he was obviously not Yeltsin's man, as he was a Gorbachev appointee, and the Union's ministers were of higher status than members of the republican Russian government. Nor did Kudryavtsev want to support the putsch led by the KGB. As Moscow was gripped in uncertainty, Kudryavtsev remained far away in Belgrade. Kudryavtsev, *Nepridumannaya Zhizn* [Not Invented Life] (Moscow: self-published, 2009).

20. Kalgin's testimony before the internal investigation conducted by the KGB, published in: Urushadze Georgy "Izbrannie mesta iz perepiski s vragami" [Selected Passages from Correspondence with Enemies] (St. Petersburg: European House, 1995), 347.

CHAPTER 3: MERLIN'S TOWER

1. Vladimir Bulgak, interview with authors, September 2014.

2. Bulgak, interview with authors, September 2014.

3. When Bulgak presented the same question to his predecessor, Kudryavtsev, he got a truthful response. Technically it could have been done, Kudryavtsev told Bulgak. The real obstacle was not money or technology but rather pressure from the KGB.

4. Larry Press, interview with authors, November 2014.

5. Anatoly Levenchuk, interviews and communications with authors, August and September 2014.

6. Mikhail Elistratov, interviews with authors, October 2014.

7. Joint order of the MGB, MVD, SVR, GUO No. N165/211/29/81, "On Approval and Enactment of the Temporary Instruction on the Organization and Tactics of Operational and Technical Measures," June 22, 1992; also, Order of the Communications Ministry No. 226, "On the Use of Means of Communication for Search Operations of the Ministry of Security of the Russian Federation," June 24, 1994.

8. Andrei Soldatov and Irina Borogan, *The New Nobility: The Restoration of the Russian Security State and the Enduring Legacy of the KGB* (New York: PublicAffairs, 2010).

9. The prosecutor's jurisdiction was limited by a stipulation in a February 1995 law, "On Organs of the Federal Security Service in the Russian Federation," Article 24: "Information regarding people who provide or have provided FSB organs with confidential assistance regarding the organization, tactics, methods, and means of implementing the activity of FSB organs shall not be subject to oversight by the prosecutor's office."

10. The statement of the State Duma on the publication of Sergei Parkhomenko, April 8, 1995, www.bestpravo.ru/rossijskoje/lj-akty/f9r.htm.

11. Sergei Parkhomenko, interview with authors, November 2014.

12. Mikhail Shevelev (chief of the political department at the time), interview with authors, October 2014.

13. Ibid.

14. Sergei Parkhomenko, "Bashnya Merlina" [Merlin's Tower], *Moscow News*, April 25, May 3, 1995.

15. Based on authors' conversation with an officer who was put in charge of "supervising" *Segodnya*.

CHAPTER 4: THE BLACK BOX

1. Vika Egorova, interview with authors, August 2014.

2. Anatoly Levenchuk, interview with authors, August 2014.

3. The document, in Russian, can be found at www.libertarium.ru/l_sorm _sormprojo.

4. Anatoly Levenchuk, interview with authors, August 2014.

5. Only one company resisted, in the southern city of Volgograd. The chief executive, Nail Murzakhanov, came under intense pressure. Eventually he left Volgograd and moved to St. Petersburg.

6. Gusev, communications with authors, August 8, 2014.

7. Decree No. 252, Ministry of Communications, the Russian Federation, signed by Vladimir Bulgak, minister of communications.

8. Boris Goldstein, interview with Borogan, September 2014.

9. Sergei Mishenkov, interview with Soldatov, August 2014.

10. We found several articles online by Vitaly Vekhov about SORM in journals close to the secret services, *Zashita informatsii Inside* [Protection of Information, Inside] and *Operativno-Rosysknoe Pravo* [Operation-Research Law: The Volume of the Volgograd Academy of the Interior Ministry]. Vekhov is a criminologist from Volgograd with a long and successful career in Russian law enforcement agencies, ending at the central apparatus of the Investigative Committee of Russia in Moscow. In all his work he repeats that "the formal emergence of SORM took place in the mid 1980s when one of the KGB's Research Institutes finalized

its tactical and technical guidelines." When we contacted Vekhov, he replied to an e-mail, confirming that development of SORM started in the 1980s. When we asked what particular KGB research facility he meant, he replied simply, "Kuchino NII of the KGB."

11. In August 1955 the chairman of the KGB, Ivan Serov, turned the Kuchino laboratory into the Central Scientific-Research Institute of Special Equipment, or, by its Russian acronym, TsNIIST.

12. KGB agents posing as laborers bugged the US Embassy in Moscow during its construction in the 1970s. When discovered in the early 1980s, it was found that even the concrete columns were riddled with bugs, and the eight-story, cubic monolith became known as an "Eight-Story Microphone." The building was abandoned and the case seemed to have no solution until 1991 when Vadim Bakatin, the head of the KGB at the time, gave an order to present US Ambassador Robert Strauss with the blueprints for the embassy bugs. In July 2000, after a complete renovation, including a new top to the building, it was finally opened.

13. On May 27, 1995, Valentin Stepankov, the general prosecutor of Russia, issued order No. 21/13/20, which established that permissions to conduct surveillance were to be issued by the general prosecutor and his deputies and main military prosecutor.

14. Based on authors' conversations with former KGB technical officers.

15. Sergei Koval, interview with authors, Speech Technologies Center, June 2009.

16. According to the testimony provided by Kalgin before the internal investigation comission of the KGB in 1991. The testimony was quoted by Andrei Uglanov, "Na Lybyanke posle putsha" [On Lubyanka After the Putsch], *Argumenti Nedeli*, Moscow, August 17, 2011.

17. Urushadze Georgy, *Izbrannie mesta iz perepiski s vragami* [Selected Passages from Correspondence with Enemies] (St. Petersburg: European House, 1995), 349–350. After the putsch Urushadze was given access to the documentation of the internal investigation of the KGB and put copies of employees' reports of the Twelfth Department in his book.

18. Kalgin's testimony before the internal investigation commission of the KGB on the events of August 1991, quoted by Andrei Uglanov, "Na Lybyanke posle putsha" [On Lubyanka After the Putsch], *Argumenti Nedeli*, Moscow, August 17, 2011.

19. The description of Stasi's wiretapping system is based on information provided by Detlev Vreisleben, an informal historian of Stasi surveillance equipment who works in Stasi archives, for our website Agentura.ru, www.agentura.ru/museum/melton/stasitapping.

CHAPTER 5: THE COMING OF PUTIN

1. On September 9, 1999, shortly after midnight, between six and eight hundred pounds of explosives detonated on the ground floor of an apartment building on Guryanova Street in southeast Moscow. The nine-story building was destroyed, killing 94 people and injuring 249. On September 13 a large bomb exploded at 5 a.m. in the basement of an apartment block on Kashirskoye Highway in southern Moscow: 118 people died, and 200 injured.

2. Boris Yeltsin, *Midnight Diaries* (New York: PublicAffairs, 2000), 289–298.

3. Elena Tregubova, *Baiki kremlevskogo diggera* [Tales of a Kremlin Digger] (Moscow: Ad Marginem, 2003), 197.

4. On the loan, the bank refused to accept the domestic currency bonds, known as OVVZs. OVVZ bonds were issued by Vnesheconombank, so the bank in fact refused to accept its own securities. Andrei Zolotov Jr., "Media Say Aides Keep Yeltsin in Dark," *Moscow Times*, July 29, 1999, www.themoscowtimes.com /sitemap/free/1999/7/article/media-say-aides-keep-yeltsin-in-dark/274376.html.

5. Tregubova, *Baiki kremlevskogo diggera*, 196–197.

6. Sergei Parkhomenko, interview with authors, November 2014.

7. NTV, "Geroi Dnya" [Hero of the Day], interview with Vladimir Putin, August 9, 1999, http://tvoygolos.forum-tvs.ru/elita/elitatext/1999.08.09.htm.

8. Nataliya Gevorkyan, Natalya Timakova, and Andrei Kolesnikov, *First Person: An Astonishingly Frank Self-Portrait by Russia's President* (New York: PublicAffairs, 2000), 83.

9. Mikhail Shevelev, interview with authors, November 2014.

10. Tregubova, *Baiki kremlevskogo diggera*, 163–166.

11. Gevorkyan, Timakova, and Kolesnikov, *First Person*.

12. Putin visited Finland October 22–23, 1999. For details, see NTV reportage, 1999, www.youtube.com/watch?v=PYMng6H7WCo.

13. Alexander Chudodeev, "Inakomislyashchy" [Dissident], an interview with Pavlovsky, *Itogi*, December 12, 2012, www.itogi.ru/spetzproekt/2012/49/184673 .html.

14. Gleb Pavlovsky, interview with authors, October 2014.

15. Tregubova, *Baiki kremlevskogo diggera*, 216.

16. Putin's statement at the FSB headquarters, December 20, 1999, YouTube (in Russian, with English subtitles), www.youtube.com/watch?v=Qb63vKtCvRo.

17. Oleg Rykov, interview with authors, August 2014.

18. The nongovernmental organization was the Russian Institute of Public Networks (ROSNIIROS).

19. Alexey Platonov, interview with authors, September 2014.

20. Alexey Soldatov, interview with authors, July–September 2014.

21. The text of the draft is available on the site of libertarium.ru, www
.libertarium.ru/gvt-names.

22. Anton Nossik, interview with authors, August 2014.

23. Platonov, interview with authors, September 2014.

24. See Anton Nossik's LiveJournal.com entry, http://dolboeb.livejournal.com
/2682401.html.

CHAPTER 6: INTERNET RISING

1. Dmitry Pavlov, "Vzyali Vladimira Gusinskogo" [Gusinsky is Caught],
Kommersant, June 13, 2000, www.kommersant.ru/doc/17059.

2. Shenderovich, interview with authors, December 2014. See also Victor
Shenderovich, *Zdes bylo NTV* [*Here Was NTV*] (Moscow: Zakharov, 2004).

3. Oleg Lurie was a good example of such journalism. He became famous in
1999 by exposing corruption in the Kremlin's renovations. In the early 2000s his
"investigations" were published by *Versiya* and *Novaya Gazeta*, and he liked to drive
a shining new BMW 7. In 2008 he was convicted and imprisoned for extortion;
he had requested $50,000 from a senator in exchange for removing kompromat
about him from the Internet. He was released in 2011 and immediately launched
the journal *Jins* (slang, a paid journalistic story).

4. Andrei Soldatov, Kremlin.com, Index on Censorship, no. 1, 2010, http://
ioc.sagepub.com/content/39/1/71.abstract.

5. Agentura.ru was inspired by the Federation of American Scientists Secrecy
Project led by Steven Aftergood and was supported by the Relcom ISP from
September 2000 to the spring of 2006.

6. A group of FSB officers arrived at the editorial offices of *Versiya* claiming
they were looking for information published in an article by Soldatov in May
2002 about the construction of residential apartment complexes on the premises
of former FSB special facilities in Moscow.

7. Andrei Soldatov, Irina Borogan, Marina Latysheva, and Anna Stavitskaya,
Journalisti i terrorism [*Journalists and Terrorism*] (Moscow: Center for Journalism
in Extreme Situations, 2008).

8. ComScore, "Worldwide Search Top 10," December 2007, Total World Age 15+,
Home and Work Locations, January 23, 2008, www.comscore.com/Insights/Press
-Releases/2008/01/Baidu-Ranked-Third-Largest-World-Wide-Search-Engine.

9. Lev Gershenzon, interview with authors, August 2014.

10. Gershenzon was summoned to the meeting with Surkov and Kostin by
Dmitry Ivanov, a projects director of Yandex. Before Yandex, Ivanov had worked

in Pavlovsky's foundation and succeeded Marina Litvinovich as chief of the FEP Internet department, when she was given Strana.ru to run.

11. Steve Gutterman, "Russia's Putin Brings 'Gray Cardinal' Surkov Back to Kremlin," Reuters, September 20, 2013, www.reuters.com/article/2013/09/20/us -russia-surkov-idUSBRE98J0VK20130920.

12. Surkov first used the term "sovereign democracy" on February 22, 2006, in a speech before the Russian political party United Russia. According to Surkov, sovereign democracy is "a society's political life where the political powers, their authorities, and decisions are decided and controlled by a diverse Russian nation for the purpose of reaching material welfare, freedom, and fairness by all citizens, social groups, and nationalities by the people that formed it." See also Masha Lipman, "Putin's 'Sovereign Democracy,'" *Washington Post*, July 15, 2006, www.washington post.com/wp-dyn/content/article/2006/07/14/AR2006071401534.html.

13. Andrei Soldatov and Irina Borogan, "A Face in the Crowd: The FSB Is Watching You!" OpenDemocracy, November 15, 2011, www.opendemocracy .net/od-russia/andrei-soldatov-irina-borogan/face-in-crowd-fsb-is-watching-you.

14. In spring 2007 Estonia had angered the Kremlin with its decision to move a Soviet war memorial out of the center of the capital. After a massive nationalistic campaign against Estonia in the Russian press, on April 27 Russian hackers launched a series of cyber attacks on the websites of the Estonian government, parliament, banks, ministries, newspapers, and broadcasters. Most of the attacks were the distributed-denial-of-service type. Estonian foreign minister Urmas Paet accused the Kremlin of direct involvement, and Estonia requested and received NATO assistance in responding to this new form of aggression. But Estonia failed to present proof of the Russian government's involvement, and in September 2007 the country's defense minister admitted he had no evidence linking cyber attacks to the Russian authorities. Two years later, in May 2009, Konstantin Goloskokov, one of the "commissars" of the pro-Kremlin Nashi movement, admitted to the *Financial Times* that he and some of his associates had launched the DDOS attacks on Estonia in 2007. See Charles Clover, "Kremlin-Backed Group Behind Estonia Cyber Blitz," *Financial Times*, March 11, 2009, www.ft.com/cms/s/0/575 36d5a-0ddc-11de-8ea3–0000779fd2ac.html#axzz3QDihM3bC. In September 2013, *Novaya Gazeta* journalists infiltrated the "trolls factory" and published the investigation. The "factory" was based in a mansion near the rail station Olgino, outside of St. Petersburg, and was led by Alexey Soskovets, once involved in Nashi and Molodaya Gvardiya. See also Alexandra Garmazhalova, "Gde zhivut trolli. I kto ih kormit" [Where the Trolls Live. And Who Feeds Them], *Novaya Gazeta*, September 9, 2013, www.novayagazeta.ru/politics/59889.html.

15. Nathan Hodge, "Kremlin Launches 'School of Bloggers,'" Wired.com, May 27, 2009.

16. These two cable operators were Akado and Stream, owned by Victor Vekselberg and Vladimir Evtushenkov, respectively.

17. Mikhail Zygar, interview with authors, August 2014.

18. Julia Ioffe, "Net Impact," *New Yorker*, April 4, 2011, www.newyorker.com /magazine/2011/04/04/net-impact.

19. Navalny blog, "Kak pilyat v Transnefti" [How They Are Sawing at Transneft], November 16, 2010, http://navalny.livejournal.com/526563.html.

20. "Pravila zhisni, Alexey Navalny" [Rules of Life, Alexey Navalny], *Esquire*, December 2011, http://esquire.ru/wil/alexey-navalny.

21. Kremlin.ru, transcripts, Speech at Meeting with Russian and Singaporean Business Communities, November 16, 2009, http://eng.kremlin.ru/transcripts /10449.

22. "Pravila zhisni."

CHAPTER 7: REVOLT OF THE WIRED

1. Transcript of the meeting of the National Antiterrorism Committee, February 22, 2011, http://eng.kremlin.ru/transcripts/1804.

2. Video of Putin's remarks in Votkinsk, YouTube, www.youtube.com/watch ?v=Tr-jIPUZPOk. Also see "Russia's Putin Sees No 'Logic or Conscience' in US Air Strikes on Libya," *Interfax*, March 21, 2001, and "Putin Likens UN Libya Resolution to Crusade Call," *RIA Novosti*, March 21, 2011.

3. Josh Halliday, "Hillary Clinton Adviser Compares Internet to Che Guevara," *Guardian*, June 22, 2011, www.theguardian.com/media/2011/jun/22/hillary-clinton -adviser-alec-ross.

4. Andrei Soldatov and Irina Borogan, "The Russian State and Surveillance Technology," *OpenDemocracy*, October 25, 2011, www.opendemocracy.net/od-russia /andrei-soldatov-irina-borogan/russian-state-and-surveillance-technology.

5. Yuri Sinodov, interview with authors, April 2011.

6. On June 2, 2010, the service invited tenders for contract No.147/I/1–133, worth up to 450,000 rubles, for the procurement of software. The contract called for an information-analysis system called "Semantic Archive," produced by the company Analytic Business Solutions.

7. Denis Shatrov, interview with authors, September 2011.

8. Natalia Sindeeva, interview with authors, August 2014.

9. Medvedev's appearance on TV Dozhd, YouTube, www.youtube.com/watch ?v=SwmvvjyhXmY.

10. Mikhail Zygar, interview with authors, August 2014.

11. Komsomolskaya Pravda radio broadcast, August 1, 2011.

12. Zygar, interview with authors, August 2014.

13. Alexander Podrabinek, "Boris Nemtsov on the Rokirovka in the Tandem: It's the Worst Scenario for Russia," RFI, September 24, 2011, http://ru.rfi.fr/rossiya /20110924-boris-nemtsov-o-rokirovke-v-rossiiskom-vlastnom-tandeme-eto -khudshii-stsenarii-dlya.

14. Nemtsov visited the United States on September 15–16, 2011, to take part in a panel at the Harriman Institute on the Russian elections. The video is available at YouTube, www.youtube.com/watch?v=ZemHhZcpKsQ.

15. Grigory Melkonyants, interview with authors, June 2013.

16. Ilya Azar, "Karusel slomalas" [Carousel Is Broken], Lenta.ru, December 4, 2011.

17. Lev Gershenzon, interview with authors, January 2015.

18. Grigory Okhotin, interview with authors, June 2014.

19. Ilya Klishin, interview with authors, October 2014.

20. This account is based on authors' interview with Parkhomenko, Klishin, and Saprykin, January 2015.

21. Stanislav Sedov, interview with authors, July 2012. See also Andrei Soldatov and Irina Borogan, "Big Brother, Little Drones—Protestors Beware," Open Democracy, July 23, 2012, www.opendemocracy.net/od-russia/andrei-soldatov-irina -borogan/big-brother-little-drones-protestors-beware.

CHAPTER 8: PUTIN STRIKES BACK

1. Nossik's post, https://dolboeb.livejournal.com/2242130.html.

2. Andrei Soldatov and Irina Borogan, "The Kremlin and the Hackers: Partners in Crime?" OpenDemocracy, April 25, 2012, www.opendemocracy.net/od -russia/irina-borogan-andrei-soldatov/kremlin-and-hackers-partners-in-crime.

3. Vadim Petrov (technical manager of Slon.ru), interview with authors, April 2012.

4. According to a report by Highload Lab company, the owners of Qrator service, posted on the site of Habrahabr, the community of geeks in Russia, http://habrahabr.ru/company/highloadlab/blog/134124.

5. For more details, see Andrei Soldatov and Irina Borogan, *The New Nobility: The Restoration of Russia's Security State and the Enduring Legacy of the KGB*, ch. 18, "Hackers" (New York: PublicAffairs, 2010).

6. "Kremlin-Backed Group Behind Estonia Cyber Blitz," *Financial Times*, March 11, 2009, www.ft.com/cms/s/0/57536d5a-0ddc-11de-8ea3-0000779fd2ac .html#axzz3QDihM3bC.

7. Eugene Kaspersky personal blog, "Vibori, vibori—ddosyat-3" [Elections, Elections, Sites Are Under DDOS-3], December 16, 2011, https://eugene.kaspersky .ru/2011/12/16/vybory-vybory-3/.

8. The transcript is available on Kot's blog, https://edvvvard.livejournal.com/56342.html.

9. Boris Nemtsov, interview with authors, February 2012. Also see Andrei Soldatov and Irina Borogan, "Who's Bugging the Russian Opposition?" OpenDemocracy, February 24, 2012, www.opendemocracy.net/od-russia/andrei-soldatov-irina-borogan/project-id-who's-bugging-russian-opposition.

10. The transcript was published in *Rossiyskaya Gazeta*, December 15, 2012, www.rg.ru/printable/2011/12/15/stenogramma.html.

11. Olga Romanova, interview with authors, March 2013. Alexey Kozlov was finally released in June 2013.

12. Grigory Okhotin, interview with authors, June 2014.

13. The impressive video setup was thanks to the efforts of Yuri Saprykin, editor of Afisha.ru, which had experience in organizing music festivals. Saprykin helped find the equipment for sound and video. Yuri Saprykin, interview with authors, February 2015.

14. Ilya Klishin, interview with authors, October 2014.

15. The Masterskaya club is owned by a prominent family, Paperny, famous among the Moscow liberal intelligentsia.

16. "FSB obeshaet ochistit Runet ot vozdeistvia zapadnikh spetszluzhb" [FSB Promises Clean Runet of Foreign Intelligence Services], *Vedomosti*, March 27, 2012, www.vedomosti.ru/technology/news/2012/03/27/fsb_obeschaet_ochistit_runet_ot_vozdejstviya_zarubezhnyh.

17. The new system of filtering was modeled on the one used to block extremist and terrorist bank accounts in Russia. Three government agencies—Roskomnadzor (the Agency for the Supervision of Information Technology, Communications and Mass Media), the Federal Anti-Drug Agency, and the Federal Service for the Supervision of Consumer Rights and Public Welfare—submit data for the government's blacklist of sites. Roskomnadzor is in charge of compiling and updating the register and is also responsible for instructing host providers to remove the URLs. If no action by the host provider follows, the ISPs are required to block access to the site within twenty-four hours. The host providers must also ensure they are not in breach of current law by checking their content against the database of outlawed sites and URLs published in a special password-protected online version of the register open only to web hosters and ISPs. Since November 2012 thousands of websites have been banned from the Russian Internet; the Internet monitoring law has had some substantial offline consequences as well. Institutions providing public access to the Internet—schools, libraries, Internet cafés, and even post offices—have been targeted for law enforcement inspections to check for computers containing software that might allow access to banned websites.

18. Irina Levova and Mikhail Yakushev (a vice president of ICANN for Russia, present at the meeting), interviews with authors, July–October 2014.

19. Ilya Ponomarev, interview with authors, September 2012. See also Agentura.ru, September 26, 2012, http://agentura.ru/projects/identification /iponomarev.

20. Andrei Soldatov and Irina Borogan, "The Kremlin's New Internet Surveillance Plan Goes Live Today," Wired.com, November 1, 2012, www.wired .com/2012/11/russia-surveillance.

21. The video was considered insulting to Muslims and includes cartoonish scenes depicting the prophet as a buffoon, a womanizer, and a greedy thug, among other things.

22. YouTube was made inaccessible in Chechnya, Dagestan, Kabardino-Balkaria, Ingushetia, Karachay-Cherkessia, North Ossetia, and the Stavropol Region.

23. For details, see Soldatov and Borogan, "The Kremlin's New Internet Surveillance Plan Goes Live Today." The mobile operators in Russia came up with the idea of traffic "shaping," a euphemism that means by using DPI technology, they could, if they wished, suppress particular services—in most cases torrents, peer-to-peer protocols, and Skype, which poses a threat to the voice-over Internet protocol services offered by the mobile operators themselves.

24. See details of the meeting in our investigation: Soldatov and Borogan, "The Kremlin's New Internet Surveillance Plan Goes Live Today."

25. Volkov and Saprykin had come to see Zygar at noon, and by 3:00 p.m., Zygar secured approval from Sindeeva, and by 11:00 p.m. of the same day, Zygar, Volkov, and Saprykin sat at the café on Nikitskaya Street to talk over the technicalities. They also invited Demian Kudryavtsev, a former CEO of Kommersant publishing house; Zygar intended to ask him to cohost the debate along with Saprykin. Kudryavtsev eagerly supported the idea.

26. Yuri Saprykin, "O teledebatakh na Dozhde" [On the TV Debates at Dozhd], *Afisha*, October 17, 2012, http://gorod.afisha.ru/archive/sluchai-saprykin -teledebaty.

CHAPTER 9: "WE JUST COME UP WITH THE HARDWARE"

1. Alexander Abashin, interview with Borogan, November 2011.

2. Konstantin Kalachev, *V kruge tretiem* [In the Third Circle]. Kalachev worked as a researcher at Marfino from 1947 to 1996, and in 1999 he wrote a history of the Marfino project. The book never made it into print and is available only on the site: http://anmal.narod.ru/kniga/kniga.html.

3. Lev Kopelev, *Utili moi pechaly* [Soothe My Sorrows] (Moscow: Novaya Gazeta, 2011).

4. In the uncensored edition of *The First Circle*, Solzhenitsyn carefully changed all the names except for the betrayed Soviet spy Koval; apparently he thought it was not a real name. As it turned out, he was wrong.

5. In June 1997 Kopelev died in Cologne. A few months before, in January 1997, in Moscow, Solzhenitsyn went back to Marfino—as a visitor. The visit needed weeks of negotiations, as it remains a highly secret facility, manned by what was then called FAPSI, the Russian electronic intelligence agency. On January 16, 1997, the gates opened to let in Solzhenitsyn's cherry-red Volvo. Solzhenitsyn was full of memories. "I never thought I could visit this place again. I walked and couldn't stop, in some rooms—incredibly!—everything is as it was then." Eventually he was shown into the large room where over five hundred employees gathered. In 1997 Marfino suffered three months' delay in payment of salaries, and the employees asked Solzhenitsyn anxiously, "What should we do? Does our country need us?" They called him a colleague. The only media report from the meeting said, "They felt in today's Solzhenitsyn an accomplice and applauded." Vladimir Umnov, "Solzhenitsyn snova v sharashke" [Solzhenitsyn Is Again in Sharashka], *Ogonyok*, January 27, 1997, www.ogoniok.com/archive /1997/4487/04–20–21.

6. Gunnar Fant, *Acoustic Theory of Speech Production* (The Hague, Netherlands: Mouton and Co, N.V. Publishers), 1960.

7. Gunnar Fant, *Akusticheskaya teoria recheobrazovania* [Acoustic Theory of Speech Production] (Moscow: Nauka, 1964).

8. Fant's autobiography on the site of the Department of Speech, Music and Hearing of KTH Royal Institute of Technology in Stockholm, founded by Fant. Gunnar Fant, "Half a Century in Phonetics and Speech Research," www.speech.kth .se/gunnarfant/halfcentury.pdf.

9. Sergei Koval, interview with authors, January 2012.

10. Vladimir Chuchupal, interview with authors, September 2014.

11. Loren Graham, conversations with authors, September 2013.

12. Anatoly Levenchuk, interview with authors, August 2014.

13. Ibid.

14. "Chuzadas no fueron hechas por el DAS: Felipe Muñoz" [Wiretappings Were Not Made by the DAS: Felipe Muñoz], *Vanguardia*, September 22, 2009, www.vanguardia.com/historico/40371-chuzadas-no-fueron-hechas-por-el-das -felipe-munoz.

15. For details, see Camilla Pease-Watkin, "DAS Scandal 'Worse than Watergate,'" *Colombia Reports*, June 18, 2010, http://colombiareports.co/us -report-das-scandal-worse-than-watergate, and the text of the report, "Far Worse than Watergate Widening Scandal Regarding Colombia's Intelligence Agency," prepared by the Latin America Working Group Education Fund, US Office on Colombia, Center for International Policy and Washington Office on Latin

America, www.lawg.org/storage/colombia/farworsethanwatergatefinalfinal.pdf, and Joshua Goodman, "Ex-Spy Chief Wanted in Colombia for Wiretaps Surrenders," Associated Press, January 31, 2015, http://abcnews.go.com/Inter national/wireStory/spy-chief-wanted-colombia-wiretaps-surrenders-28625517.

16. "Chuzadas no fueron hechas por el DAS: Felipe Muñoz" [Wiretappings Were Not Made by the DAS: Felipe Muñoz]. See also SpeechPro's press release, "STC Expert Helped Justifying Colombian Security Department," October 6, 2009, http://speechpro.com/media/news/2009–10–06.

17. Chris Kraul, "Colombia Spy Chief Works to Clean Up Agency," *Los Angeles Times*, April 22, 2010, http://articles.latimes.com/2010/apr/22/world/la -fg-colombia-das-qa-20100423.

18. William Romero, a former senior official of Colombia's DAS security service, told radio stations that he received orders from then DAS director Maria del Pilar Hurtado—who went into exile in Panama in the summer of 2014—to spy on Supreme Court justices. He also said that the main intended recipient of transcripts of the intercepted communication was ex-President Álvaro Uribe. For details, see EFE, "Uribe Ordered Illegal Wiretaps, Former Colombian Spy Says," *Latin American Herald Tribune*, August 1, 2014, www.laht.com/article.asp ?ArticleId=381815&CategoryId=12393.

19. "WikiLeaks: The Spy Files," www.wikileaks.org/the-spyfiles.html.

20. Vadim Sekeresh, interview with authors, December 2011.

CHAPTER 10: THE SNOWDEN AFFAIR

1. "Glava Roskomnadzora na peredache Hard day's night" [Head of Roskomnadzor at the Broadcast of Hard Day's Night], TV Dozhd, November 20, 2012, http://tvrain.ru/articles/glava_roskomnadzora_ob_obyskah_u_malofe eva_ekspertah_po_detskoj_pornografii_i_chernyh_spiskah_interneta-333188.

2. YouTube was blocked in the mostly Muslim republics of Chechnya, Dagestan, Kabardino-Balkaria, Ingushetia, Karachay-Cherkessia, North Ossetia, and the Stavropol Region.

3. The account is based on Alexey Afanasyev, interviews with authors, September and October 2014.

4. Konstantin Poleskov, "Eto bylo nechto!" [It Was Something!], *Novaya Gazeta*, April 8, 2013, www.novayagazeta.ru/society/57539.html.

5. Ilya Azar, "I Don't Appeal to Build a Dictatorship," interview with Kaspersky, Lenta.ru, October 1, 2013.

6. Andrei Soldatov, "What Russia Censored in March," Index on Censorship, April 30, 2013, http://uncut.indexoncensorship.org/2013/04/what-russia-censored -in-march.

7. "Administratsia Twittera aktivno vkluchilas v sotrudnichestvo s Reestrom zapreshennoi k rasprostaneniyu v Rossii informatcii" [Administration of Twitter Actively Involved in Cooperation with the Register of Information Forbidden to Disseminate in Russia], Roskomnadzor statement, March 19, 2013, http://06.rkn.gov.ru/news/news48104.htm.

8. Andrew E. Kramer, "Russians Selectively Blocking Internet," *New York Times*, March 31, 2013, www.nytimes.com/2013/04/01/technology/russia-begins-selectively-blocking-internet-content.html.

9. M. Ksenzov remarks, enlarged meeting of the board of Roskomnadzor, May 14, 2013, http://rkn.gov.ru/press/developments/speech/news19962.htm.

10. A. A. Zharov remarks, enlarged meeting of the board of Roskomnadzor, May 14, 2013, http://rkn.gov.ru/press/developments/speech/news19962.htm.

11. Jeffrey Peterson, "Safe Internet League Established in Russia," *EWDN*, February 11, 2011, www.ewdn.com/2011/02/15/safe-internet-league-established-in-russia.

12. "LBI: Russkoyazichny segment interneta stanovitsa chishe" [The Safe Internet League: The Russian Segment of the Internet Is Getting Cleaner], Refnews.ru, March 2, 2015, www.refnews.ru/read/article/1061481.

13. The official site of the project is http://mediagvardia.ru.

14. Statement by Edward Snowden to human rights groups at Moscow's Sheremetyevo airport, WikiLeaks, July 12, 2013, https://wikileaks.org/Statement-by-Edward-Snowden-to.html.

15. Transcript of the press conference of Vladimir Putin with president of Finland Sauli Niinistö, June 25, 2013, http://eng.kremlin.ru/transcripts/5646.

16. News conference following the working meeting of the Gas Exporting Countries Forum (GECF) summit, the transcript on the site of the Kremlin, July 1, 2013, http://eng.kremlin.ru/transcripts/5666.

17. Andrew E. Kramer, "Rights Group Says Its Researcher in Moscow Is Threatened," *New York Times*, October 4, 2012, www.nytimes.com/2012/10/05/world/europe/human-rights-watch-says-its-moscow-researcher-threatened.html.

18. The account below is based on Tanya Lokshina, interview with authors, August 2014.

19. The e-mail was provided to authors by Lokshina.

20. Sergei Nikitin, interview with authors, August 2014.

21. Andrew Roth and David M. Herszenhorn, "Russian Authorities Raid Amnesty International Office," *New York Times*, March 25, 2012, www.nytimes.com/2013/03/26/world/europe/russian-authorities-raid-amnesty-international-office.html?_r=0.

22. On May 12, 2007, the FSB's Public Relations Center announced that the agency had created a "Public Council" to be geared toward "developing cooperation between security agencies and academic organizations and Russian

citizens in providing national security, protecting the rights and freedoms of Russian citizens as well as the constitutional order." Nikolai Patrushev, then FSB director, said the task of the council is to provide cooperation between the FSB and NGOs as well as Russian citizens. In reality the Public Council has no power and was intended to be a purely consultative body. Apparently the main task of the Public Council is to improve the image of the FSB, as was confirmed to Andrei Soldatov by Andrei Przhedomsky, a member of the Council. For details, see "Public Council at the FSB Established," Agentura.ru, www.agentura.ru/english/timeline/2007/publiccouncil.

23. Ekaterina Grigorieva, "Rossia profinansiruet evropeiskuyu demorkatiyu" [Russia Will Fund the European Democracy], *Izvestia*, October 29, 2007, http://izvestia.ru/news/330162. For details in English, see Nikola Krastev, "In the Heart of New York, Russia's 'Soft Power' Arm Gaining Momentum," Radio Free Europe /Radio Liberty, February 14, 2015, www.rferl.org/content/In_The_Heart_Of _New_York_Russias_Soft_Power_Arm_Gaining_Momentum/1493429.html.

24. Miriam Elder, "Russia Needs to Reclaim Its 'Digital Sovereignty' from US, says MP," *Guardian*, June 19, 2013, www.theguardian.com/world/2013/jun /19/russia-digital-soveriegnty-nsa-surveillance.

25. Interview to Channel One and Associated Press news agency, the transcript on the site of the Kremlin, September 4, 2013, http://eng.kremlin.ru/transcripts /5935.

26. Vladislav Novy, "Spetsluzbi ne vpisalis v traffik" [Secret Services Didn't Make into Traffic], *Kommersant*, October 24, 2013, www.kommersant.ru/doc /2326973.

27. Andrei Soldatov, "Russia's Spying Craze," *Moscow Times*, October 31, 2014, www.themoscowtimes.com/opinion/article/russias-spying-craze/488773.html.

28. The roundtable on SORM at the MSK-IX conference, with Vartan Khachaturov, deputy director of the infrastructure department at the Ministry of Communications and Mass Media of the Russian Federation, present, December 10, 2013, YouTube, www.youtube.com/watch?v=JuqiBGhJBtA.

29. Transcript, "Direct Line with Vladimir Putin," Kremlin, April 17, 2014, http://eng.kremlin.ru/news/7034.

30. Ibid.

31. Edward Snowden, "Vladimir Putin Must Be Called to Account on Surveillance Just Like Obama," *Guardian*, April 18, 2014, www.theguardian.com /commentisfree/2014/apr/18/vladimir-putin-surveillance-us-leaders-snowden.

32. Marina Zhunich, YouTube, July 18, 2012, www.youtube.com/watch?v=76 KrOhZNsEo.

33. Marina Zhunich, conversations with authors, December 2014.

34. Irina Yusbekova, "Google [Has] Begun to Relocate the Servers to Russian Data-Centers," April 10, 2015, RBC Daily.

CHAPTER 11: PUTIN'S OVERSEAS OFFENSIVE

1. "Developments in the Field of Information and Telecommunications in the Context of International Security," introduced by Russia as a draft resolution in the First Committee of the UN General Assembly, A/RES/53/70, January 4, 1999.

2. Vladimir Markomenko, "Nevidimaya Zatyazhnaya voina" [Invisible Protracted War], *Nezevisimaya Gazeta*, August 16, 1997. Markomenko was then the first deputy director of FAPSI.

3. Doctrine of the Information Security of the Russian Federation, Russian Security Council, www.scrf.gov.ru/documents/6/5.html.

4. The diplomat who reported this was US chargé d'affaires Hugh Neighbour, reporting March 16, about a meeting in Vienna. "U.S.-RF Cybersecurity Bilateral on Margins of Osce Cyber Workshop," March 25, 2009, WikiLeaks, https://wikileaks.org/plusd/cables/09USOSCE66_a.html.

5. In 2010 Kaspersky Lab discovered Stuxnet, the US-Israeli worm that wrecked nearly a thousand Iranian centrifuges. Two years later it exposed Flame, which attacked computers running the Microsoft Windows operating system; the program is being used for targeted cyber espionage in the Middle Eastern countries. Based on Kaspersky Lab's investigation, experts and journalists found additional evidence that the United States was behind the development of Stuxnet and Flame. For details, see Kaspersky Lab, "Stuxnet Worm: Insight from Kaspersky Lab," *Virus News*, September 27, 2010, www.kaspersky.com/about/news/virus/2010/Stuxnet _Worm_Insight_from_Kaspersky_Lab. Andrey Krutskikh referred to Stuxnet at the meeting in Garmisch, 2012; see Adrian Croft, "Russia Says Many States Arming for Cyber Warfare," Reuters, April 25, 2012, www.reuters.com/article/2012/04/25 /germany-cyber-idUSL6E8FP40M20120425, and Krutskikh remarks at London Cyber conference on November 11, 2011, the conference Kaspersky also attended: www.rusemb.org.uk/article/112.

6. In January 2011 Krutskikh welcomed Andrey Yarnikh, head of Government Relations at Kaspersky Lab, into the Russian delegation at the intergovernmental group on cyber crime of the UN Office on Drugs and Crime. Open-ended intergovernmental expert group on cybercrime, UNODC, January 21, 2011, www.unodc.org/documents/treaties/organized_crime/EGM_cybercrime_2011 /UNODC_CCPCJ_EG4_2011_INF_2_Rev1.pdf.

7. Eugene Kaspersky blog, "Call for Action: Internet Should Become a Military-Free Zone," November 25, 2011, http://eugene.kaspersky.com/2011/11/25 /internet-military-free-zone.

8. The account is based on authors' interviews with Russian and American participants of the conference who preferred not to be named.

9. John Markoff, "At Internet Conference, Signs of Agreement Appear Between U.S. and Russia," *New York Times*, April 15, 2010, www.nytimes.com/2010/04/16/science/16cyber.html?_r=0.

10. George Sadowsky, interview with authors, January 2015.

11. Markoff, "At Internet Conference."

12. "Prime Minister Vladimir Putin Reaffirms the Russian Federation's Support for ITU," *ITU News*, November 5, 2011, https://itunews.itu.int/En/1444-Prime-Minister-Vladimir-Putin-reaffirms-the-Russian-Federation%C2%92s-support-for-ITU.note.aspx; Jerry Brito, "The Case Against Letting the UN Govern the Internet," *Time*, February 13, 2012, http://techland.time.com/2012/02/13/the-case-against-letting-the-united-nations-govern-the-internet; and Leo Kelion, "US Resists Control of Internet Passing to UN Agency," BBC, August 3, 2012, www.bbc.com/news/technology-19106420.

13. "Prime Minister Vladimir Putin Reaffirms the Russian Federation's Support for ITU."

14. Vinton G. Cerf, "Keep the Internet Open," *New York Times*, May 24, 2012, www.nytimes.com/2012/05/25/opinion/keep-the-internet-open.html?_r=0.

15. Richard Lardner, "A Battle for Internet Freedom as UN Meeting Nears," Associated Press, June 22, 2012, http://bigstory.ap.org/article/battle-internet-freedom-un-meeting-nears-0.

16. The Russian proposal is dated November 17, 2012, wcitleaks.org, http://files.wcitleaks.org/public/S12-WCIT12-C-0027!R1!MSW-E.pdf.

17. Brian Murphy, "Clashes Over Internet Rules to Mark International Conference," Associated Press, December 3, 2012, www.komonews.com/news/tech/Clashes-over-Internet-rules-to-mark-Dubai-meeting-181860811.html.

18. The account is based on authors' interviews with participants of the conference who preferred not to be named.

19. Ambassador Terry Kramer, US Head of Delegation, "Development and Progress of the World Conference on International Telecommunications Currently Being Held in Dubai, United Arab Emirates Until December 14, 2012," Special Briefing, World Conference on International Telecommunications, Via Teleconference, December 6, 2012, www.state.gov/e/eb/rls/rm/2012/201637.htm.

20. The document is available at wcitleaks.org, http://files.wcitleaks.org/public/Merged%20UAE%20081212.pdf.

21. Dave Burstein and Grahame Lynch, "WCIT Bombshell: Russia Withdraws Internet Regulation Push, Apparently Under ITU Pressure," Commsday.com, December 10, 2012, www.commsday.com/commsday-australasia/russia-combines-with-china-arab-states-on-dramatic-internet-regulatory-push.

22. AFP, "Confusion on Internet Future After UN Treaty Split," December 16, 2012, www.securityweek.com/confusion-internet-future-after-un-treaty-split.

23. Eric Pfanner, "U.S. Rejects Telecommunications Treaty," *New York Times*, December 13, 2012, www.nytimes.com/2012/12/14/technology/14iht-treaty14.html ?pagewanted=1&_r=1&.

24. The White House, Office of the Press Secretary, "Fact Sheet: U.S.-Russian Cooperation on Information and Communications Technology Security," June 17, 2013, www.whitehouse.gov/the-press-office/2013/06/17/fact-sheet-us-russian -cooperation-information-and-communications-technol.

25. Ewan MacAskill, "Putin Calls Internet a 'CIA Project' Renewing Fears of Web Breakup," *Guardian*, April 24, 2014, www.theguardian.com/world /2014/apr/24/vladimir-putin-web-breakup-internet-cia.

26. Minkomsvyaz Rossii, "Rabota nad itogovimi documentami NETmundial-2014 neprozrachna" [The Ministry of Communications of Russia: The Work on Resulting Documents of NETmundial 2014 is Nontransparent], April 25, 2014, http://minsvyaz.ru/ru/events/30026.

CHAPTER 12: WATCH YOUR BACK

1. Andrew Mitrovica, "The Troublemaker," *UofTMagazine*, Autumn 2009, www.magazine.utoronto.ca/autumn-2009/profile-of-u-of-t-citizen-lab-founder -professor-ron-deibert.

2. The copy is in authors' possession.

3. UK Office of National Statistics, "Visits to the UK for the London 2012 Olympic Games and Paralympics," April 19, 2013, www.ons.gov.uk/ons/rel/ott /travel-trends/2012/sty-visits-to-the-uk.html.

4. Eli Lake, "Why the FBI Didn't Make Much of Russia's Request to Probe Boston Bomber," *Daily Beast*, April 22, 2013, www.thedailybeast.com/articles/2013 /04/22/why-the-fbi-didn-t-make-much-of-russia-s-request-to-probe-boston -bomber.html.

5. "Kremlin: Russia, US to Step Up Counter-Terrorism Cooperation," Reuters, NBC, April 20, 2013, http://worldnews.nbcnews.com/_news/2013/04 /20/17836295-kremlin-russia-us-to-step-up-counter-terrorism-cooperation.

6. David Wise, "The FBI-Russia Connection," Reuters, May 9, 2013, http:// blogs.reuters.com/great-debate/2013/05/09/the-fbi-russia-connection.

7. "Britain to Provide Security for Sochi Olympics," News24 Online, May 11, 2013, http://news24online.com/britain-to-provide-security-for-sochi-olympics.

8. The Presidential Executive Order No. 686, "On Peculiarities of Applying Enhanced Security Measures During the XXII Winter Olympic Games and the XI Winter Paralympic Games in Sochi in 2014." On January 4, 2014, Putin signed Executive Order "On Amendments to the Order 686," and the amendments allowed the protests during the Games but in a specially designated place—in

the park twelve miles from the city and only after they agreed with the Interior Ministry and the FSB. See Kremlin, http://eng.kremlin.ru/news/6491.

9. Fred Weir, "Russia's Sochi Games: Why You May Want to Leave Your Laptop at Home," *Christian Science Monitor*, October 7, 2013, www.csmonitor.com/World /Europe/2013/1007/Russia-s-Sochi-Games-Why-you-may-want-to-leave-your -laptop-at-home.

10. "Let's Just Put Some Random Words: FSB, Sochi, Spying," *Voice of Russia*, October 9, 2013, http://sputniknews.com/voiceofrussia/2013_10_09/Let -s-just-put-some-random-words-FSB-Sochi-spying-4373.

11. Nikita Sorokin, "Don't Be Scared of Phone Tapping During Sochi-2014, It's for Your Own Safety—Experts," *Voice of Russia*, October 10, 2013, http:// sputniknews.com/voiceofrussia/2013_10_10/Dontt-be-scared-of-phone-tapping -during-Sochi-2014-its-for-your-own-safety-experts-5489.

12. Ibid.

13. The decree No. 1003 "Ob osobennostyakh okazania uslug svyazi i o poryadke vzaimodeistvia operatorov svyazi s upolnomochennimi gosudar-stvennimi organami, osushestvlyaushimi operativno-razysknuyu deyatelnost, na territorii g. Sochi v period provedenia XXII Olimpiyskikh zimnikh igr i XI Paralimpiyskikh zimnikh igr 2014 goda v g. Sochi" [Details of the Provision of Telecommunications Services, and on the Interaction of Operators with the State Authorities Conducting Operational Search Activities on the Territory of Sochi During the XXII Olympic Winter Games and XI Paralympic Winter Games of 2014 in Sochi], *Rossiyskaya Gazeta*, November 8, 2013, www.rg.ru/2013/11/13/ opera-site-dok.html.

14. Shaun Walker, "MEPs Raise Concerns Over Sochi Winter Olympics Surveillance Plans," *Guardian*, November 13, 2013, www.theguardian.com/world /2013/nov/13/meps-concerns-sochi-winter-olympics-surveillance.

15. "Islamic Group Claims Volgograd Attacks and Threatens Sochi Visitors," Associated Press, January 20, 2014, www.theguardian.com/world/2014/jan/20 /islamic-group-claims-volgograd-threatens-sochi.

16. Nataliya Vasilyeva, interview with authors, March 2014.

17. Nikolai Levshits, "Sochi-2014: Zaslon dlya ne loyalnikh" [Sochi 2014: The Wall for Not Loyal], *New Times*, January 27, 2014.

18. Paul Sonne, Gregory L. White, and Joshua Robinson, "Russian Officials Fire Back at Olympic Critics," *Wall Street Journal*, February 6, 2014, http://www .wsj.com/articles/SB10001424052702304680904579366712107461956.

19. Umberto Bacchi, "Sochi Winter Olympics: Circassian Protest Website NoSochi2014 Hacked on Games' Eve," *International Business Times*, February 7, 2014, www.ibtimes.co.uk/sochi-winter-olympics-circassian-protest-website -nosochi2014-hacked-games-eve-1435553.

20. The account is based on Anastasia Kirilenko, interview with authors, March 2014.

21. Joshua Yaffa, "The Waste and Corruption of Vladimir Putin's 2014 Winter Olympics," Bloomberg, January 2, 2014, www.bloomberg.com/bw/articles/2014 –01–02/the-2014-winter-olympics-in-sochi-cost-51-billion; and Thomas Grove, "Special Report: Russia's $50 Billion Olympic Gamble," Reuters, February 21, 2013, www.reuters.com/article/2013/02/21/us-russia-sochi-idUSBRE91K04M20130221.

CHAPTER 13: THE BIG RED BUTTON

1. On April 4, 2014, Ukraine's Foreign Ministry sent a note to Moscow demanding to clarify the circumstances of presence of FSB Colonel-General Sergei Beseda in Kiev on February 20 and 21. The next day the Russian news agency Interfax, citing security sources, confirmed that Sergei Beseda was indeed in the Ukrainian capital on February 20–21, "Russia's FSB Says Top Officer Went to Kiev for 'Security,'" AFP, April 5, 2014. For details, see James Marson, "Russia Fails to Make Deeper Inroads in Ukraine—For Now," *Wall Street Journal*, April 10, 2014, www.wsj.com/articles/SB10001424052702303603904579491641537737078.

2. Kathy Lally, Will Englund, and William Booth, "Russian Parliament Approves Use of Troops in Ukraine," *Washington Post*, March 1, 2014, www .washingtonpost.com/world/europe/russian-parliament-approves-use-of-troops -in-crimea/2014/03/01/d1775f70-a151–11e3-a050-dc3322a94fa7_story.html.

3. The archive of NTV coverage is available on the site of NTV, March 1, 2014, www.ntv.ru/2014/03/01.

4. Roskomnadzor news, "Po trebaniyu Generalnoy Prokuraturi prekrashen dostup k soobshestvam urkainskikh nationalisticheskikh organizatciy v socialnoy seti 'VKontakte'" [At the Request of the General Prosecutor's Office Access Discontinued to Communities of Ukrainian Nationalist Organizations in the Social Network 'VKontakte'], March 3, 2014, http://rkn.gov.ru/news/rsoc/news 24185.htm.

5. "Russia Lenta.ru Editor Timchenko Fired in Ukraine Row," BBC, March 12, 2014, www.bbc.com/news/world-europe-26543464; Roskomnadzor statement could be found here: http://rkn.gov.ru/news/rsoc/news24418.htm.

6. Address by president of the Russian Federation, March 18, 2014, Kremlin .ru, http://eng.kremlin.ru/transcripts/6889.

7. "Ogranichen dostup k ryadu internet-resursov, rasprostranyavshikh prizyvi k nesanktcionirovannim massovim meropriatyam" [Access Restricted to a Number of Internet Resources, Distributing Calls to Unauthorized Mass Event], Roskomnadzor news, March 13, 2014, http://rkn.gov.ru/news/rsoc/news24447 .htm.

8. Nikita Likhachev, "Genprokuratura zablokirovala blog Navalnogo, saiti Echa Mosckvy, Grani.Ru, Kasparov.Ru I Ezh.Ru" [General Prosecutor's Office Has Blocked Navalny Blog, the Sites Echo of Moscow, Grani.ru, Kasparov.ru, and EZh.ru], Tjournal.ru, March 13, 2014, http://tjournal.ru/paper/kasparov-grani-ej.

9. Viktor Shenderovich, "Putin I devochka na konkakh" [Putin and a Girl on Skates], Ej.ru, February 10, 2014, http://ej.ru/?a=note&id=24384.

10. Agora, a human rights group based in Kazan that provides legal advocacy for victims of suspected human rights abuses, with a focus on journalists, political activists, bloggers, and NGOs, provided a lawyer, Damir Gainutdinov, to help the blocked sites in court, but eventually, despite all efforts, they failed.

11. Nikita Likhachev, "Polzovateli pozhalovalis na blokirovku saita LifeNews" [Users Complained of the Blocking by the Site LifeNews], Tjournal, March 17, 2014, http://tjournal.ru/paper/lifenews-block.

12. Ruslan Leviev, interview with authors, August 2014.

13. Leviev's post on LiveJournal, "Kak rabotaet mechanism blokirovok Roskomnadzora" [How the Mechanism of Blocking by Roskomnadzor Works], April 22, 2014, http://ruslanleviev.livejournal.com/34401.html.

14. Ksenia Boletskaya, "Roskomnadzoru pokazivayut kotyat vmesto saita Navalnogo" [Roskomnadzor Is Shown Kittens Instead of the Site of Navalny], *Vedomosti*, April 21, 2014, www.vedomosti.ru/technology/articles/2014/03/21/roskomnadzoru-pokazyvayut-kotyat-vmesto-sajta-navalnogo.

15. "70th Anniversary of Lifting of Siege of Leningrad," Kremlin.ru, January 27, 2014, http://eng.kremlin.ru/news/6573.

16. Natalia Sindeeva, interview with authors, August 2014.

17. Natalia Krainova and Anna Dolgov, "Cable Providers Drop Independent Dozhd TV Amid Pressure," *Moscow Times*, January 29, 2014, www.themoscowtimes.com/news/article/cable-providers-drop-independent-dozhd-tv-amid-pressure/493576.html. See also Will Englund, "Russian TV Channel Takes Flak Just for Asking: 'Should Leningrad Have Surrendered?'" *Washington Post*, January 30, 2014, www.washingtonpost.com/world/europe/russian-tv-channel-takes-flak-just-for-asking-should-leningrad-have-surrendered/2014/01/30/c1455812–89c0–11e3–833c-33098f9e5267_story.html.

18. Sindeeva, interview, August 2014.

19. "Peskov: telekanal Dozhd pereshev vse grani dopustimogo" [Peskov: TV Dozhd Crossed the Line of the Permissible], Interfax, January 29, 2014, www.interfax.ru/russia/354742.

20. "Putin—Dozhdu: Ya sdelayu vse, chtobi izbavit vas ot izbitochnogo vnimania kontroliruyushikh organov" [Putin—Dozhd: I'll Do Anything to Save You from Excessive Attention to Regulatory Bodies], TV Dozhd, April 17, 2014, http://tvrain.ru/articles/putin_dozhdju_ja_sdelaju_vse_chtoby_izbavit_vas_ot_izbytochnogo_vnimanija_kontrolirujuschih_organov-367069.

21. "Putin—Dozhdu: I ne daval kommandu kabelshikam prekrashat rabotu s vami" [Putin—Rain, I Did Not Command Cable Manufacturers to Stop Working with You], TV Dozhd, June 6, 2014, http://tvrain.ru/articles/putin_dozhdju_ja_ne_daval_komandu_kabelschikam_prekraschat_rabotu_s_vami-369587.

22. The TV Dozhd staff found the new premises only in 2015, at the former factory of Flakon.

23. Glenn Kates, "Moscow Freaks Out About Federalization Rally . . . In Siberia," Radio Free Europe/Radio Liberty, March 6, 2014, www.rferl.org/content/russia-separatism-rally-siberia/26515418.html.

24. BBC World Service statement regarding interview with Artem Loskutov, BBC Media center, August 5, 2014, www.bbc.co.uk/mediacentre/statements/artem-loskutov.

25. "Roskomnadzor dobralsya I do ukrainskikh SMI" [Roskomnadzor Reached Ukrainian Media], BBC Ukrainian service, August 4, 2014, www.bbc.co.uk/ukrainian/ukraine_in_russian/2014/08/140804_ru_s_roskomnadzor_restricting_access.

26. Miriam Elder, "Russia Threatens to Ban BuzzFeed," BuzzFeed.com, December 6, 2014, www.buzzfeed.com/miriamelder/russia-threatens-to-ban-buzzfeed#.wy34B5ad.

27. VKontakte was also under pressure. Pavel Durov's brother Nikolai, who also used to work in VKontakte, posted a message on his page on Sunday, December 22, that on this day alone VKontakte got fifty-three requests from Roskomnadzor to block events, groups, and pages where the word Navalny is mentioned. For details, see http://geektimes.ru/post/243309.

28. Ilya Kuvakin and Daria Luganskaya, "V Facebook zablokirovali stranitsu gruppi v podderzhku" [Facebook Blocked a Group Page in Support of Navalny], RBC, December 20, 2014, www.rbc.ru/rbcfreenews/5495b98a9a7947bb5e5f3e5a.

29. Andrew Roth and David M. Herszenhorn, "Facebook Page Goes Dark, Angering Russia Dissidents," *New York Times*, December 22, 2014, www.nytimes.com/2014/12/23/world/europe/facebook-angers-russian-opposition-by-blocking-protest-page.html?_r=0.

30. "Istochniki Dozhdya: Facebook and Twitter otkazalis blokirovat stranitsi storonnikov Navalnogo" [Sources of Dozhd: Facebook and Twitter Refused to Block Pages for Supporters of Navalny], TV Dozhd, December 22, 2014, http://tvrain.ru/articles/istochniki_dozhdja_facebook_i_twitter_otkazalis_blokirovat_stranitsy_storonnikov_navalnogo-379720.

31. Maria Tsvetkova, "Kremlin Critic Navalny Given Suspended Sentence, Brother Jailed," Reuters, December 30, 2014, www.reuters.com/article/2014/12/30/us-russia-crisis-navalny-idUSKBN0K80AA20141230.

CHAPTER 14: MOSCOW'S LONG SHADOW

1. Sasha Romantsova, interview with authors, September 2014.

2. Andrew E. Kramer, "Ukraine's Opposition Says Government Stirs Violence," *New York Times*, January 21, 2014, www.nytimes.com/2014/01/22/world /europe/ukraine-protests.html?_r=0, and Heather Murphy, "Ominous Text Message Sent to Protesters in Kiev Sends Chills Around the Internet," *New York Times*, January 22, 2014, http://thelede.blogs.nytimes.com//2014/01/22/ominous-text -message-sent-to-protesters-in-kiev-sends-chills-around-the-internet.

3. Andrew E. Kramer, "Russia Defers Aid to Ukraine, and Unrest Persists," *New York Times*, January 29, 2014, www.nytimes.com/2014/01/30/world/europe /ukraine-protests.html.

4. In April 2007 Estonia provoked the Kremlin with its decision to move a Soviet war memorial out of the center of the capital. After a massive nationalistic campaign against Estonia in the Russian press, a series of DDOS attacks was launched on the websites of the Estonian government, parliament, banks, ministries, newspapers, and broadcasters. In June 2008 Lithuania came into Russia's crosshairs when lawmakers voted to ban the public display of Nazi German and Soviet symbols. Some three hundred websites, including those of public institutions such as the National Ethics Body and the Securities and Exchange Commission as well as a string of private companies, had found themselves under cyber siege. Their websites' content was replaced with images of the red flag of the Soviet Union alongside anti-Lithuanian slogans. In August 2008 the military conflict with Georgia in South Ossetia also included cyber attacks against Georgia's Internet infrastructure, compromising several Georgian government websites and prompting the government to begin hosting its sites in the United States. Georgia's Ministry of Foreign Affairs, in order to disseminate real-time information, was forced to move to a BlogSpot account.

5. "Na UNIAN vedetsya mashtabnaya DDoS-ataka" [UNIAN Is Under Massive DDOS Attack], UNIAN, March 3, 2014, www.unian.net/politics/892159 -na-unian-vedetsya-masshtabnaya-nepreryivnaya-ddos-ataka.html.

6. Pavel Sedakov and Dmitry Filonov, "Pervy Ukrainsky kiberfront: kto i zachem obiavil IT-mobilizatiu?" [The First Ukrainian Cyberfront: Who and Why Announced IT Mobilization?], *Forbes* Russia, March 4, 2014, www.forbes.ru /tekhnologii/internet-i-svyaz/251623-pervyi-ukrainskii-kiberfront-kto-i-zachem -obyavil-it-mobilizatsi.

7. The tactics were not completely abandoned, though, and in two weeks, on March 15, DDOS attacks disrupted access to some NATO sites. They focused on the main NATO public site, www.nato.int, knocking it offline for long periods, and a pro-Russian Ukrainian hacktivist group, Cyber Berkut (clearly echoing

the name of the riot police Berkut), claimed responsibility for the attacks. But they were not very serious, and John Bumgarner, a spokesman for the US Cyber Consequences Unit, which assesses the impact of cyber attacks, compared it with "kicking sand into one's face." Naked Security, "DDoS Attack Takes Out NATO Websites, Ukraine Connection Claimed," Sophos, March 17, 2014, https:// nakedsecurity.sophos.com/2014/03/17/ddos-attack-takes-out-nato-websites -ukraine-connection-claimed. Also see Mark Piggot, "Ukraine Crisis: Pro-Russian Hackers Attack Nato Websites," *International Business Times*, March 16, 2014, www .ibtimes.co.uk/ukraine-crisis-pro-russian-hackers-attack-nato-websites-1440497.

8. Chris Elliot, "The Readers' Editor On . . . Pro-Russia Trolling Below the Line on Ukraine Stories," *Guardian*, May 4, 2014, www.theguardian.com /commentisfree/2014/may/04/pro-russia-trolls-ukraine-guardian-online.

9. Ilya Klishin, "Maksimalny retvit: Laiki na Zapad" [Maximus Retweet: Likes on the West], *Vedomosti*, May 21, 2014, www.vedomosti.ru/newspaper/articles/2014 /05/21/lajki-na-zapad.

10. Konstantin Kostin's interview to TV Dozhd, July 1, 2013, http://tvrain .ru/articles/eks_glava_upravlenija_vnutrennej_politiki_kremlja_konstantin _kostin_navalnomu_opasno_idti_na_vybory_karera_nemtsova_zakonchilas _na_vyborah_mera_sochi-346962/?video.

11. Ibid.

12. Anton Butsenko, "Trolli iz Olgino pereekhali v noviy chetyrekhatazhny office na Savushkina" [Trolls from Olgino Moved to a New Four-Story Office on Savushkina], DP.ru, October 28, 2014, www.dp.ru/a/2014/10/27/Borotsja _s_omerzeniem_mo.

13. Dmitry Volchek and Daisy Sindelar, "One Professional Russian Troll Tells All," Radio Free Europe/Radio Liberty, March 27, 2015, www.rferl.org/content /how-to-guid-russian-trolling-trolls/26919999.html.

14. The other was of a conversation between Helga Schmidt, deputy secretary general for the External Action Service at the European Union, and Jan Tombinski, an EU representative in Ukraine.

15. The account is based on Christopher Miller, conversation with authors, March 2015.

16. Christopher J. Miller, "'Fuck the EU,' Frustrated Nuland Says to Pyatt, in Alleged Leaked Phone Call," *Kyiv Post*, February 6, 2014, www.kyivpost.com /content/politics/fuck-the-eu-frustrated-nuland-says-to-pyatt-in-alleged-leaked -phone-call-336373.html.

17. "Ukraine Says Not Investigating Bugging of U.S. Diplomats Phone Talk," Reuters, February 8, 2014, www.reuters.com/article/2014/02/08/us-ukraine-call-id USBREA170G020140208.

18. For details, see Andrei Soldatov and Irina Borogan, "In Ex-Soviet States, Russian Spy Tech Still Watches You," Wired.com, December 21, 2012, www.wired .com/2012/12/russias-hand.

19. "Turchinov pomenyal vse rukovodstvo SBU" [Turchinov Changed the Entire Leadership of the SBU], *Vesti Reporter*, March 7, 2014, http://vesti-ukr.com /strana/41511-turchinov-pomenjal-vse-rukovodstvo-sbu.

20. "Kadrovie peremeni: Poroshenko naznachil nachalnikom Departamenta operativno-technicheskikh meroptiyatiy SBU Frolova" [Personnel Changes: Poroshenko Appointed as Head of Operational and Technical Measures SBU Frolov], Ukranews, http://ukranews.com/news/129796.ru.

21. Over two years we ran a joint investigation along with our friends at Citizen Lab (Canada) and Privacy International (UK) called "Russia's Surveillance State." We found that many countries that won their independence in 1991 still live in the shadow of Soviet surveillance practices. In August 2012 the Kyrgyz's State Committee of National Security put on its website the draft of a national regulation on SORM, which was almost identical to the Russian interception system. The Kyrgyz parliament's Defense and Security Committee stated in an economic analysis of the proposed SORM legislation that the Russian-made connection device linking SORM equipment and the PU would be three times cheaper than that of the Israeli firm Verint. Moscow hardly missed these opportunities to extend its intelligence positions on the soil of the former Soviet Union, but that option was considered as a minor evil by these countries' governments. In November 2012 the Radio Liberty's Kyrgyz Service reported that Russian-made interception equipment could have been used to intercept phone conversations of Kyrgyz politicians leaked online two years ago. The Kyrgyz "telephone gate" scandal greatly embarrassed the provisional government, as it exposed how the positions and money were distributed. Making matters worse, the Russian producers' tapping gear—Moscow's Oniks-Line and Novosibirsk's Sygnatek—were accused of retaining back doors in the equipment. "We shipped the interception equipment to Kyrgyzstan—it was an intergovernmental decision," Sergei Pykhtunov, deputy director of the Sygnatek, admitted to us. But he said he was not aware of the scandal and dismissed the accusation. Sergei Bogotskoi, CEO of Oniks-Line, took the same line. The scandal did not cause the Kyrgyz government to change its approach to the national interception rules.

CHAPTER 15: INFORMATION RUNS FREE

1. On October 26, 2011, in a filing with the US Trade Representative's (USTR) office, the Recording Industry Association of America (RIAA) outlined how

VKontakte and its unlicensed music service is increasingly undermining the growth of the international legitimate music marketplace. According to the RIAA's filing, the service's music functionality is "specifically designed to enable members to upload music and video files, hundreds of thousands of which contain unlicensed copyright works." "RIAA Highlights Russian Service VKontakte, Others in Report to U.S. Government About Markets Rife with Music Theft," RIAA, www.riaa.com/newsitem.php?contentselector=newsandvie ws&news_month_filter=10&news_year_filter=2011&id=B966B360–22F9 -C11E-B7A3–50777A8122E7. For details, see Delphine d'Amora, "Record Firms Sue Social Network VK for Piracy," *Moscow Times*, April 4, 2014, www .themoscowtimes.com/business/article/record-firms-sue-social-network-vk-for -piracy/497473.html; Kathryn Dowling, "VKontakte Case Puts Russian Music Piracy into Spotlight," BBC, August 11, 2014, www.bbc.com/news/business -28739602; and Martech Social, "Russian Social Network VKontakte Sparks Piracy Worries," January 22, 2015, www.martechsocial.com/russian-social-net work-vkontakte-sparks-piracy-worries.

2. Alexandra Bayazitova, "Pavel Durov May Face a Criminal Case for His Expenses," *Izvestia*, March 5, 2014, www.izvestia.ru/news/566840.

3. "Media Forum of Independent Local and Regional Media," Transcripts, Kremlin.ru, April 24, 2014, http://eng.kremlin.ru/transcripts/7075.

4. Ibid.

5. Leonid Bershidsky, "How Putin Crashed a Russian Internet Stock," *Bloomberg*, April 25, 2014, www.bloombergview.com/articles/2014–04–25/how -putin-crashed-a-russian-internet-stock.

6. Vsevolod Pulya, "Yandex Reacts to Putin Comments About Foreign Influence as Share Price Falls," the press release of Yandex (in Russian), *Russia Beyond the Headlines*, April 28, 2014, http://rbth.com/business/2014/04/28/yandex _reacts_to_putin_comments_about_foreign_influence_as_share_pri_36283.html.

7. Maxim Stulov, "Yandex Seeks Putin's Ear With German Gref Board Appointment," *Moscow Times*, May 27, 2014, www.themoscowtimes.com/business /article/yandex-seeks-putins-ear-with-german-gref-board-appointment/500969 .html.

8. "Russian Lawmaker Motions to Probe Internet Giant Yandex," RAPSI, May 15, 2014, http://rapsinews.com/news/20140515/271323235.html.

9. Jason Bush and Alissa de Carbonnel, "Russia Launches Fraud Case Against Backers of Putin Critic Navalny," Reuters, May 23, 2014, www.reuters.com/article /2014/05/23/us-russia-navalny-idUSBREA4M05H20140523.

10. Kaspersky refused to give an interview with the authors.

11. "UPDATE 2—Kaspersky to Buy out US Investors, Rules Out IPO," Reuters, February 3, 2012, www.reuters.com/article/2012/02/03/kaspersky-idUS L2E8D3ETO20120203.

12. About Kaspersky Lab: "Today Kaspersky Lab is the world's largest privately held vendor of endpoint protection solutions, with a holding registered in the United Kingdom," www.kaspersky.com/about.

13. Kaspersky Lab corporate news, "Laboratoria Kasperskogo prisoedinyaetsa k rabote Ligi Bezopasnogo Interneta" [Kaspersky Lab Joins the Safe Internet League], Kaspersky, February 8, 2011, www.kaspersky.ru/news?id=207733419.

14. "The Cyberguard," Safe Internet League, www.ligainternet.ru/en/liga/activity-cyber.php.

15. The primary backer of the League is businessman Konstantin Malofeev, a prominent Orthodox business and political leader who has enjoyed increasing influence since 2012 as conservative and Orthodox beliefs have grown in popularity. In 2014 Malofeev was put under sanctions by the EU and Canada, as Ukraine's government accused him of financing the rebels in eastern Ukraine on behalf of the Russian government. Both Alexander Borodai, the former prime minister of the self-proclaimed Donetsk People's Republic, and Igor Strelkov, formerly one of the main commanders of the rebel forces, are ex-Malofeev employees. For details, see Courtney Weaver, "Konstantin Malofeev, Marshall Capital Partners," *Financial Times*, September 8, 2013, www.ft.com/intl/cms/s/0/569e533e-051c-11e3-9e71-00144feab7de.html#axzz3UGtNNZEy, and Joshua Keating, "God's Oligarch," *Slate*, October 20, 2014, www.slate.com/articles/news_and_politics/foreigners/2014/10/konstantin_malofeev_one_of_vladimir_putin_s_favorite_businessmen_wants_to.single.html.

16. Statistics 2013, the Russian Association for Electronic Communications, June 10, 2014, http://raec.ru/times/detail/3472.

17. At the time, Boris Dobrodeyev was rumored to become the new CEO of VKontakte; he got the position in September 2014. "Son of State Media Chief Appointed CEO of Russia's VKontakte," *Moscow Times*, September 19, 2014, www.themoscowtimes.com/article/son-of-state-media-chief-appointed-ceo-of-russias-vkontakte/507411.html.

18. "Internet Entrepreneurship in Russia Forum," transcripts, Kremlin.ru, June 10, 2014, http://eng.kremlin.ru/transcripts/22470.

19. "Yandex Is Included in the Register of the Organizers of Dissemination of Information," Rublacklist, September 12, 2014, http://rublacklist.net/8598.

20. See www.blog.yandex.ru/post/77678.

21. Andrei Kolesnikov, interview with authors, September 2014.

22. International Telecommunication Union, Internet Exchange Points (IXPs), World Telecommunication Policy Forum, May 14–16, 2013, www.itu.int/en/wtpf-13/Documents/backgrounder-wtpf-13-ixps-en.pdf.

23. Ivan Pavlov (Davydova's lawyer), interview with authors, March 2015.

EPILOGUE

1. "Lifenews Publishes New Secret Phone Conversations of Nemtsov," Lifenews.ru, December 20, 2011, www.lifenews.ru/news/77529.

2. Christopher Hill, *The World Turned Upside Down* (London: Penguin Books, 1991), 17.

INDEX

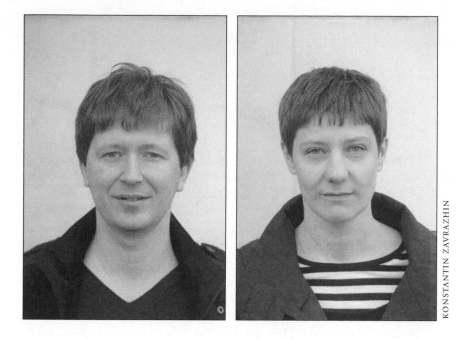

KONSTANTIN ZAVRAZHIN

Andrei Soldatov and **Irina Borogan** are cofounders of Agentura.ru and authors of *The New Nobility: The Restoration of Russia's Security State and the Enduring Legacy of the KGB*. Soldatov and Borogan worked for *Novaya Gazeta* from 2006 to 2008. Agentura.ru and its reporting have been featured in the *New York Times*, the *Moscow Times*, the *Washington Post*, Online Journalism Review, *Le Monde, The Christian Science Monitor*, CNN, Federation of American Scientists, and the BBC. The *New York Times* called it "A Web Site That Came in From the Cold to Unveil Russian Secrets." Irina and Andrei live in Moscow, Russia.

PublicAffairs is a publishing house founded in 1997. It is a tribute to the standards, values, and flair of three persons who have served as mentors to countless reporters, writers, editors, and book people of all kinds, including me.

I. F. STONE, proprietor of *I. F. Stone's Weekly*, combined a commitment to the First Amendment with entrepreneurial zeal and reporting skill and became one of the great independent journalists in American history. At the age of eighty, Izzy published *The Trial of Socrates*, which was a national bestseller. He wrote the book after he taught himself ancient Greek.

BENJAMIN C. BRADLEE was for nearly thirty years the charismatic editorial leader of *The Washington Post*. It was Ben who gave the *Post* the range and courage to pursue such historic issues as Watergate. He supported his reporters with a tenacity that made them fearless and it is no accident that so many became authors of influential, best-selling books.

ROBERT L. BERNSTEIN, the chief executive of Random House for more than a quarter century, guided one of the nation's premier publishing houses. Bob was personally responsible for many books of political dissent and argument that challenged tyranny around the globe. He is also the founder and longtime chair of Human Rights Watch, one of the most respected human rights organizations in the world.

•   •   •

For fifty years, the banner of Public Affairs Press was carried by its owner Morris B. Schnapper, who published Gandhi, Nasser, Toynbee, Truman, and about 1,500 other authors. In 1983, Schnapper was described by *The Washington Post* as "a redoubtable gadfly." His legacy will endure in the books to come.

Peter Osnos, *Founder and Editor-at-Large*